FACTS
REVEALED

ANSWERS TO FANS' CURIOUS QUESTIONS

Disney FACTS REVEALED

ANSWERS TO FANS' CURIOUS QUESTIONS

BY DAVE SMITH

CHIEF ARCHIVIST EMERITUS
OF THE WALT DISNEY ARCHIVES

EDITIONS

LOS ANGELES • NEW YORK

Editorial Director: Wendy Lefkon
Editor: Jennifer Eastwood
Cover design by Alfred Giuliani
Interior design by Arlene Schleifer Goldberg

This book's producers would like to thank Jennifer Black, Elena Blanco, Christopher Caines, Jackie DeLeo, Monique Diman, Dennis Ely, Winnie Ho, Warren Meislin, Robert Oelslager, Humaira Shaikh, Marybeth Tregarthen, Dushawn Ward, and Jessica Ward.

ISBN 978-1-4847-4202-0
FAC-026988 -16078
Printed in the United States of America
First Edition, May 2016
10 9 8 7 6 5 4 3 2 1
Visit www.disneybooks.com

D23
The Official Community for Disney Fans
Disney.com/D23

SUSTAINABLE FORESTRY INITIATIVE Certified Sourcing www.sfiprogram.org SFI-00993

THIS LABEL APPLIES TO TEXT STOCK

TABLE OF CONTENTS

ASK DAVE

For over thirty years, I have had a column in *Disney Channel Magazine* and *Disney Magazine*, along with various company Web sites, in which I have answered Disney questions sent in by readers. It constantly intrigues me that fans can come up with the most detailed and interesting questions. Several friends and colleagues persuaded me to collect my "Ask Dave" questions in a book, leading to *Disney Trivia from the Vault* in 2012. The almost one thousand questions published in that book ranged from 1983 to 2010, but my column has continued, now on the D23 Web site, and there have been many more questions. The questions from today are, if anything, more unique and interesting, partly because of the Internet providing quick answers to most of the easier questions. The questions sent to me are thus the ones where the readers were unable to find an answer in normal sources. So, this book contains another thousand questions, primarily dating from 2010 to 2014, and also includes some subject categories not included in the first book. While it is not designed as an ordinary trivia book in which readers quiz their friends with questions and look for a response, this book provides a wealth of obscure Disney facts that should intrigue even the most in-the-know and up-to-date Disney fans.

Dave Smith

Chief Archivist Emeritus
Walt Disney Archives

ACKNOWLEDGMENTS

My deepest thanks go to the many people who helped me with this book, especially Walt Disney Archives staff members Becky Cline, Robert Tieman, Alesha Reyes, Mike Buckhoff, Edward Ovalle, and Kevin Kern. Special thanks go to my good friend and colleague Steven Vagnini, who spent countless hours reading the manuscript and providing advice. Additional thanks go to friends and colleagues, including Bruce Aguilar, Tony Anselmo, Justin Arthur, Matt Bond, Keith Burrell, Rob and Zinnia Cress, Tyson Ervin, Ruston Harker, John Johnson, Ryan Letts, Paula Sigman Lowery, Julian Lowy, Michael Maney, Brainard Miller, Matt Pilla, Russell Schroeder, Moises Torres, Melody Dale Vagnini, Michael Vagnini, Alex Williams, and James Wilson. Family members Jean Marana, Kathy Eastman, and Gil and Val Eastman provided welcomed support. I also extend my gratitude to Wendy Lefkon and Jennifer Eastwood at Disney Editions. And, above all, thank you to all the Disney fans who took the time to write in their questions.

Dave "Ask Dave" Smith

Burbank, CA

ANIMATED
FEATURES

Q In *The Little Mermaid*, Ursula's hench-eels are Flotsam and Jetsam. Which one is which? I know they both have a yellow eye; one's left eye is yellow, while the other's is on the right? Normally I'm good at telling which Disney character is which, but this is one I don't know the answer to. Think you know the answer, Dave? Bobby, Banning, CA

A —It is generally agreed that Flotsam has a glowing left eye, and Jetsam has a glowing right eye. Otherwise, they are meant to be identical.

Q What year was *The Little Mermaid* made? Sharon, Senatobia, MS

A —*The Little Mermaid* was released in 1989, but Disney animators had started work on a film with that title way back in the 1930s. Famed book illustrator Kay Nielsen did some of the preliminary sketches.

Q Please tell me what is Bambi's mother's name. My wife and I have been going back and forth on this question. She said that they never gave her a name, and I swear I remember someone calling her by name like Enna or Ella. Please let us know who is right. Keith, Tamarac, FL

A —We never gave Bambi's mother a name, but Aunt Ena is the name of Faline's mother. (Faline was Bambi's girlfriend.)

Q One of my favorite artists of all time is the great Eyvind Earle. I love his work, especially the background art and styling that he did for Walt Disney's *Sleeping Beauty*. How did Walt Disney find Earle? Courtney, Mesa, AZ

A —Eyvind Earle, born in 1916, had been working as an artist, but then went back to school (at the Art Center School) to take more art classes in 1950. That same year, he applied for a job at the Disney Studio and was hired as a background painter in October. He remained at Disney until 1958.

Q

I have some pictures from 1996 of a parade in New Orleans. There are floats themed to *Toy Story* and *Mary Poppins*. The caption says that the parade was in celebration of *The Hunchback of Notre Dame*'s release and that it was the first time Disney held a parade outside of the Parks. Know anything about this? Alex, St. Augustine, FL

A

—Disney often likes to try something unique when premiering a major motion picture, such as holding the 1995 premiere for *Pocahontas* in New York's Central Park. For *The Hunchback of Notre Dame*, Disney's marketing staff decided to have the premiere in New Orleans. It was held at the Superdome, and the film was projected on six enormous screens on June 19, 1996, two days before the film's national release; the showing was preceded by a Disney parade through the French Quarter, beginning at Jackson Square. The parade utilized floats and Cast Members from Walt Disney World, including the restored horse-drawn steam calliope which has been seen in so many Walt Disney World parades. The following year, a parade and premiere were held in New York City for *Hercules*.

Q

Were any of the songs in *The Three Caballeros* original? Jeremiah, Fairfax, VA

A

—Only one of the songs in the film was original: "Mexico" by Charles Wolcott and Ray Gilbert. The other songs came from Brazilian and Mexican composers, such as Augustín Lara and Ary Barroso, but had English lyrics written by Ray Gilbert. One song, "Os Quindins de Yaya," by Barroso, kept its Portuguese lyrics.

3

Q Who is the artist who drew Grumpy? Michael, Chicago, IL

A —A number of different artists were involved with the animation of Grumpy in *Snow White and the Seven Dwarfs*. Some of the major ones were Fred Moore, Bill Roberts, Bill Tytla, Dick Lundy, Eric Larsen, and Fred Spencer.

Q Who was the narrator for the 1967 movie *The Jungle Book*? Judy, Andrews, TX

A —That would have been Sebastian Cabot, who also provided the voice of Bagheera in the film. Cabot narrated a number of Disney films, including *The Sword in the Stone* and *The Many Adventures of Winnie the Pooh*.

Q Who animated Casey Jr. the circus train in *Dumbo*? Justin, Appling, GA

A —Most of the animation of Casey Jr. was done by animators Don Tobin, Paul Kossoff, and Don Patterson.

Q Thank you for all the time you spend answering our questions! Here's my question: I'm watching *Dumbo* and one of the elephants sounds exactly like Minnie Mouse. Is the person that did the voice work for Minnie Mouse the same as the elephant? Thank you again for your time. ☺ Salvador, Oxnard, CA

A —None of the actresses who did the voices of the elephants in *Dumbo* had also voiced Minnie Mouse. The uncredited actresses were Verna Felton, Noreen Gammill, Dorothy Scott, and Sarah Selby. Felton played the elephant known as Matriarch; Gammill was Fidgity; Scott was Giddy; and Selby was Prissy—and good luck to anyone who knows which elephant is which.

Q Dave, in a recent answer to a question about the actors who provided voices for the *Dumbo* animated feature, you mentioned the elephants Matriarch, Fidgity, Giddy, and Prissy, and then said, "Good luck to anyone who knows which elephant is which." That answer, of course, begs this question: Do you know which is which? Jim, Cape Canaveral, FL

A —In doing more research, I see that the elephants have not always been referred to by the same names. Fidgity and Giddy were also called Catty and Giggles. According to John Grant in his *Encyclopedia of Walt Disney's Animated Characters*, at the beginning of the film, Matriarch has the pink-violet headdress, Catty has the yellow, Giggles the blue, and Prissy the red. Matriarch is the leader of the group; when the stork asks if she is the one receiving the baby, she haughtily replies, "Certainly not." Prissy replies, "The very idea!" Later on, when the elephants first see Dumbo's huge ears, Catty is the one who says in an undertone, "Just look at those E-A-R-S," with Giggles responding, "Those what? Oh, ears!"

Q Which is the shortest of all the Disney animated movies? Justin, Appling, GA

A —That would be *Saludos Amigos* at forty-two minutes. Normally, a film of that length would be called a featurette, but *Saludos Amigos* has always been counted as one of Disney's animated feature films.

Q Which cartoon or film has some reference to Italy (like the spaghetti scene from *Lady and the Tramp*)? Diletta, Rome, Italy

A —The main one, of course, is *Pinocchio*, whose story is set in Italy. There is a scene in Italy in *Cars 2*, and one of the Scat Cats in *The Aristocats* is an Italian cat.

Q Can you tell me at which cinema in London, England, the Disney film *The Rescuers* premiered? I'm doing some research on Disney's first-time releases in London. Thanks. Robert, London, England

A —The Royal European Premiere of *The Rescuers* was held on October 13, 1977, at the Odeon Theatre, St. Martin's Lane, in London, in the presence of Princess Margaret. The premiere was a benefit for Girl Guides, a group that's similar to Girl Scouts in the United States.

Q At the end of *Brave*, the movie was dedicated to Steve Jobs. Why? Jeff, Tampa, FL

A —Steve Jobs, who had become involved with Pixar Animation Studios in 1986, passed away while *Brave* was in production.

Q I remember watching a live-action *Snow White and the Seven Dwarfs* on VHS that had the same songs as the cartoon. Is that by Disney, and where can I find it? Anonymous

A —This stage show was taped from a 1979 presentation at Radio City Music Hall in New York City. It was released on video and shown on Disney Channel in the 1980s, but it is unavailable at the present time.

Q I know that the name of the demon in *Fantasia*'s "Night on Bald Mountain" is Chernabog, but I was wondering where the animators came up with this name. Thanks for your help! Catherine, Las Vegas, NV

A —Chernabog was actually a name from Slavonic mythology, meaning "black god" or "god of evil."

Q **Has Pixar ever helped with any Disney animated movies?**
Kobe, Delaware, OH

A —John Lasseter, chief creative officer of Pixar Animation Studios,
is also chief creative officer of the Walt Disney Animation
Studios. Ed Catmull, president of Pixar Animation Studios, is also
president of Walt Disney Animation Studios. So, yes, the two
groups consult with each other.

Q **Is it true that Ilene Woods didn't remember she voiced**
Cinderella **by the time she died? That just sounds so sad.**
Taylor, Hillsboro, OR

A —Perhaps you are referring to her quote: "Seeing it [*Cinderella*]
in its new form was breathtaking for me. It's so beautiful. The
color is magnificent, it just took my breath away; it was so
wonderful. I sort of forget when I'm watching the movie that
I had anything to do with it." Ilene Woods died in 2010 from
causes related to Alzheimer's disease, so it is possible that by
then she had forgotten her role because of her affliction.

Q **My siblings and I recently helped my parents, now in their**
eighties, unpack items that have been in storage for many years.
We discovered two original hand-painted movie cels. They
both have a circular stamp with the written letters *WM* **in the**
middle. The first is of Eeyore and says it's from the 1977 *Winnie*
the Pooh **movie. The other has less information. It's of Mickey**
Mouse inside a house with a bare-boned Christmas tree on a
barrel, wood floors, a wooden chest, and a table with a bowl
and spoon. Only Mickey is in color. We are hoping you can help
us determine their value and their history. Leslie, Burlington, VT

A —Your second cel is from *Mickey's Christmas Carol* (1983).
During the 1970s and 1980s, when these films were made, Disney

7

was selling cels through art dealers throughout the country. The initials *WM* stand for Wendall Mohler, who was one of the Disney executives in charge of the cel-sale program. You can check eBay to find out what similar cels are bringing at auction.

Q **Dave, do you have a favorite Disney villain? Joseph, Nevada City, CA**

A —This might seem like a strange answer, because the character is not very well known, but I would say the Horned King in *The Black Cauldron*. For years before that film came out, many Disney animated villains tended to be funny villains; you would tend to laugh at Captain Hook or Cruella De Vil or Madam Mim or Prince John or Madame Medusa. The Horned King was the first in ages who was truly evil.

Q **What Disney movies/fairy tales have begun with the opening of a book? I know my favorite *Sleeping Beauty* does, with that beautiful jeweled book. Are the books real or animated? Barbara, DeWitt, MI**

A —The technique of using a book to open an animated feature was a favorite of Walt Disney's. The three books that the Walt Disney Archives has are the ones from *Snow White and the Seven Dwarfs*, *Cinderella*, and *Sleeping Beauty*. They are actual books. Others have included *The Sword in the Stone*, *Robin Hood*, *The Jungle Book*, *The Adventures of Ichabod and Mr. Toad*, *The Many Adventures of Winnie the Pooh*, and *Enchanted*.

Q **In *Cinderella*, the Grand Duke yells after Cinderella as she loses her slipper. Why does he call her "*señorita*"? Melanie, Northfield Center, OH**

A —The Grand Duke, in trying to stop Cinderella, who is fleeing from the castle, says, "Oh, I say, young lady, wait! *Mademoiselle . . .*

señorita . . . uh . . . uh. . . ." Since she does not respond, he is calling out to her in French and Spanish, not knowing anything about her, including her native language.

Q **Hey, Dave! Do you know when *Snow White and the Seven Dwarfs* is set? I know this is sort of a silly question, but it just bugs me not knowing the answer. And another small question: how did Disney compensate for the money he lost in the early 1940s? Was it through his animated shorts? Thanks a million, Dave! Mohammad, Anaheim, CA**

A —*Snow White and the Seven Dwarfs* is a fairy tale first published by the Brothers Grimm in 1812, so it obviously takes place before that, but I don't think the Grimms (or Walt Disney) ever determined exactly when the story is supposed to be set. During the postwar years of the 1940s, Walt Disney kept his company afloat by producing educational films, short cartoons, and package features (groups of shorts and featurettes tied together and released as features), as well as by licensing merchandise. By the start of the 1950s, he had a hit with *Cinderella*, had started his True-Life Adventures, and was about to embark in the fields of TV and theme parks.

Q **What is Sebastian's full name from *The Little Mermaid*? Kobe, Delaware, OH**

A —It is Horatio Felonious Ignacious Crustaceous Sebastian.

Q **Is there any truth to the rumor that Disney had once considered adapting *The Lord of the Rings* as an animated feature? Jeremiah, Fairfax, VA**

A —There were preliminary discussions, but Disney never bought the film rights.

Q I really like Will Rogers, and I'm wondering if the animators made Pecos Bill after Will? Pecos Bill looks like Will: the same hair, face, and love of the lariat! Who was the animator for that short? Thanks! Kelly, Hollywood, CA

A —The Pecos Bill story about a cowboy hero comes from the folklore of the Old West and was first printed in a magazine by Edward O'Reilly in 1917. (Some have suggested that O'Reilly actually made up the stories.) There was probably no connection in the minds of the Disney artists with the humorist Will Rogers. The character was animated in *Melody Time* by Ward Kimball and Milt Kahl.

Q What was the last Disney film to be completely hand drawn? Larry, Churchton, MD

A —The last fully hand-drawn animated feature was *Winnie the Pooh* (2011).

Q Is the rumor that Snow White's prince's name is Ferdinand true? If not, do you know how the rumor started? Alex, Austin, TX

A —The rumor is untrue. It may have started way back in 1939 when Shirley Temple presented a special Academy Award to Walt Disney in honor of *Snow White and the Seven Dwarfs*. In her speech, she called Walt "the daddy of *Snow White and the Seven Dwarfs*, Mickey Mouse, Ferdinand, and all the others." But the Ferdinand she was referring to was not the Prince but Ferdinand the Bull, star of a 1938 cartoon of the same name, which also received an Academy Award.

Q The movie *DuckTales: the Movie* that was released in theaters never got a DVD release date; are there any plans for releasing in the United States? Allan, Agawam, MA

A —*DuckTales: the Movie, Treasure of the Lost Lamp* was released on DVD as a Disney Movie Club Exclusive in 2006; copies have been available on eBay. It had been released earlier on VHS and laser disc in 1991.

Q Hi, Dave. Well, after going to the D23 event a couple of weeks ago, I am confused. They mentioned that Marc Davis drew the first Tinker Bell. And I've gone to a lot of Disney events and met with Margaret Kerry, who said she was the first model for Tinker Bell. So was she the first, or did Marc draw the first? D23 never mentioned Kerry. Thanks, Dave. Joann, Kildeer, IL

A —Marc Davis was the artist who developed and refined the character of Tinker Bell; Margaret Kerry was the actress who modeled for him. Marc was not the first to draw the character— other artists, including Bianca Majolie, were doing concept work on her by the early 1940s.

Q Dear Dave, I noticed that Charles Muntz, the villain in Disney·Pixar's *Up*, shares a name remarkably similar to that of Walt Disney's Universal distributor, Charles Mintz. Is there any direct relationship, or is this sheer coincidence? Also, is it true that the character was based off of Errol Flynn? Jared, Terre Haute, IN

A —According to designer Albert Lozano, "If you were to blend Errol Flynn, Clark Gable, Howard Hughes, and Walt Disney into one heroic 1930s man," you would come up with Charles Muntz. I have never heard that the name was based on Charles Mintz.

Q I really enjoy the music from the films, especially the deleted songs. I have fallen in love with the deleted songs from *Cinderella* and absolutely love the *Lost Chords* albums, which have the original demo and an orchestrated recording for several songs. Do you have a list of all of the deleted songs from *Cinderella,* and do you know why some of them weren't put onto the newest album, including one of the work songs? Mitchell, Roseville, CA

A —No one has compiled a list of all the deleted songs. Perhaps you are aware that bonus material on the 2005 Platinum Edition of *Cinderella* included some deleted songs, one being the alternate "Cinderella Work Song." I checked with Russell Schroeder, the author of the two-volume book set *Disney's Lost Chords* (available on Amazon). While volume 1 of his set includes eight deleted songs from *Cinderella,* two of these were never recorded: "Horse-Sense" and "Raga-Daga-Day." The only other *Cinderella* songs Schroeder is aware of are "Pretending" (Larry Morey/Charles Wolcott) and "Tee Hee Hee, You Can't Scare Me" (Mack David/Al Hoffman/ Jerry Livingston). Neither has been published or recorded.

Q Where did the idea for *Wreck-It Ralph* come from, and were there early versions of the story that were rejected? Daniel, Bergenfield, NJ

A —The idea came from Rich Moore, who made his feature film directing debut for Walt Disney Animation Studios on the film. The story taking place in the world of video games was one of three ideas that Moore pitched to Disney. He wanted to portray how arcade game characters have no free will. "They're programmed to do one thing day in and day out; they don't have a choice in the matter," Moore once said. One early working title was *Reboot Ralph.*

Q Recently I have become very interested in the behind-the-scenes of *The Black Cauldron* and have come across sources that say there were twelve minutes of film that were cut out of the movie at the last minute because some of the scenes were too scary. Can you give me detailed information about all of these scenes please? Mitchell, Roseville, CA

A —You can find discussions of some of the cut scenes on the Internet. The production of *The Black Cauldron* was troubled, and its release was scheduled just about the time that Michael Eisner and Jeffrey Katzenberg came to the Studio. After seeing an early version of the film, which had been started under the previous Studio administration, Katzenberg had definite ideas on what would improve it, so he was the one who ordered the cuts. Many of them concerned the scary Cauldron Born, the army of zombielike creatures brought forth by the Horned King.

Q Hello, Dave. First-time questioner here. A few people say that in *Sleeping Beauty*, at the part during "Once Upon a Dream" when Aurora and Phillip are dancing next to the water, that the reflection is of Ariel and Eric! Not only do I not see the resemblance, but seeing as this film was made thirty years before Ariel and Eric were even designed, I find this hard to believe. Nevertheless, I'd feel better if *you* would look into it and prove it once and for all. Thank you. (And do hurry. These people are driving me crazy!) Sheila, Conestoga, PA

A —You are entirely correct, in that *Sleeping Beauty* was made in 1959, and *The Little Mermaid* in 1989. There would certainly be no subtle references to the later characters in the former film since indeed they had not yet been created.

Q I recently saw some production cels from *Snow White and the Seven Dwarfs*. How many production cels were needed for an animated film before the digital age? And thanks for your recent book; loved reading it. D.J., Dallas, TX

A —This is hard to count. There are twenty-four frames per second, but some cels are held over for two frames. Also, if there are several characters in a scene, they are sometimes painted on separate cels. So *Snow White and the Seven Dwarfs*, as a guess, might have had in the neighborhood of a hundred thousand cels.

Q I see this rumor pop up so often that I figured I should ask Dave himself. A lot of people insist that Ariel's character design (at least the facial structure and characteristics) is inspired by Alice's. I'm not convinced, but does this rumor hold any water? Joseph, Nevada City, CA

A —Ariel's lead animator, Glen Keane, has said, "I was supposed to animate Ursula, but when I heard Jodi Benson sing 'Part of Your World,' I said, 'I have to draw that character!' I talked to [directors] Ron [Clements] and John [Musker] and said, "I've gotta draw Ariel.' They asked, 'Can you draw a pretty girl?' I said, 'Oh, I've been drawing my whole married life, and I think I can!' I did a lot of design study drawings on my wife and used her for my inspiration for Ariel. And she's kind of got this girl-next-door kind of a look; she actually looks very much like Ariel."

Q I heard from someone that Snow White has a sister. Is this true? If so, what is the story? Nicholas, Silver Spring, MD

A —There is another Snow White fairy tale from the Brothers Grimm in which a girl named Snow White has a sister named Rose Red, but that is a different story than the one used by Disney.

Q What was the reason for Arthur from *The Sword in the Stone* to be voiced by three different people? Taylor, Hillsboro, OR

A —Since an animated feature takes so long to make, boys hired to do the voices grow up and their voices change, and the filmmakers have to find someone else who sounds like the young boy to continue with the role. In this case, the two replacements were sons of the director, Wolfgang Reitherman.

What is the history of *The Lion King*? Anna, Perris, CA

—This story originated in the Animation Department at Disney, where it was known as *King of the Jungle* throughout much of its production. Disney artists traveled to Africa to get ideas for the locale of the film, and live animals were brought to the Disney Studio so that the animators could study their movements. After several years of production, the picture opened in June 1994 and became one of the highest-grossing films of all time.

What year did the Walt Disney's *Cinderella* picture disc with songs by Mack David, Al Hoffman, and Jerry Livingston come out? Carolyn, Stoutsville, OH

—The animated motion picture *Cinderella* was released in 1950; the picture disc (phonograph record) came out in 1981.

Is it true that someone counted out 6,469,952 black dots in the *One Hundred and One Dalmatians* movie? Marlee, Decatur, AL

—That is the number given in the publicity materials for the film, though I assume it is an educated guess. How would one count all the spots, especially on moving Dalmatians?

Is Bambi a girl or boy? Cheryl, Linden, MI

—Bambi is male; he has a girlfriend, Faline. People do get confused, because Bambi is a name given to girls these days.

Q Dear Sir, I think I read somewhere that Walt had figurines made to give the animators a better idea as to how the characters should look in 3-D. Is this true? And where can I learn more on these? I think I have one but am unable to find any information. Thanks. Stephen, Salisbury, NC

A —Back in the late 1930s, Disney set up a Character Model Department, which made plaster figurines of some of the characters, beginning with those in *Pinocchio*, to aid the animators in their work. The number made of each character depended on how many animators were animating the character, but there were rarely more than half a dozen or a dozen. We still do models today, but they are now made of resin. The Walt Disney Archives has an inventory of most of the different character models made.

Q Hi, Dave. How are you today? I'm doing very well. The reason for my question is that on the D23 Web site it states that *Aladdin* was released on November 11, 1992. But on my D23 Disney Undiscovered Calendar it says November 25, 1992. So which is it? Thanks. Todd, North Hampton, NH

A —Both dates are correct. *Aladdin* had an initial release in a few theaters on November 11, but its general release did not come until November 25.

Q As D23 members, we saw an advanced screening of *Winnie the Pooh* at the El Capitan in Hollywood and were lucky enough to talk to the animators after the show. We have now purchased the DVD and are wondering what typeface was used for the story text in the movie as Winnie and his pals climb up and down the text. The animators were unable to identify the font. Can you help us out? Many thanks! Florian, Santa Clarita, CA

A —I asked Stephen Anderson, one of the movie's directors, and his response was, "The font for the Pooh book pages is Adobe Caslon Pro, which is a Photoshop font."

Q Hi, Dave. I am currently researching the 1940 classic *Fantasia* for my undergraduate music dissertation. Do you have any information regarding the meeting between composer Paul Hindemith and Walt Disney during the production of *Fantasia*? Thank you! Kayleigh, Glasgow, Scotland

A —I refer you to the essay "Paul Hindemith Meets Walt Disney," by Donald Draganski (*http://www.michaelbarrier.com/Essays/ Hindemith/Hindemith.html*).

Q My name is Sunny. I come from China and am a visiting scholar at UCSB [University of California—Santa Barbara] right now. I am writing a paper about Disney's screenwriters; specifically, how they work out wonderful stories, why they rewrite fairy tales, and what are the procedures when they cooperate with the Disney company. I wonder whether you can provide me with some documents and information for these questions. Thank you very much. Sunny, Santa Barbara, CA

A —I refer you to several books by John Canemaker, including *Before the Animation Begins: The Art and Lives of Disney Inspirational Sketch Artists* and *Paper Dreams: The Art and Artists of Disney Storyboards*. Also, in recent years there have been books about the making of each of our animated features.

Q I'm a student and need some clarification. There are some films that are computer animated but have no credit of being a Disney·Pixar film. What sets a Disney·Pixar film apart from other computer-animated Disney films? Kaitlynn, West Burlington, IA

A —Disney has released all of the animated features made by Pixar Animation Studios, a company founded in the San Francisco Bay area in 1986 to produce computer-generated films, beginning with *Toy Story* in 1995. Disney purchased Pixar in 2006. While all of the features from Pixar have used computer animation, and have been known as Disney•Pixar films, Walt Disney Animation Studios has done some of its own films using computers, including *Chicken Little*, *Meet the Robinsons*, *Bolt*, *Tangled*, *Wreck-It Ralph*, *Frozen*, *Big Hero 6*, and *Zootopia*.

Q **Is it true that Bruce from *Finding Nemo* is named after the shark in the famous movie *Jaws*? Joshua, Ivanrest, MI**

A —This may be true, but there is also speculation that Bruce was used because it is often the name for a generic Australian male. The shark in *Jaws* had no name, but the crew on the film nicknamed its mechanical models Bruce, according to some sources, after Steven Spielberg's lawyer, Bruce Raiman.

Q **Is there any way to see the entire font collection for *Aladdin*? I am planning on getting a tattoo of "A Diamond in the Rough," and I want it to be in the same font, but I can only find fake fonts and the original title's few letters. Jocilyn, Levittown, PA**

A —No full-alphabet fonts exist for most movie-title treatments. Unless there is some need (marketing, advertising, etc.), the creative artists who come up with individual title fonts don't bother creating alphabet letters that aren't used in the title.

Q **Does The Walt Disney Company still put hidden Mickeys in their movies? Veronica, Anaheim, CA**

A —I am unaware of many hidden Mickeys deliberately being placed in Disney films, other than cameo appearances (for example, the Disney characters in Sebastian's audience in *The Little Mermaid*).

Q **I was watching *Toy Story 3* and saw an address on the bottom left-hand corner of a letter that said STATE UNIVERSITY on the top row and EMERYVILLE, CA, and I think the numbers 34608 on the bottom row and also the address 1215 45TH STREET on the line above. Is that an address for the Pixar Animation Studios? (Found this info eleven minutes, fifteen seconds into the movie.) Kobe, Delaware, OH**

A —That is indeed the address for Pixar Animation Studios in Emeryville, CA 94608. (They are not open to the public.)

Q **Why was *Saludos Amigos* counted as one of Disney's animated features when *The Reluctant Dragon* was not? I'm curious because both films integrate substantial live-action sequences with animation. Andrew, Nissequogue, NY**

A —*The Reluctant Dragon* has always been considered primarily a live-action film. Besides the eponymous cartoon, its animated sequences are relatively short. *Saludos Amigos* has a much larger percentage of animation.

Q **I have a sixtieth-anniversary edition DVD of *Dumbo* that I've had ever since I was little. One of the bonus features promotes the sequel *Dumbo II*. When I was little, I thought that this movie would be released on DVD, but it never was. I think that it was shelved, but I would like to know why, and why it was promoted if it never came about. Linda, Alva, OK**

A —The sixtieth-anniversary *Dumbo* DVD came out in 2001. At that time, Disney was planning a direct-to-video *Dumbo II*. However, John Lasseter, who became the chief creative officer of Walt

Disney Animation Studios in 2006, felt that such sequels tarnished the classics, so he put a stop to this one, as well as several others that were being considered.

Q **Our small school is interested in producing two presentations of *Beauty and the Beast*. Please direct us to a contact person to get permission. Thanks. Dan, Branford, FL**

A —*Beauty and the Beast* and *Beauty and the Beast Jr.* are both distributed by MTI (Music Theatre International). You can check their Web site.

Q **Is Mittens from *Bolt* meant to be a particular kind of cat? Or is she based on more than one type? Fred, Placentia, CA**

A —Mittens was not meant to be any specific type of cat.

Q **We have a question for you about *Fantasia* and Fantasound: When we purchased the home video of *Fantasia*, the stereo effect is heard at times as the whole music track sweeping from left to right, for example. My father feels that conductor and collaborator Leopold Stokowski would never have approved such an effect and would have only agreed to participate if a natural stereo effect was the intent, and that the Studio altered the original stereo track for the video release. My opinion is that Stokowski may have made an exception, and that indeed, if you would have seen *Fantasia* in a theater equipped with Fantasound, you would have heard the panning effects. Who is right? Jim, Anaheim, CA**

A —Stereophonic sound was so new to films in 1940 that Fantasound was a tremendous novelty to audiences who were able to experience *Fantasia* in its original version. The Fantasound effects did indeed include the sound following the action across the screen, and at times even around the theater, and Stokowski would have been involved in the planning.

As far as Jiminy Cricket being *Pinocchio*'s good conscience and his initials being J.C., did that have any correlation at all to Jesus Christ and His initials being J.C.? Alan, Anaheim, CA

—The slang expression *Jiminy Cricket* existed long before it became the name of the cricket in *Pinocchio*, and in fact can be heard in the dialogue of *Snow White and the Seven Dwarfs*. According to the *Partridge Dictionary of Slang and Unconventional English*, "Jiminy Cricket! used as a mild expletive. Extended from obsolete 'jiminy!'; 'gemini!', etc., which may derive from Jesu domine; modern use is probably intended to be a euphemism for JESUS CHRIST! US, 1848." Since the character was a cricket and needed a name, it is likely that some story man (or perhaps even Walt himself) suggested using Jiminy as his first name since it was a common expression (as opposed to using the more typical alliteration in naming animated characters and calling him Christopher Cricket or something else starting with a C).

I just finished watching *The Princess and the Frog* recently, and I noticed that at the end of the movie, when Lou the crocodile is playing with the jazz band, the bass drum reads THE FIREFLY FIVE + LOU. Is that paying homage to the Dixieland band the Firehouse Five Plus Two that used to play at Disneyland in the 1950s and was made up of Walt's animators? Philip, Valhalla, NY

—Yes, indeed, the animators working on *The Princess and the Frog* included that shout-out to the Firehouse Five Plus Two, the Dixieland band started by Disney animator, and one of Walt's Nine Old Men, Ward Kimball.

Q I was looking for the sheet music to the music Donald used to move the llama in *Saludos Amigos*. My daughter plays in the school band and is always looking for something fun to play on solo night to see how many Disney fans are in the audience. Is there a place to get any of these older hidden treasures? Benjamin, Westminster, MA

A —The music has not been released on sheet music. The tune is known simply as "Llama Theme," composed by Disney composer Charles Wolcott.

Q I've asked this question a few times around the Parks and to some of the management while I worked at Disneyland, and I have never gotten a definitive answer. I always wondered why the sound track to Disney's *Robin Hood* has never been released. As a child, it was one of my personal favorites, and I always enjoyed the songs and occasionally whistle the intro when I walk around. I know a few songs were released on the *Classic Disney* five-disc set, but I want the whole thing. It seems like songs from *Song of the South* are more known and obtainable on discs, and that hasn't even had a DVD release! I believe *Robin Hood* has now had two. I would really appreciate a response as I do admire your books and input. Thank you very much. Samson, Brooklyn, NY

A —While there has been no CD sound track of *Robin Hood* released, there was a long-playing phonograph record that came out with the film in 1973, featuring music and dialogue from the sound track. The Disneyland Record number is ST-3810.

Q For almost fifty years I have been trying to locate a copy of the sheet music for "Painting the Roses Red" from *Alice in Wonderland*. Does it even exist? The song is never included in any of the Disney sheet music books. As Alice would say, "Curiouser and curiouser!" Barry, New Cumberland, PA

A —As far as I can tell, the song was never released on sheet music or in a song folio in the United States. There was a simple single page of sheet music of the song sold in Britain for one shilling in 1950.

Q There is currently a debate about Snow White's eye color . . . several people believe that when they saw the film in theaters years ago, her eye color was blue, not brown as normally depicted. Surviving cels, etc. seem to indicate that her eyes were originally brown, but someone located a Golden Book from 1962 called *Walt Disney's Story Land*, in which she is depicted with blue eyes. Did Disney ever produce material, or authorize material, in which Snow White had blue eyes? Brian, Littleton, MA

A —Snow White's eyes in the original film were brown. It is possible that in later uses—movie posters, books, merchandise—she might sometimes have been given blue eyes.

Q Hello. I was just wondering. I have what I was told is a "cutting" or "continuity" script for *Pinocchio*. It is about two hundred pages, and I think eleven by seventeen inches. Would you know how many of these existed? Also, how and when they were used? I think I have something fairly unique here. What do you think? Thanks so much. Jaimie, Chilliwack, BC, Canada

A —Cutting continuities are prepared in a very limited edition for all films after they are completed. The continuities indicate the exact length of each scene, a description of the action, and any dialogue. They are used in many different departments at Disney, for such purposes as sound dubbing, foreign releases, selecting film clips for publicity, etc. Since they are primarily an internal document, there would be few outside the company, so you have a nice item. It would not have much monetary value, however.

Q **Why did animators make Cruella's hair half black and half white? Avi, Irvine, CA**

A —The original book, by Dodie Smith, features Cruella with the dual-colored hair. It gave her a distinctive look.

Q **Disney has done amazing jobs interpreting stories, such as those about Snow White, Peter Pan, and Rapunzel. What was the *first* Disney movie that was based on an original idea from Disney? Avi, Irvine, CA**

A —If you don't count *Fantasia*, it would be *Saludos Amigos*, followed by *The Three Caballeros*.

Q **I hear many things about characters that to the big Disney fans are unnamed, though others give them names. It's been confirmed here [on the Ask Dave Web site] that Adam is not the name of the Beast, and Ferdinand is not the name of the Prince in *Snow White and the Seven Dwarfs*. Lately I've been hearing that Scar's name, from *The Lion King*, was Taka before he got the scar on his face. Can you confirm or deny this rumor? Dana, New York, NY**

A —That name appeared in a 1994 book series about *The Lion King*, and is not recognized as an official name of the character.

Q **Was *Snow White and the Seven Dwarfs* Walt Disney's *first* option to make an animated movie, or were there other options? Avi, Irvine, CA**

A —As early as 1932, Walt Disney was considering *Alice in Wonderland* and *Bambi* for features; in fact *Alice* would have been partially live action and partially animated, and Mary Pickford was anxious to play the role. But Walt settled on *Snow White* as his first feature in 1933.

Q **Were there any songs from the movie *Frozen* that were cut from the movie? Avi, Irvine, CA**

A —Yes, there were some songs cut; demos of some of them are available on the two-disc CD containing the *Frozen* sound track. Some of the song titles include "We Know Better," "More Than Just the Spare," "You're You," and "Life's Too Short."

Q **Was there or is there a way to get the *Three Caballeros* sound track? I want to find a recording of "Bahia" from the movie but don't know if it was ever released. Rebecca, Santa Maria, CA**

A —The first recording of music from *The Three Caballeros* was released on 78-rpm records in 1944 by Decca; that record was never rereleased in LP or CD format. Disney's own recording, released in 1959, was produced by Louis Oliveira in Brazil. But the sound track is unavailable separate from the film.

Q **I have had this photo of a *Sleeping Beauty* background scene for many years, and it's my favorite early Disney film. I have always wondered who painted the original scene of the castle battlements. In the credits at the end of the film, there are ten artists listed. I would like to know if it's possible to find out the name of the artist. Mark, Los Angeles, CA**

A —It is not usually possible to determine which particular artist did which background for a film. The primary styling of the film was done by Eyvind Earle, and other artists, including Art

Riley, Thelma Witmer, Frank Armitage, Walt Peregoy, Al Dempster, Dick Anthony, and Ralph Hulett, who contributed backgrounds in his style.

Q **One of my all-time favorite Disney movies, *The Adventures of Ichabod and Mr. Toad*, has been announced to be released on Blu-ray. Mr. Toad is one of my favorite characters, and it makes me crazy like the Toad Hall owner that I cannot find any information on the making of this movie anywhere! Could you share some interesting facts about the movie most Disney fans would not know? Thanks, and I hope you have a kind of day where you can't open your mouth without a song jumping right out of it! Trent, Minneapolis, MN**

A —During the 1940s with the Disney Studio having financial problems due to the war, Walt decided to release a bunch of feature packages that were made up of two or more shorter films. *The Adventures of Ichabod and Mr. Toad* was the last of those package films. It juxtaposed a famous American tall tale, by Washington Irving, with an even better-known British tale by Kenneth Grahame. Bing Crosby and Basil Rathbone were hired to narrate the two segments. The film took more than two years to complete and, at sixty-eight minutes, is still one of the shorter Disney animated features.

Q **I have seen several "complete" lists of Disney films floating around online (including the one on this D23 site), and none of them ever mention *Aladdin and the King of Thieves* or *Return of Jafar*. Is there a reason for this? Courtney, Muncie, IN**

A —The published lists of Disney films normally include only theatrical releases; the two films you cited were produced for video release.

Q I was wondering if there was anywhere to find a list of when films went into production. I am doing some research on *The Black Cauldron* and its correlation to historical events occurring at the time. I am looking to understand "the why" behind when stories were told. Thanks again for all that you do! Kaitlyn, Orlando, FL

A —Animation began on *The Black Cauldron* in 1981, but story work had begun years earlier, in 1973.

Q When did Disney's Animation Studios start on *Frozen*? Jessica, Flagler Beach, FL

A —Early concepts for an animated film based on Hans Christian Andersen's *The Snow Queen* date back to the 1930s, even before *Snow White and the Seven Dwarfs* was finished. The project was shelved until the 1990s, with a number of different story ideas proposed over the next decade. But none were viable. Finally, a script was approved and the *Frozen* film was announced in 2011.

ANIMATED
SHORTS

Q **I was wondering if the father-and-son team of wolves in old Pluto cartoons such as *Camp Dog* and *Pests of the West* have names. What's the history behind these characters? Allyson, Rowlett, TX**

A —They are actually coyotes. We simply called them Bent-Tail (because of his characteristically bent tail) and Bent-Tail Junior. Bent-Tail had made his debut in *The Legend of Coyote Rock* in 1945 (his son was not featured in that one); the two of them were together first in *Sheep Dog* (1949). *Camp Dog* and *Pests of the West* were their only other appearances.

Q **When did Disney regain the rights to Oswald the Lucky Rabbit after losing them to Charles Mintz? Roy, Portland, OR**

A —It wasn't until 2006 that Disney regained the rights, after losing them seventy-eight years earlier. Disney CEO Robert Iger arranged a deal with NBC Universal, which then owned the rights, trading them ESPN and ABC sportscaster Al Michaels in return. The deal relates to the rights to the character and to the Oswald cartoons made by Walt Disney from 1927 to 1928, but not to the later cartoons, which were made by Walter Lantz.

Q **What happened to the thirteen lost Oswald the Lucky Rabbit cartoons? Reece, Durham, NY**

A —Like many films from the silent era, no one cared about them, so they were left to deteriorate and then be discarded. In some cases, they were destroyed to extract the silver content from the film stock. Sometimes films thought to be lost turn up in unexpected places, such as movie theater basements or foreign film archives, so we continue to harbor the hope that more of the Oswalds will eventually be found.

Q I have heard that the first Oswald cartoon made, *Poor Papa*, has been found. Is that true? If yes, then have any of the other twelve missing 'toons been found? Ryan, Annapolis, MD

A —*Poor Papa* 16 mm prints came up for auction in 2013, and Disney acquired that title. The most recent discovery has been *Empty Socks*, found in Norway. At the present time, Disney is missing three Laugh-O-grams, twenty-one Alice Comedies, and six Oswalds.

Q Has Disney ever allowed their cartoon shorts to be shown with non-Disney movies? Steven, Houston, TX

A —Yes, in the days when short cartoons were normal fare in movie theaters, Disney cartoons would often be shown when other companies' features were on the bill.

Q I know Huey, Dewey, and Louie have a mother named Dumbella, but I heard somewhere that her husband is Daisy Duck's brother. Is this true? Catherine, Las Vegas, NV

A —We never created a husband for Dumbella in the cartoons. In fact, she never appears either; just a postcard written by her to her "brother" Donald Duck in *Donald's Nephews*.

Q Why does Donald Duck wear a towel around his waist, and yet he doesn't wear pants? Pamela, Anaheim, CA

A —Probably just because it fit the particular story the animators were trying to tell in a cartoon. It may be simply used to indicate modesty or embarrassment, or to show that the character is coming out of a bath.

Q In *Donald Duck and the Gorilla*, the radio broadcasts end with "That is all. Breckinridge." I've heard that this is a standard way for police broadcasts in the 1930s and 1940s to end, and that Breckinridge would be the dispatcher's name. Any idea where this name came from, or was it just random? This question has been bugging people for years. John, Verona, PA

A —We assume that the Breckinridge name was selected simply because it sounded funny (apologies to all you out there named Breckinridge). According to one writer, the gag was a takeoff on an old radio show, *Calling All Cars*, which was broadcast in Los Angeles for eight years. The show used a real-life officer, Jesse Rosenquist, as the "opening police radio" voice to set the scene for each week's crime. He would sign off by saying, "That is all. Rosenquist."

Q I know that Fauntleroy is Donald Duck's middle name, but do any of the other characters in the fab five (Mickey, Minnie, Goofy, and Pluto) have middle names? I also was wondering if there has ever been a book published that details the families of the characters and their backstories? Rachel, Littleton, CO

A —No, the other characters have not been given middle names. The most comprehensive book on the history of the characters is John Grant's *Encyclopedia of Walt Disney's Animated Characters*. Perhaps your local library might have it.

Q I am a Minnie Mouse fan and am curious about how and when Figaro the cat became associated with her. I believe he made his debut as Geppetto's cat in *Pinocchio*. Was he always Minnie's cat, and is Figaro her official pet? Breanne, Sacramento, CA

A —The first cartoon in which Figaro appeared with Minnie Mouse was *First Aiders* (1944), four years after his debut in *Pinocchio*. He would continue to appear with Minnie and Pluto in a few more cartoons, ending with *Pluto's Sweater* (1949). So, at least during that five-year period, he could be deemed Minnie's pet.

Q I came across a picture of a sandman. He is holding a bag and sprinkling something over a child. It is marked DISNEY, and is in soft pastel colors. Can you tell me more about this? I have never seen it before. It looks like part of it is brushed. Maybe it used to glow in the dark? Julie, Windham, ME

A —The luminous picture shows characters from the Disney Silly Symphony *Lullaby Land*. It was made and distributed by Henry A. Citroen of New York City, who was licensed by Disney from 1944 to 1946.

Q How many movies and shorts and shows has Roger Rabbit been in? I have a cel of Roger Rabbit from an unknown film; can you help me? John, Montgomery, NY

A —Besides his appearance in *Who Framed Roger Rabbit*, the title character also appeared in three short cartoons—*Roller Coaster Rabbit*, *Tummy Trouble*, and *Trail Mix-up*.

Q Hi, Dave. I'm looking for a short movie that was produced about a guy that was pinstriping a car and was interrupted by a phone call while in the middle of doing such detailed work. While he is talking on the phone, the two pinstripes take off racing. When he comes back from the call, the car is totally striped out. It is from the late 1960s. I remember seeing this as a kid and would love to see it again to show my kids. Neil, Calgary, AB, Canada

A —You may be recalling the title sequence for *Dad, Can I Borrow the Car?* (1970). It was last released on videocassette in the 1990s; it has not been released on DVD.

Q Have Mickey and Oswald ever been in a comic or a cartoon together? Cora, Navarre, FL

A —Not in a comic book, comic strip, or animated cartoon, but they are together in the *Epic Mickey* video game.

Q What is the original name of Oswald the Lucky Rabbit's feline girlfriend? Is it Sadie or Ostensia? Michael, Vancouver, BC, Canada

A —In *Epic Mickey*, it is Ortensia. Fanny and Sadie were names used for girlfriends during the production of the Oswald cartoons in the 1920s

Q Hi, I recently received from Disney Vacation Club/D23 a limited-edition lithograph reproduction of Walt Disney's Mickey Mouse *Hawaiian Holiday* poster. I was wondering if Walt was the one who did the original art for this particular piece. Thanks! James, Van Nuys, CA

A —No, Walt Disney was not doing any artwork by that time.

Q I was fortunate to see a short animated film by Salvador Dalí at the Hollywood Bowl with the orchestra playing the especially commissioned music. I understand this was commissioned by Disney for the original *Fantasia*, but not included in the final work. It is a masterpiece. Is there any hope it might be released on DVD?

A —The short, *Destino*, was based on concepts and designs by Salvador Dalí, who came to work at the Disney Studio on the project six years after *Fantasia*. *Destino* was released in 2010 as bonus material on the Blu-ray set of *Fantasia* and *Fantasia/2000*.

Q I recently re-watched *Goliath II* and I always wondered how a perfectionist like Walt Disney released an animated short with so many sketch lines left on some of the characters. Why didn't he have the clean-up artists fix the drawings before they were printed on film? Laura, Casper, WY

A —*Goliath II* (1960) was the first time that the Xerox process was used to transfer the animators' drawings to cels. Since the animators' original pencil drawings were used, rather than drawings with inked lines, the cels had a more sketch-like quality than usual. You see a similar look in *One Hundred and One Dalmatians* from 1961.

Q Before she died, I had the pleasure of meeting Disney Legend Ginny Tyler. Among her many Disney credits she was supposed to have voiced Witch Hazel in the 1952 Donald Duck cartoon *Trick or Treat*. Many sources on the 'net credit June Foray. Is this true? Which witch is which? Boo! And Happy Halloween! John, Seattle, WA

A —Witch Hazel was indeed voiced by June Foray in the 1951 *Trick or Treat* cartoon. Ginny Tyler did the voice for a *Trick or Treat* record album years later, which she also narrated.

Q Hey, Dave! I'm a huge fan of your work. Your encyclopedic knowledge of Disney is amazing! Anyway, I just wanted to know the name of the music that plays in the beginning of the 1932 classic *Flowers and Trees*. I must have searched for an hour without results. Please answer; if anyone can do it, it's you! Thanks in advance! Mohammad, Sacramento, CA

A —That piece is "Kamennoi Ostrow" by Anton Rubenstein. Other works included in the cartoon are Schubert's song "Der Erlkönig," Mendelssohn's *Ruy Blas* Overture and Wedding March, Rossini's

William Tell Overture, Margis's "Valse Bleue," and Chopin's Funeral March.

Q **I have heard that Donald's birthday is on a Friday the thirteenth. Is that true? I know Disney keeps track of the "births" of Mickey, Minnie, and Donald. Kobe, Delaware, OH**

A —The birthday we use for Donald Duck is June 9, 1934, the release date of *The Wise Little Hen*, his first film appearance. His birthday was sometimes celebrated on Friday the thirteenth in comics and storybooks.

Q **If you could, do you think you could put together a list of everyone who has ever voiced Mickey Mouse? Possibly a list of how long they voiced him to go with it? Krista, Hillsboro, OR**

A —There have, up to now, been four people who were the official voices of Mickey Mouse. Walt Disney was the first (1928–1946), followed by Jim Macdonald (1946–1977), Wayne Allwine (1977–2009), and Bret Iwan (2009–present). Chris Diamantopoulos began doing the Mickey Mouse voice for the new series of Mickey cartoons that debuted in 2013. Additionally, composer Carl Stalling did Mickey's voice in a few early cartoons when Walt was busy.

Q **Hi, Dave. In watching the 1950 short *Crazy Over Daisy*, one can't help noticing that the tune used in the feature (credited to Oliver Wallace) is the same music that would eventually become "Meet Me Down on Main Street." Did Oliver Wallace write the lyrics for "Meet Me Down on Main Street" as well? Was it written specifically for The Mellomen to record, or was it written for a special on Disneyland? Craig, Avondale, AZ**

A —Oliver Wallace wrote both the words and music for "Daisy Mae" to be used in the *Crazy Over Daisy* cartoon in 1949.

He then adapted his song in 1956 as "Meet Me Down on Main Street," with lyrics by Tom Adair. The latter may have first been used, without lyrics, in the Main Street, U.S.A. segment of the 1956 People and Places series film *Disneyland, U.S.A.* and on the "Walt Disney Takes You to Disneyland" record album (WDL 4004, released May 1, 1956). The Mellomen's recording came out in 1957 as WDL 3012.

Q **What is your favorite piece of Mickey memorabilia from the Archives, and what is your favorite Mickey cartoon? Alex, Muskegon, MI**

A —My favorites are the Mickey Mouse items that aren't normally saved as collectibles. Such items are quite scarce, but often not expensive when they do turn up: things from the 1930s like a Mickey Mouse toothbrush, underwear, sweatshirt, matching scarf and purse. My favorite Mickey Mouse cartoon is *Brave Little Tailor*.

Q **When did Mickey lose his tail, and when did they bring it back? John, Conway, SC**

A —He has always had it; it is just inside his pants. ☺

Q **Hi, Dave! Let me begin by saying thank you for sharing your wealth of knowledge with the world so we can all feel like a part of the Disney magic. I do have a question for you. I'm a hopeless romantic and huge Disney fan, and a friend told me once that the actors who play the voices of Mickey and Minnie are married in real life. Is this true? I know many voice actors have portrayed Mickey and Minnie, so I'm not certain if that was ever the case. Krystina, Avondale, AZ**

A —Russi Taylor, who did the voice of Minnie Mouse, and Wayne Allwine, who did the voice of Mickey Mouse, were indeed married.

Wayne sadly passed away in 2009, the year after he was named a Disney Legend. Russi is still active in voice recording.

Q **Considering that the Oscars are right around the corner, I have an appropriate question. I have searched and searched but can't locate the source of the following: I read somewhere that Disney was so upset at the Academy for refusing to consider *Fantasia* worthy of a Best Picture nomination that he pulled all his cartoon shorts from consideration for the 1940 Best Cartoon awards. Indeed, not a single Disney cartoon was nominated for 1940—this after Disney dominated the category the first eight years prior and, skipping 1940, in the two years following, winning every time. So what he did would explain the total absence of his work from the 1940 awards. Is this true? Michael, Irvine, CA**

A —I cannot imagine that this is true. By 1940, Academy voters had become accustomed to Walt Disney winning the Best Cartoon Oscar each year, so perhaps they felt others should be given a chance. In fact, by then, many of the other studios had improved their cartoon-making capabilities so much that they had some films that would give Walt Disney some definite competition. The winner at the 1941 ceremony was former Disney animator Rudolf Ising's *The Milky Way* for MGM. No animated feature was nominated for Best Picture until *Beauty and the Beast* (1991).

Q **Dear Dave, thank you for all the time you take answering so many questions sent in by your fans and Disney devotees. I wanted to ask you about the song "Minnie's Yoo Hoo." It is my favorite of all Disney songs. It's the song that plays on my alarm clock, and it's my ringtone, yet I have no idea of its history. Can you please enlighten me on the story behind this clever and whimsical little tune? I'd be most grateful. Leo, Santa Maria, CA**

A —"Minnie's Yoo Hoo" was actually the first Disney song to be published, in 1930, as sheet music—both for general sale and as a giveaway at Mickey Mouse Club events in theaters (it was the club's official theme song). The authors listed were Walt Disney and Carl Stalling. The song originally appeared in the Mickey Mouse cartoon *Mickey's Follies* (1929).

Q **Hi, Dave! I was just wondering, who were the artists who first drew Donald Duck and Goofy? Obviously, Walt was the first to draw Mickey. Sometimes I feel he's credited as coming up with Donald and Goofy because they're "Disney characters," but was he really the one who came up with and the first to draw them for their first cartoons, *The Wise Little Hen* and *Goofy and Wilbur*? Dean, Nampa, ID**

A —The names of the first artists to draw the characters are usually unknown, but we can tell you the first animators to actually animate them in their debut cartoons: it was Tom Palmer doing Goofy in *Mickey's Revue*, and Art Babbitt and Dick Huemer doing Donald in *The Wise Little Hen*. Mickey was first drawn by animator Ub Iwerks, with Walt's collaboration.

Q ***The Art of Walt Disney* by Christopher Finch says that Mickey Mouse's last black-and-white cartoon was *Mickey's Service Station*. But other sources say that *Mickey's Man Friday* was the last one. Which one is the last Mickey Mouse cartoon? Christopher, Lolo, MT**

A —The last one in black and white was actually *Mickey's Kangaroo*. Even though *The Band Concert*, the first one in color, was released in early 1935, two black-and-white ones followed it: *Mickey's Service Station* and *Mickey's Kangaroo*. From then on, all the rest of the Mickey cartoons were in color.

Q Hi, Dave! One of my all-time favorite classic Disney shorts is *Johnnie Fedora and Alice Bluebonnet*. After watching the short time and time again and purchasing some merchandise with his likeness on it, I've noticed some inconsistencies with the spelling of Johnnie's name. The title before the short spells his name JOHNNIE. Any merchandise I've come across, including the Little Golden Book and sheet music from the song, spells his name JOHNNY. I am a Disney purist (I like to make sure I know everything about my favorite characters), which is why I'm wondering what the proper spelling of Johnnie's name is. Thank you, Dave, for helping me solve a mystery! Emily, Celebration, FL

A —Both spellings were used at the time the film was released in 1946. Usually we go by the spelling on the film itself, but in this case, the other spelling was a lot more common. As you noticed, the JOHNNY spelling was used on contemporary merchandise and sheet music. So, there really is no definitive answer to your question; Disney used both spellings.

Q I was going through a box of home movies and found a Disney short called *Jealous Mickey*. The box has HOME MOVIES and MADE IN HOLLYWOOD CALIF. on it. It has ENTERPRISES INC. on the end flap. The number is 1525-A. This must have been purchased by my parents when I was little. It appears to be in great condition and was probably only run once or twice. Is there a market for this? Barbara, Camarillo, CA

A —When shortened home-movie versions of the Disney cartoons were released in 8 mm and 16 mm versions, they were often given different titles by Hollywood Film Enterprises, the licensee. Thus, *Jealous Mickey* is their title for a part of *Mickey's Rival* (1936). They had cut the cartoon into several parts and gave each part a new title. These films have little or no value, since the cartoons have been released in their complete form on video and DVD.

Q **Dave, I have two 6 mm or 9 mm films. They are titled *Mickey's Rough Ride* (1609-z) and *Donald Duck in Ducking Out* (1552- A). The boxes also say WALT DISNEY'S MICKEY MOUSE & SILLY SYMPHONY CARTOONS. My question is: what can you tell me about these two films? I can't seem to find anything about them on the Internet. Thank you. Kathy, Schenectady, NY**

A —These are segments of Disney theatrical cartoons released for home use in 8 mm by Hollywood Film Enterprises. They would cut a cartoon into multiple parts, then put their own title on each part. I can tell you at least that *Donald Duck in Ducking Out* is from *Orphan's Picnic* (1936). These short films have little or no value, as the old film would be brittle, and all of the full cartoons have been released on VHS or DVD.

Q **The animal origins of most Disney characters are pretty clear: Mickey is a Mouse, Goofy and Pluto are dogs, Donald is a duck, and so forth. But what exactly is/was Peg Leg Pete? Randy, Lithia Springs, GA**

A —John Grant, in his authoritative *Encyclopedia of Walt Disney's Animated Characters*, refers to him as a "rogue cat." According to Grant, this differs from his earliest appearances in the Alice Comedies before his look was changed, where he was "most probably a tail-less rat or oversized mouse."

Q **I was wondering if you could tell me, who is the singer on the Silly Symphony *Goddess of Spring*? We thought it sounded like Dick Powell. Collin, Okotoks, AB, Canada**

A —The voice credits we have for that film are Kenny Baker (singing narrator) and Tudor Williams (Pluto).

Q When is Pluto's birthday? I heard people saying it is September 5, 1930. It also says on some Web sites that it is September 5, 1930. And other Web sites say it is August 18, 1930. I was wondering which one is correct. I have also seen conflicting birthdays for Goofy and Daisy Duck. Can you also tell me the correct dates for them? David, Seminole, FL

A —The Walt Disney Company only celebrates "birthdays" for Mickey Mouse, Minnie Mouse, and Donald Duck. The other characters do not have official birthdays.

Q I was watching the Silly Symphony called *The Cookie Carnival* and I was wondering if Mae Questel was the voice of the Cookie Queen. The only voice from the short I managed to get was Pinto Colvig as the Gingerbread hobo. Abby, Agoura Hills, CA

A —We do not have a record as to who voiced the Cookie Queen, but supposedly Mae Questel did not do any Disney voices until Betty Boop in *Who Framed Roger Rabbit*.

Q We have a small Disney character that is white, has an elongated head with a big red nose, and has red polka dots over the rest of his body. The bottom of the character reads DISNEY 1999. Can you tell me the character's name, as we have looked all over the Internet and can't come up with one? Frank, Levittown, PA

A —That is most likely a Woozle, a character that first appeared in the Academy Award-winning *Winnie the Pooh and the Blustery Day*.

Q I'm sixty-five years old and a member of Disney Vacation Club for ten years. I have had many happy vacations with my adult children and especially grandchildren. When I was a kid, I would watch Disney cartoons along with any other Disney show on TV. I was fascinated with how Donald Duck talked. After some practice, I could talk like him also. When there aren't any adults around, I have fun talking like Donald Duck to my grandchildren. Could you give me some information on how this voice came about, and who was the person with the original voice? Dennis, Lansing, IL

A —Walt Disney heard a recording of Clarence Nash doing a voice which he felt would be perfect for Donald Duck, so he was hired to do the voice for Donald's debut in *The Wise Little Hen*. Nash continued doing the voice for many years; he passed away in 1985, shortly after helping the character celebrate his fiftieth anniversary.

Q I know that Walt was the first voice of Mickey Mouse, but did he also provide Mickey's whistling of the tune "Steamboat Bill" in *Steamboat Willie*? Mike, Atlanta, GA

A —We do not know for sure, but I would guess that he did not. He recorded the film in New York City and hired sound effects artists there to perform on the sound track. Mickey had no dialogue in that cartoon. Occasionally in the first year or so, Carl Stalling, who composed most of the musical scores for the cartoons, stepped in to do Mickey's voice.

Q Dave, it's great to see more and more of the older Disney animated shorts available online. I was watching *Ye Olden Days*, which was in black and white, and assumed that the original drawings must have been done in color, but were filmed in black and white. Is that the way it was done, and if so, are the color

drawings/cels preserved such that you could go back and film them in color if there was a desire to? Jim, Cape Canaveral, FL

A —The early Disney shorts were not animated in color; usually only the movie poster was in color. It was only in the days after the Disney cartoons began being released in color (1932 for the Silly Symphonies, 1935 for the Mickey Mouse cartoons) that the artwork (backgrounds and cels) were prepared in color.

Q I know that Goofy was originally called Dippy Dawg before he went from being a minor player in Mickey Mouse shorts to a star in his own right. My question is, how did the change come about? Why did they decide to rename him? How exactly did he go from being an obnoxious laugh in the crowd to sharing the spotlight with Mickey and Donald? Templeton, Louisville, KY

A —After the first appearance of Dippy Dawg in *Mickey's Revue* (1932), the staff at the Disney Studio felt that he would be a good character to develop. As he was used in more cartoons, he became popular with movie audiences. It was not just the character that was notable but the distinctive laugh and voice provided by Pinto Colvig. I do not recall ever seeing anything on the reasons for the name change, which evolved from Dippy Dawg, to Dippy the Goof, and then Goofy.

Q I have a question about the Disney short *How to Swim* from 1942, starring Goofy. About a minute into the cartoon, the narrator states that "with the aid of a piano stool, we learn the basic strokes of swimming." Right after that, he goes on: "breathing is of first importance." At that moment there is an absolutely lovely melody in the background. Was it from a known work, or was it just a creation for the cartoon? If you do find out, please reply. Stephane, Sterling, VA

A —The composer of the score for *How to Swim* was Disney staffer Paul Smith. Besides his own compositions, he also used three other pieces of music in the cartoon. While I am not sure where these appeared in the film, they were (in this order): "Rocked in the Cradle of the Deep" (by Joseph Knight), "Over the Waves" (by Juventino Rosas), and "Frankie and Johnnie" (traditional).

Q **Hi, Dave! I have a question about the Alice Comedies. How exactly did they pull off having a live-action girl in a land of animated characters, because green screens, I think, didn't exist way back then. Lauren, Austin, TX**

A —There is a device called an optical printer that allows filmmakers to combine two separate pieces of film (for the Alice Comedies, it would be one featuring the live-action girl, and one the animated film) onto a single new strip of film by the use of two projectors and a camera. The Alice live-action bits were filmed in front of a plain white sheet, which would then "disappear" when combined with the pencil drawings (also done on white paper).

Q **Dear Dave, I am in my mid-fifties. I remember seeing Disney "educational" films when I was in middle and high school. One had Goofy in it and it was about safe driving. Another one taught about colors and the mixing of colors. I've been trying to locate the color one for years because I teach art in my classroom. Do you know anything about these films? Thank you. Lori, Woodland Hills, CA**

A —The Goofy cartoon was *Motor Mania*. Ludwig Von Drake gave a comic lesson on color in the 1961 Disney TV show entitled *An Adventure in Color/Mathmagic Land*, in which the color segment was combined with *Donald in Mathmagic Land*. The TV show, which was Disney's first to be aired in color, was released on videocassette in 1986, but it is no longer available for sale. *Donald in Mathmagic Land* is still available.

Q **I have always heard that Mickey's birthday was November 18, but I have a vinyl album in my collection that celebrates Mickey, and on the back it reads that *Steamboat Willie*'s big debut was actually September 19, 1928, at the Colony Theater in New York. The album was made by the Disney company. So why am I hearing two different dates? Thank you, Dave! Alex, Fortville, IN**

A —Mickey's birthday has always been determined to be the date that *Steamboat Willie* opened at the Colony Theater. We have a program from that theater in the Archives from the actual date. It was November 18, 1928, not September 19. Before I discovered that date in the early 1970s, a number of dates had been used as "Mickey's birthday," usually a convenient Saturday in the fall when they could get a lot of kids into a theater for a Mickey birthday party.

Q **Years ago, I remember Donald's nephews being in a scout troop. They were led by a scout leader (human cartoon) who was rather rotund and had a small upper body and head, and had a strange voice. He did wear a campaign hat and some sort of uniform. What was his name, and where can I locate a photo/statue of him? I have seen a set of statues at Walt Disney World with Daisy and the nephews dressed as Junior Woodchucks. Mike, Byron, IL**

A —The chubby guy was Ranger J. Audubon Woodlore, who appeared in a number of cartoons. John Grant's book *Encyclopedia of Walt Disney's Animated Characters* is a good source for photos and information about the Disney characters.

Q I've always loved the character Ranger Woodlore, but I don't know who, specifically, created him. Was it just one person, or were several involved, and what were their names, if you know? Joseph, Nevada City, CA

A —The creation of a Disney character can only rarely be attributed to a single person. Ranger J. Audubon Woodlore first appeared in the cartoon *Grin and Bear It* (1954). The character would have come out of meetings held with the director, Jack Hannah, and the writers, David Detiege and Al Bertino. The artist who animated the ranger's scenes in that cartoon was Bill Justice.

Q Growing up, Donald movies were my favorite, and I watched them all the time! I have memories of a collection of Donald shorts with a "scary" theme. The only one I can really recall from that movie though is one with Donald and a gorilla that escaped from the zoo. What is it? Please help! Jaime, Albuquerque, NM

A —The title of that cartoon is actually *Donald Duck and the Gorilla*, originally released in 1944.

Q Hello, Dave. On a recent visit to Tokyo Disney Resort, I noted a large amount of merchandise, from figurines to jigsaw puzzles, relating to the marriage of Mickey and Minnie. Is there an official backstory behind this particular form of merchandise that appears in Japan? Keith, Sydney, NSW, Australia

A —At least in the United States, Disney does not recognize that Mickey and Minnie are "married."

Q Why is the 2013 Mickey animated short called *Get a Horse!*? What's the inspiration behind it? Avi, Irvine, CA

A —For an answer, I went to the director of the cartoon, Lauren MacMullan. Here is her reply: "As the Mickey short was being made, I decided I wanted a title that sounded decidedly unmodern—as if it was named in 1928, not 2013. 'Get a horse!' is actually a phrase from the early days of the auto. As cars started venturing out of the city into the country, the newfangled contraptions would spook farmers' horses, who had never seen anything like it and often reacted badly. But the cars themselves often broke down, or had tire troubles; and when this happened, the farmers would ride by and make fun of the drivers by yelling, 'Get a horse!' As the short has Mickey and Horace facing off against Pete and his car, I thought this would be a fine title."

Q When my father was a young boy, he delivered newspapers here in Yuma, Arizona. In the mid-1950s, he won a contest doing this, and first prize was a trip to a place called Disneyland in California. Is it possible there might be a photo or videos of this event? Mark, Yuma, AZ

A —Photos are usually not available of individual Disneyland contest winners. I also won a pass to Disneyland when I was a newspaper boy (for the Pasadena, California, *Star-News*) in the 1950s; there are no photos of my visit.

Q I first went to Disneyland in 1955. For the longest time I remember that the Autopia roadway did not have a central rail. When was this safety feature installed? Marc, Broken Arrow, OK

A —The center rail was added to the Autopia track in 1963.

Q Is the train station at Disneyland modeled after a real station, or is it a composite of train stations? George, San Diego, CA

A —It is a composite of many stations; most of the drawings of the station and the rest of Main Street, U.S.A. were by Imagineer Harper Goff, who grew up in Fort Collins, Colorado, and had fond memories of that historic town. Walt's childhood memories of Marceline, Missouri, also figured in the street's design.

Q Is the train station at Disneyland modeled after a real station? I thought I saw a plaque at the train station in or near Salt Lake City claiming it to be the inspiration for the Disneyland station. Thank you! George, San Diego, CA

A —The Disneyland Railroad Station was not based on any particular station. Disney Imagineers studied the designs of many stations from the turn of the century in coming up with a station that would match the rest of the architecture of Main Street, U.S.A. Main Street and its buildings derived from Walt Disney's memories of small-town life in Marceline, Missouri, but also the memories that the Main Street designer, Imagineer Harper Goff, had of his boyhood town of Fort Collins, Colorado.

Q **I wanted to ask you if Disneyland really has two or three levels? Because I always wondered how fast a Cast Member gets from one area to another with all the crowds. Brian, [No city provided], CA**

A —The Walt Disney World Magic Kingdom is on the second level, with the first level consisting of tunnels called Utilidors, storerooms, and offices. Disneyland has only one short tunnel, built primarily for use by entertainers at the Tomorrowland Terrace, though backstage areas practically surround the Park, making it possible for Cast Members to enter onstage near their work location.

Q **How many days before the official opening of Disneyland was the press opening? What was available to the press to see and do at that event? Kathy, Ellicott City, MD**

A —The Disneyland press opening was on July 17, 1955; the Park opened to the public the next day. There were twenty attractions open on July 17. A few others that were not quite ready (such as Casey Jr. Circus Train, Dumbo Flying Elephants, and Rocket to the Moon) opened within the next few weeks.

Q **At the end of a production season (I guess you could call it) of a parade, what happens to the floats? Clearly they're too large to fit into the archive area. Do they all get dismantled, and are some parts kept? Are they entirely destroyed, or do they get reused elsewhere? Cameron, New York, NY**

A —Many of the Disney Park floats get reused. Sometimes there are only a few changes in color or decor; other times only the drive chassis is saved and a new superstructure is constructed. One example of a float that has been preserved intact is the Castle in the Sky finale float seen in recent parades at Walt Disney World; that float first premiered in the early 1980s at Disneyland and has been used in most of the Walt Disney World parades ever since. For some new parades, completely new floats are designed, such as those that appeared in Mickey's Soundsational Parade at Disneyland.

Q I've noticed that in the Haunted Mansion, there is a small hole in the glass panel separating the Doom Buggies from the birthday party scene below—the hole is mostly obscured by a spider and web. I've heard numerous rumors on how the hole got there, from teenagers and BB guns to a foreign dignitary's guards. Where did the hole come from, and why was the glass not replaced? Christy, San Diego, CA

A —The story I have heard is that someone shot a BB through the huge plate glass window, and because they would have to take off the roof to replace a glass panel of that size, the Disneyland Maintenance crew simply painted a spider web around the hole to disguise it. It has been there for decades, almost back to the time when the attraction opened.

Q I was an employee of Disneyland in the 1980s. There used to be an alumni club with promotions and special Disney events for alumni employees. Is there anyone I can contact who would have information about this? It is not Disney style to forget those who helped the dreams come true! Tamra, Watertown, SD

A —Disneyland still has an active alumni club. Former Cast Members can join through their Web site at *www.disneylandalumni.org.*

Q **Which pirates were on the original murals inside the Pirates of the Caribbean ride queue? Who did Jack Sparrow and the others replace on the queue murals? Sheryl, Riverside, CA**

A —The caricatures on the interior walls are based on some of Imagineer Marc Davis's earliest renderings of the nautical personages Sir Francis Verney, Ned Low, Sir Henry Mainwaring, Anne Bonny and Mary Reed, and Captain Charles Gibbs. Captain Jack Sparrow and Captain Barbossa were added in 2006; these two were new and did not replace any previous art.

Q **Years ago, my wife and I both remember a ride that looked like flying saucers. From what I remember it was powered by air coming up from the ride's floor, and you would steer it with a stick in the center of the saucer. Do you know if this ride existed, when they built it, and when it was removed? Brian, Arcadia, CA**

A —The Flying Saucers attraction was in Tomorrowland at Disneyland from 1961 to 1966; it was removed because of overwhelming maintenance issues.

Q **I heard from a friend that years ago, for a few years, there used to be actual Cast Members within the Haunted Mansion as part of the attraction. Is any of this true? Tommy, Huntington Beach, CA**

A —At various times in the past, Disneyland did indeed experiment with having Cast Members inside the Haunted Mansion stationed at various locations (one was in a suit of armor) to scare guests.

Q I recently saw you on the D23's *Armchair Archivist* talking about when Japan sent Disney a prop so that the Park could have a Japanese ghost in the mansion. Do you know if this ghost does exist in any of the Haunted Mansions, and if so in what room? Sean, Tokyo, Japan

A —No, she is not in any of the Haunted Mansions; she is in a case in the Archives. Her name is O-Iwa, a representation of a ghost from perhaps the most famous Japanese ghost story of all time. She is so scary looking that many former Archives employees did not want to go near her.

Q Wasn't Disneyland called the Happiest Place on Earth? Manny, Anaheim, CA

A —Yes, Disneyland has been called the Happiest Place on Earth since its debut in the 1950s. A member of the Disneyland marketing team came up with the phrase.

Q Did Walt personally plant all the bonsai trees in the Storybook Land Canal Boats attraction? Joyce, Anthem, AZ

A —Walt Disney would not have personally planted any of the trees in the attraction; that would have been the job of his landscaping staff. Actually, the decision was made not to use bonsai trees, because they would have required constant care and were very expensive. Instead, the staff found dwarf pine trees in a "pygmy forest" near Mendocino, California. They were confined in their original containers to help retain their diminutive size and received periodic pruning and shearing.

Q I seem to remember back in the late 1970s as a kid that the Monorail went up to the Disneyland Hotel. Having never ridden it or stayed at the hotel, I didn't know for sure. I just remember seeing the hotel and Monorail station in front of it from the parking lot (now Disney California Adventure). Did the hotel or Monorail station move when Downtown Disney was built? Brett, Tijeras, NM

A —The Disneyland Monorail, which had opened in 1959, was extended to the Disneyland Hotel in 1961. Some of the original two-story buildings at the Disneyland Hotel, which fronted on West Street (now Disneyland Drive), including the Monorail station, were removed when Downtown Disney was built (2001), and a new Monorail station was built.

Q While walking through the French Quarter in Disneyland, I noticed there is a terrace with seating on the second floor of the building that sits between the Pirates of the Caribbean and the Jack Skellington shop. As I admired the detail of the iron grates that surround the deck, I noticed a brass *WD* and *RD* in the middle of two center panels. Could you tell me the significance of these initials? Leo, Santa Maria, CA

A —Those are the initials of Walt Disney and Roy O. Disney. When that area was originally built, it was meant to be an apartment for the Disney family, but that never happened. The balcony was part of the Disney Gallery for many years and later became part of the Dream Suite during the Year of a Million Dreams, which started in 2006.

Q Hi, Dave! My husband and I love discovering all of the personal touches around Disneyland that honor individuals who made Disney what it is today. Among other things, we have noticed Disney's family crest above the castle and a nod to his father, plus other animators and Imagineers on windows on Main Street, U.S.A. Are there any other hidden treasures around the Park that honor his wife, daughters, brothers, or any other family members? Crystal, Reseda, CA

A —Here are some: if you look above New Orleans Square, you will see *WD* and *RD* in the wrought iron of the balcony. The special parlor car on the train is named the Lilly Belle after Walt's wife, Lillian. There used to be a WILLARD P. BOUNDS BLACKSMITH AND U.S. MARSHAL sign in Frontierland, named for Lillian's father. There is also on display the chunk of a petrified tree that Walt gave Lillian for their wedding anniversary. And, of course, there is the bronze statue of Walt with Mickey in the center of the hub.

Q **I recently came across a photo in an envelope with a preprinted return address reading** FUN PHOTO GALLERY, DISNEYLAND ANAHEIM, CALIF. **The photo (probably a Polaroid) shows a group posing in a frame labeled** HONORED GUESTS. **I have never heard of this and am wondering where the "Gallery" was located, what is there now, and, if possible, how long it operated there. Thank you very much. Jennifer, Fremont, CA**

A —There was the Art Gallery and Photo Studio on Main Street, U.S.A. from 1955 to 1959. Beginning in 1957, the shop offered plywood cutout flats behind which you could pose. Then the operation moved to Tomorrowland, from 1959 to 1967; it was first known there as Photo Gallery, and then Fun Fotos. One paid $1 for a black-and-white Polaroid photo.

Q **The earliest picture of the Disneyland marquee that I have found is from August 1959, and the video footage from opening day does not show a marquee at Disneyland. Did Disneyland have a marquee prior to August 1959? Anakaren, Glendale, AZ**

A —That is a big unanswered question. We have not found any pictures of a Disneyland marquee or sign from the early years (1955–1958), so if anyone took a picture of one on a family trip, we would love to see it. We know that the original large marquee at Disneyland was constructed in 1958. It was forty-two feet high and had seven flags at the top, and read DISNEYLAND–PARK & HOTEL ENTRANCE. A message board was added in the mid-1960s, and the subtitle was replaced by THE HAPPIEST PLACE ON EARTH in the mid-1970s. That original marquee was replaced by a new, larger one, at sixty-seven feet high, in 1989. That marquee was removed in 1999 and replaced by an arch over the entry road.

Q **I recently watched the *Disneyland After Dark* DVD and loved the segment with Louie Armstrong, Kid Ory, and Johnny St. Cyr. I know that Johnny was a regular musician at the Park, but was Kid Ory? I've seen some handbills for shows he played in there, but was he a regular Disneyland Cast Member or just a guest musician from time to time? Ethan, New York, NY**

A —Famed jazz trombonist Edward "Kid" Ory (1886–1973) started performing at Disneyland with Johnny St. Cyr and his Young Men from New Orleans in the September 30, 1961, Dixieland at Disneyland show. That was the show filmed for *Disneyland After Dark*, which aired on TV in 1962. Ory, while not a Cast Member, was fond of appearing at Disneyland and would return for a number of performances in subsequent years.

Q **My son, who is thirty-nine years old, is a yo-yo expert and has traveled the world as a demonstrator. I've always been involved with it too and have met *many* other *yo-yologists* in the world and produced a couple of contests in the past. I heard that Donald Duncan Jr. held a National Yo-Yo Contest at Disneyland in California in approximately 1962, 1963, and/or 1964. Can you find out if it is true? Jeannie, Stockton, CA**

A —I wasn't having any success in finding an answer until I discovered that the Duncan National Yo-Yo Contest was held not at Disneyland Park but across the street at the Disneyland Hotel, which was owned by Jack Wrather. The first contest, with Donald

Duncan Jr. in attendance, was held at the hotel in 1962, with a $5,000 prize. The next two contests, in 1963 and 1964, included spin-tops as well as yo-yos; 1964 was the last year that the contest was held.

Q

We know that Walt gathered inspiration for Disneyland from lots of sources. I understand that one of the parks he visited was Children's Fairyland in Oakland, California. Is there any record of Walt's visit to this park? It would be fabulous to see a photo! Is it true that he hired away the park's first director, Dorothy Manes, as an early employee of Disneyland? Chris, Alameda, CA

A

—No specific evidence turned up in the Walt Disney Archives that Walt or his designers ever visited Children's Fairyland, but he, along with Nat Winecoff and C. V. Wood, did fly to San Francisco on Disneyland business on April 17, 1954. It is possible that they headed over to Oakland. It is indeed true that Walt hired Dorothy Manes. She began working at Disneyland in the 1950s, in charge of youth activities, and continued in that position until 1972.

Q

I was wondering, who are the voices behind some of the attractions? For instance, I found out that Paul Frees is the voice behind the Haunted Mansion Ghost Host; I was wondering, who are all the others? Maybe it's a Disney secret they don't want to give away. I could understand that. I wouldn't want to give away the magic either. Debra, Manalapan, NJ

A

—Disney has generally not publicized the actors whose voices have been used in the Park attractions, though some of the Haunted Mansion actors have indeed become well known: Paul Frees, Thurl Ravenscroft, and Eleanor Audley, to name three.

Royal Dano provided the voice of Abraham Lincoln for attractions at the Walt Disney World Magic Kingdom and Disneyland Park. Pete Renaday has done voices for a number of attractions. You can find Web sites that list other Disney Park voices.

Q **The King Triton statue that used to sit in Ariel's Grotto over in the Disneyland Resort has been removed. Is it the same one that is now on top of The Little Mermaid—Ariel's Undersea Adventure? If not, where is it now? Cooper, Salt Lake City, UT**

A —Yes, that is the same King Triton statue.

Q **Is it true that there was once a walk-through miniature "ride" at Disneyland? I was told that it was so popular, people would stay and gaze at the dollhouses for so long that it had to be shut down, since it proved impractical. If there was such a thing, are there any photos? I'm a thirty-plus-year-old miniaturist, and I would love to see pictures! (I was told this info by a former Disneyland employee; I hope it's true!) Anonymous**

A —Walt Disney was a collector of miniatures, and he originally envisioned a series of settings in which miniatures could be displayed. He even built Granny's Cabin, a pioneer farm home filled with miniature furniture and other pieces, which was exhibited at a 1952 Festival of California Living show in Los Angeles. But he soon realized that capacity per hour would be extremely low for such an attraction, so one was never built at Disneyland.

Q **I, like many people, have always presumed that the animals on the Jungle Cruise and other such rides were Audio-Animatronics figures. I've heard a couple of different people now say they are not, because they act on a mechanical loop and are not technically Audio-Animatronics figures. What is the**

official Disney definition of Audio-Animatronics, and which types of attraction characters qualify? Thank you. Russell, Antelope, CA

A —The definition of Audio-Animatronics in a 1960s WED Enterprises press release states it is "a unique concept in entertainment which electronically combines and synchronizes voices, music, and sound effects with the movement of animated objects." Disney first used the name for animals in advertisements for Nature's Wonderland (1960), though the mechanical characters there did not really fit the definition. The first authentic Audio-Animatronics show was the Enchanted Tiki Room in 1963.

Q **I remember reading somewhere that you could purchase the Disney red rose to plant. Could you please tell me if the rose is still available to order or purchase? A Disney fan who wants to keep Disneyland memories alive at home. Phyllis, La Mesa, CA**

A —The Disneyland Rose (PP#15,114), the official rose of the Disneyland Resort, is an orange-pink floribunda rose. It was introduced for sale through Jackson & Perkins, and can be found through their Web site, and sometimes at local nurseries.

Q **This is a *Where is she now?* question. I was just watching the *Disneyland 10th Anniversary* DVD. In it, Julie Reihm, a Guest Jockey, was Disneyland Miss Tencennial. How did her life go? Tim, Anthem, AZ**

A —She is now Julie Reihm Casaletto, living with her husband in Virginia. She returned to college after her year as the first Disneyland Ambassador and never rejoined the Disneyland payroll, henceforth only returning to Disney for occasional special events. She was named a Disney Legend in 2015.

Q Could you please tell me the date that the Lovin' Spoonful played at Tomorrowland in the 1960s? Thank you. Kim, Sacramento, CA

A —The Lovin' Spoonful performed at Disneyland during Easter week beginning April 8, 1968. Also performing in Tomorrowland were the Cowsills, the Mustangs, and the Baja Marimba Band, along with several of Disneyland's regular performing groups, such as the Clara Ward Gospel Singers and the Young Men from New Orleans.

Q We recently stayed at the Disneyland Hotel for the first time in January 2012. It is now one of our favorite Disney hotels. What is the story behind Walt Disney not owning the property when the Park opened? When did Disney acquire the property? J.R., Richmond, VA

A —Walt Disney was hard pressed for cash in the 1950s, so he asked a friend of his, Jack Wrather, if he would build and operate a hotel on Disney property in Anaheim. Wrather did so, and the Disneyland Hotel, which opened several months after Disneyland Park in 1955, became one of the prime hotels in Orange County. Disney purchased the hotel from the Wrather Corporation in 1988. For more information, you might like to pick up Don Ballard's book, *Disneyland Hotel: The Early Years, 1954–1988*.

Q I am confused. How many different versions of Great Moments with Mr. Lincoln are there, and when/where did each appear? The LP of the show claims that it is the version "exactly" as it appeared at the 1964–1965 New York World's Fair. However, the version on the recent World's Fair CD set seems to be abbreviated in certain ways and different in others, and the version on the fiftieth anniversary of Disneyland CD set is even shorter. Then there is the shorter version that currently runs at Disneyland with the folk song in the middle. Was this always the version at the Park, or was it once the longer World's Fair version? (I didn't start frequenting the Park until 1983.) And finally, there is the notorious version with the stereophonic headphones. These are just the ones I know of. . . . Larry, Thousand Oaks, CA

A —The original version of the show that ran at the 1964–1965 New York World's Fair is the one that was brought to Disneyland, where it opened in July 1965. It was a duplicate Audio-Animatronics Lincoln, because the original one was still running at the fair. The show continued until it was replaced by The Walt Disney Story in 1973. It returned in 1975 as The Walt Disney Story Featuring Great Moments with Mr. Lincoln. A new Lincoln slide show and animation was added in 1984, and in 2001 the show was changed to focus on the Civil War, with Lincoln reciting the Gettysburg Address. The show closed from 2005 to 2009, for a Disneyland fiftieth-anniversary attraction, but when Lincoln returned, a shortened version of the original speech was featured.

Q I have several items from Club 33, and I was wondering about the Club 33 logo. Can you tell me who designed it and any background about how the design came about? Has it been the same design since the club opened? Thank you very much for continuing to answer our questions even in your retirement. Barry, Oceanside, CA

A —Jack Sayers, who first headed the work on the club, asked artist Rex Goode to work on the Club 33 logo, which was finalized in January 1967. It has remained pretty much the same through the years until the club's 2014 renovation and expansion, for which a new logo was introduced.

Q Hey, Dave! When I was a kid I used to go to the Monorail Café at the Disneyland Hotel. Or *near* the Disneyland Hotel. It's been many years. From what I read, the Monorail Café closed in 1999, but I was wondering what year it opened. Thanks. Joseph, Nevada City, CA

A —The fondly remembered Monorail Café opened in 1986, taking the place of an earlier restaurant called simply the Coffee Shop/ Coffee House. That earlier restaurant had opened in 1956.

Q I have two questions. The first is, today I was playing Kinect Disneyland and, this is going to sound kind of stupid, but I overheard one of the guests ask his father, "Goofy's a dog, right?" I couldn't help but wonder what Goofy really is. Is he a dog, or something else? My other question is, what was Sleeping Beauty Castle called before *Sleeping Beauty* was released? Seeing as the film *Sleeping Beauty* was released in 1959, and Disneyland was opened four years prior . . . Katy, Sherwood, OR

A —Goofy is portrayed as a human character with doglike features; his original name was Dippy Dawg. Sleeping Beauty Castle has always had that name, as the film was in production when the Park opened and Walt obviously wanted to promote his upcoming animated feature. (Before the Park was built, Walt did once mistakenly refer to the castle as Snow White's Castle on a TV show, but that was never its name.)

Q I have heard there is a tradition at the Disney Parks: when one ride is replaced with another, the Imagineers save something from the former ride somewhere in the new ride. This may not always be easily visible to guests. I have seen the Melvin, Buff, and Max from Country Bears in the Winnie the Pooh ride in Disneyland. How did this get started, and what is the most unusual item saved from one ride to the next? Is there any source, similar to Hidden Mickey books, that shares where these can be found? Thank you! Leslie, Newbury Park, CA

A —While this may not be an official tradition, some designers have wanted to honor the former attractions somewhere in the new ones. Besides the instances you cite, others at Disneyland have included: (1) parts of the town of Rainbow Ridge from the Mine Train Through Nature's Wonderland reused at Big Thunder Mountain Railroad; (2) the Mighty Microscope from Adventure Thru Inner Space in the Star Tours preshow film; (3) ride vehicles from past Tomorrowland attractions in the preshow for Rocket Rods; (4) a car from Midget Autopia along the Autopia track; and (5) the Gullywhumper of Mark Fink Keel Boats and a mine train from Mine Train Through Nature's Wonderland added as props along the Rivers of America. Walt Disney World has a number of such attraction tributes also.

Q Dave, there has been an ongoing conversation (argument really) with my friends and family in regards to what "lands" the Matterhorn Bobsleds and It's a Small World belong to in the Disneyland Resort. Is the Matterhorn part of Fantasyland? Or Tomorrowland? Or is it on the "borderline" between both lands as a "stand-alone" attraction? Same question about It's a Small World. Is it part of Fantasyland or Mickey's Toontown? Your answer could settle this long-held "discussion," as it comes up every year when we visit Disneyland for the new year. Leo, Santa Maria, CA

A —The Matterhorn Bobsleds are officially a part of Fantasyland, as is It's a Small World.

Q Do you know if the Walt Disney Archives, or perhaps some backstage area at Disneyland or Walt Disney World, has any recognizable parts of former Monorail generations? I read

somewhere that Bob Gurr has a Mark I Monorail red door. Robert, Kissimmee, FL

A —I went to former Imagineer Bob Gurr with your question. He responds that Walt Disney World had a display case with a front left door from a yellow Disneyland Mark I Monorail. Bob has a red panel from a Mark I; it is currently on display in Walt's barn at the Los Angeles Live Steamers area in Griffith Park, and previously had been shown at the Richard Nixon Presidential Library. Bob also has two panels from the Mark I blue Monorail.

Q **Have you ever been to Disneyland? If so, what's your favorite memory of your visit? Avi, Irvine, CA**

A —Since I grew up in Southern California, I have been to Disneyland many times over the past six decades. At first, my parents were reluctant to go, instead wanting to wait until all the attractions were finished and everything was running smoothly. Then I discovered that my grandmother had gone to Disneyland. Before I did! I was sure perturbed but was able to use that evidence to get my parents to take me. One of my favorite memories as a teenager was running into Walt Disney walking through the Park and getting to speak with him briefly.

Q **Did Disneyland ever have amusement rides called the Rocket Ride, Moon Orbit, and Space Wheel? They were Walt Disney Tomorrowland Space Toys made in the 1960s by Wen-Mac. If these did exist, are there any pictures or movies of the actual rides? Roy, Birdsboro, PA**

A —There were no attractions with those names. The Wen-Mac toys were simply meant to be reminiscent of the type of attractions in Tomorrowland.

Q In July 1975, when I was a teenager, my family and I drove to Disneyland from Red Deer, Alberta, Canada, and stayed at the Disneyland campground in our holiday trailer. I remember the campground as being very close to the Disneyland Hotel. This was a trip of a lifetime for our family! I have been back to Disneyland several times since then and I always wonder where the campground was. When was the campground closed and what is now standing on the land where it was located? Peggy, Calgary, AB, Canada

A —Disney's Vacationland campground was north of the Disneyland Hotel on West Street (now Disneyland Drive), in the place where the current Mickey & Friends Parking Structure is located. It was open from about 1971 to 1996.

Q When did Date Night at Disneyland return in the 1960s with Benny Goodman? Matthew, North Hollywood, CA

A —Goodman played at Disneyland on Memorial Day weekend (May 27–29) in 1961, then returned the next week (June 3) for the start of Date Night; he performed also on June 10 and 30, and July 1.

Q Someone told me that the Rancho del Zocalo restaurant in Frontierland was listed on the original sign over Frontierland. However, I've tried to research it and come up empty-handed. Can you explain the history, if any? Thanks! Jon, Laguna Hills, CA

A —Disneyland has had a restaurant featuring Mexican food almost from the beginning. The Casa de Fritos (sponsored by Fritos) opened in August 1955 in a site near the current River Belle Terrace, but in 1957 it moved to the present site. It was renamed Casa Mexicana in 1982 and closed in 1999

to make way for the completely redesigned Rancho del Zocalo.

Q **How many rides have remained at Disneyland ever since its opening, if there are any? Lexi, Orlando, FL**

A —Even though most have been revised and/or renamed, the only attractions still at Disneyland today that were there on opening day, July 17, 1955, are: King Arthur Carrousel, Peter Pan's Flight, Mad Tea Party, Snow White's Adventures, Mr. Toad's Wild Ride, Autopia, Santa Fe and Disneyland Railroad, Horse-drawn Streetcars, Main Street Cinema, Jungle Cruise, *Mark Twain* Riverboat, and Penny Arcade.

Q **I have noticed that Bo Peep was removed from Toy Story Midway Mania. Was this because of the fact that she no longer had a very major role in *Toy Story 3*? Jeremy, Los Angeles, CA**

A —Games in Toy Story Midway Mania were swapped out to incorporate new characters from *Toy Story 3*.

Q **Why was the Hatbox Ghost removed from the Haunted Mansion ride, and where is it now? Avi, Irvine, CA**

A —Supposedly the special effect never worked well enough. The original ghost's current location has never come to light, which means that most likely he was destroyed. There is a Web site about him: www.thehatboxghost.com. As part of the celebration of Disneyland's sixtieth anniversary in 2015, the Hatbox Ghost returned to the Haunted Mansion in an updated form.

Q **Back in the 1980s, Disneyland offered for purchase a lifetime pass for senior citizens: is this true? Donald, Huntington Beach, CA**

A —No, Disneyland has never offered a lifetime pass.

Q **I remember seeing Patti Page at Disneyland. I believe it was in Tomorrowland. I believe in was the late 1960s. Do you know the exact date or any details? Melissa, Yucaipa, CA**

A —We are aware of Patti Page visiting Disneyland on September 6, 1960, and again in the summer of 1968, when she was photographed with Goofy and Pluto. See *http://disneyparks. disney.go.com/blog/2013/01/remembering-singer-patti-pages-visit-to-disneyland-park/*.

Q **We have been enjoying your sharing of Disney knowledge for many years now and have a question we hope you can answer for us. There is a clock hanging in the walkway through Sleeping Beauty Castle at Disneyland that has stopped. Some have said the stopped time refers to the time Walt Disney passed away or the time of his Disneyland inauguration speech. Both ideas have been dismissed by Disney fans. Is there a special reference for the time on this beautiful timepiece? Thank you for helping us solve this mystery! Matthew and Cynthia, Damascus, MD**

A —There is plenty of discussion of this clock chandelier on the Internet. The clock doesn't seem to always be stopped at the same time, but recently it was around 12:23, and another time at 1:25, so two suggested rumors would be incorrect—that the time relates to the time of Walt's death (which was 9:30 a.m.) or to the time Walt gave his Disneyland dedication speech (which would have been mid- to late afternoon). The position of the clock's hands actually is just random; there is no significance to the time on which it has stopped. According to Walt Disney Imagineering, the clock was installed in a 1996 refurbishment, and has never worked since it was acquired.

Q   **In 1959, I was at Disney World and I got a colored-chalk hand drawing of Donald Duck by an artist, name of Roy. I would like to know if it could have been Roy E. Disney? Joe, Dixon, IL**

A   —No, Roy E. Disney was not an artist. In 1959, it would have been at Disneyland, not Walt Disney World. Roy was Roy Williams, better known as the Big Mooseketeer on the *Mickey Mouse Club* TV series. He enjoyed doing drawings for guests at Disneyland.

Q   **Hi, Dave! I was recently accepted to the Disney College Program at Disneyland. Is there anything special I should do while I'm there? Jonathan, Albany, NY**

A   —Congratulations on your acceptance into the program. The Disney College Program, at both Disneyland and Walt Disney World, is an excellent program for college students who want to learn more about The Walt Disney Company and how it operates. Take advantage of the seminars, lectures, and tours (some visit the Walt Disney Archives) that are offered, and if you are interested in an eventual Disney career, arrange some one-on-one informational interviews with company leaders in your field. Hopefully your time in the College Program will bring you much satisfaction.

Q   **There's a myth going around that Tom Sawyer Island is actually part of Missouri, because Walt Disney convinced the governor of Missouri to annex it, and that no snacks can be sold on the island due to that. I don't think this is true. What's the real story? Jonathan, Universal City, CA**

A   —The whole thing about Tom Sawyer Island being part of Missouri came from what was essentially a publicity stunt at the opening ceremonies in 1956. Phil Donnelly, the governor of Missouri, sent a tongue-in-cheek letter to Governor Goodwin Knight of California asking him "to take appropriate action which will cause the Tom Sawyer Island in Disneyland, Calif. to be deeded to the Sovereign State of Missouri, the only true and rightful possessor of any and all Tom Sawyer Islands in the world." Snacks were indeed sold on the island; as early as 1957, Nesbitt's operated a refreshment stand there, and there was a canteen in Fort Wilderness that sold hot dogs, cider, and candy.

Q **What year did the plaques (HERE TODAY . . .) above the Disneyland tunnel entrances go up? I was looking at some early 1955 photos and noticed the plaques weren't there. Bob, Thousand Oaks, CA**

A —We do not know the exact day the plaques were installed, but we have a memo in the Walt Disney Archives dated June 22, 1955, sent to Walt Disney for approval of the text, stating that they would be "ready for opening."

Q **What became of the Mary Blair murals that used to be in Tomorrowland at Disneyland? I cannot remember if they were tile or paint; were they simply painted over, or was some attempt made to preserve them in some way? Heather, Santa Clarita, CA**

A —The two tile murals were covered over in 1986 and 1997. According to Walt Disney Imagineering's Marty Sklar, "Mary Blair's murals were not damaged or painted on, but the decision was made for cost reasons to leave them in place—hidden treasures at Disneyland!"

Q **Back on Memorial Day weekend either in 1965 or 1966, as a teenager, a girlfriend and I saw "The Golden Horseshoe Revue." We went back after equipping ourselves and had a squirt gun fight with the man portraying Pecos Bill. He and the woman playing Sluefoot Sue were perplexed but played along.**

The piano player that day said it was the funniest thing he ever saw. I have wondered for years if those actors and piano player remember that. Thank you. Sue, Atascadero, CA

A —Unfortunately, the actors, Wally Boag and Betty Taylor, are no longer living. A number of different piano players were used through the years that the show was performed.

Q In Disney California Adventure, there is a statue, *Storytellers*, featuring Walt and Mickey. We're told that the statue, and in fact the entire Buena Vista Street, represents 1923, when Walt arrived in California. I'm wondering why Mickey is depicted, since he wasn't even conceived until that fateful train ride in 1928. Teri, Anaheim, CA

A —Very good question; it has been raised by many people. Perhaps Mickey is just there to depict Walt's dreams of what is to come. Hollywood certainly did not change very much between 1923 and 1928, when Mickey was created.

Q Good morning, Dave. In the line for Buzz Lightyear Astro Blasters at Disneyland, there are murals showing the ride vehicles. The "scores" shown on these vehicles look like dates. Can you tell us what they represent? Teri, Anaheim, CA

A —There was only one birthday put into a mural by the designers, but there is another tribute. The names of the designers are hidden on graphics as planet names in the attraction.

Q Watching some old *Mickey Mouse Club* footage of cartoonist Roy Williams, I noticed a striking similarity (especially in his profile shot) of him to figures used in the Pirates of the Caribbean attraction. Knowing that the Imagineers have used real-life models for some of the pirates (Sid Caesar comes to mind as one), do you know if Roy Williams's image was used as well, or is it just an amazing coincidence in looks? Any other information you can provide on real-life models for popular Disney Parks attractions? Kevin, Encino, CA

A —The pirates were all composites of people that Blaine Gibson and other Imagineers knew or saw on the street. They were constantly making note of particular noses, or chins, or ears, or hair that they felt they could use. In an interview with Scott Wolf on his Mouse Clubhouse Web site, Blaine said, "One of the cases where I did one based on a guy at Disney's, this particular guy wasn't working where I was working; he happened to be a man working outside. And it wasn't like I was knocking or trying to belittle a laborer because I was a laborer much of my early life, and you don't belittle laborers. It was because he had the most wonderful face that I'd ever seen. George Snowden was a sculptor that was on my team. He was older; he was the same age as Walt was. A wonderful guy. He said, 'Blaine, you'd better be careful with that one. It looks exactly like him.' Well, it was more exaggerated, but when you look at it you think, 'Yes, it looks like him,' but in a good, exaggerated character. But I didn't really change it because each one was costumed differently and he did turn out to be an interesting character."

Q How did X. Atencio come up with the title song "Grim Grinning Ghosts"? Avi, Irvine, CA

A —While X. Atencio did not consider himself a songwriter, Walt Disney was very pleased with the lighthearted lyrics he came up with for Pirates of the Caribbean. When work was progressing on the Haunted Mansion, X. felt that a simple song would lighten up the mood in that attraction also. So he wrote the lyrics for "Grim Grinning Ghosts"; the alternate title was "The Screaming Song." He never revealed how he came up with the song's title.

Veteran studio composer Buddy Baker wrote the music. Different arrangements of the song were used throughout the attraction. According to Jason Surrell in his book on the Haunted Mansion, "In order to make the Graveyard scene a true showstopper, X. and Buddy did everything they could to give those music cues an even more otherworldly quality, including detuning the instruments and recording the music backward and combining it all in the final mix."

Q   **A long time ago, I heard that the Haunted Mansion was to be a "walk-through" attraction. If so, why did Imagineering (WED) decide to use the Doom Buggies? Christopher, League City, TX**

A   —The Doom Buggies were used to create a constant flow of guests through the Haunted Mansion. It was felt that if guests were walking through the attraction, many would stop to look at effects, creating bottlenecks.

Q   **Dave, did Walt and the Disney company use a lot of the same voices for ride attractions at Disneyland in the early days? The narrator of the original Haunted Mansion sound track and the narrator of the Monsanto Adventure Thru Inner Space sound like one and the same. Keith, Port Orchard, WA**

A   —Yes, those two attractions both had the same narrator, Paul Frees. Walt Disney had some voice actors whom he especially liked, so he tended to pick them when he had a project that could use their talents.

Q   **There are so many great ideas that The Walt Disney Company comes up with that they shelve. Do they ever decide to do a project again after it's been decided not to do it? Lexi, Seattle, WA**

A   —No Disney project is forgotten completely; great ideas never really go away. For example, a DisneySea nautical-themed Park,

planned in the early 1990s for Long Beach, California, finally
came to fruition as Tokyo DisneySea in 2001.

Q

**Hi, Dave! What's going on with the Disney Galleria these days?
I have not been to Disneyland for almost a year now . . .
the last I heard the galleria had been closed and was being
redone (but I can't remember for what . . . must be the age
thing kicking in for me, LOL!). Anyway, I was wondering if the
galleria was reopened and if people could still go through it
and view the wonderful artwork. . . . Oh, and we used to be
able to purchase a variety of things at the gift store within the
galleria. I'm planning on visiting Disneyland next month and
would love to know the status of the wonderful galleria! Thank
you! Barbara, Citrus Heights, CA**

A

—You are probably referring to The Disney Gallery, which was
located above Pirates of the Caribbean since opening in 1987.
It closed twenty years later, and the Disney Dream Suite took
its place. However, a new Disney Gallery opened in the former
bank location on Main Street, U.S.A. in 2009 and later moved to
the Great Moments with Mr. Lincoln lobby; it features changing
exhibits of Disney art.

Q

**When I was young, my mom and dad took me to Disneyland,
and I just fell in love with it; I went many years for a long time.
Then I grew up and stopped going until I had kids. I told them
about the many rides I went on as a kid and remembered one
and sadly it is gone. Can you help me with the name so I can
show it to my kids if there is a picture? It was a ride where a
car went up a telescope and you got to see outer space on the
ride. On the outside, as you watched the cars go in the ride, it
looked like the cars were getting smaller as they passed in the
scope. Thanks in advance, Dave, for your help, and keep up
the good work. Terry, Colorado Springs, CO**

A —You are thinking of Adventure Thru Inner Space, sponsored by Monsanto, and located in Tomorrowland from 1967 to 1985. In the attraction, you were given the impression of being miniaturized and able to explore the inside of an atom.

Q **What were some of the original in-Park bands that performed live at Disneyland? Chelsea, Fullerton, CA**

A —In its early years, Disneyland did not have the atmosphere bands that are used today. In fact, in 1955 there was only the Disneyland Band and the small band in the Golden Horseshoe. The Firehouse Five Plus Two occasionally played, and there was a barbershop quartet and the Coke Corner pianist on Main Street, U.S.A. Guest bands from local high schools and colleges would perform for a day. It would be several years before other bands appeared on a regular basis: 1960 saw the Gonzalez Trio and the Yachtsmen Trio; Kay Bell and the Spacemen first performed in 1961; and the Elliott Bros. Band and the Young Men from New Orleans came in 1962.

Q **In the Enchanted Tiki Room's "Tiki, Tiki, Tiki Room" song, there is a line concerning a "Herr Schmidt" who is "follically challenged." What was the inspiration and who was the reference about when the lyric was penned? Adam, Skokie, IL**

A —While we do not know for sure, Wally Boag, the comedian at the Golden Horseshoe, wrote the script for the Enchanted Tiki Room, and he happened to be bald. One of the funniest parts of the Golden Horseshoe show was when Wally removed his toupee.

Q **Who came up with the idea of Disneyland Park's Fantasy Faire? Paul, Evanston, IL**

A —Tony Baxter and his team at Walt Disney Imagineering found that the prime Plaza Gardens area of Disneyland was underutilized and thought that it would make for a nice expansion to Fantasyland. Tony recruited Dutch ride designer Michel Den Dulk, formerly from Europa Park, to join Walt Disney Imagineering and become creative director of Fantasy Faire.

Q **What was the story of the idea of the busts in the Haunted Mansion that follow you when you walk by; I understand that the effect was discovered when Imagineers were working on Great Moments with Mr. Lincoln. Avi, Irvine, CA**

A —According to Jason Surrell, in his book on the Haunted Mansion, "The moving bust illusion was one of [Imagineer] Rolly Crump's so-called happy accidents. As part of their research and development for The Hall of Presidents [which had been going on since the late 1950s], the Imagineers had created a mold of Abraham Lincoln's face, an artificial life mask of sorts. One day Rolly and Yale [Gracey] happened to stroll past the backside of the face, and as they did so, realized that from the reverse angle it appeared as though Honest Abe's eyes were following their every move."

Q **Dave, I would like to find more information about Holidayland. My grandfather has a couple of pictures that show Disney artists with sketches of Holidayland; some even have Walt Disney in them. Mark, Irvine, CA**

A —Holidayland was a picnic area, operating from 1957 to 1961, under a circus tent outside the Disneyland berm. Companies could rent the area for company picnics; then the guests could enter Disneyland itself.

Q **I have really vague memories of some kind of temporary theme in Disneyland related to the Disney Afternoon. I think I remember these from when I was very young (I was born in**

1986). I looked online about these memories and only found a name: Disney Afternoon Avenue. But I don't know if it's all true. Once again, these are very vague memories of mine, and I could have just dreamed them for all I know. Know anything about this, Dave? Thanks! Joseph, Nevada City, CA

A —The only Disney Afternoon theme at Disneyland was indeed Disney Afternoon Avenue, for eight months in 1991. The area in front of It's a Small World was decorated with building fronts modeled after the ones in the Disney Afternoon TV shows, and costumed characters interacted with guests. The Fantasyland Autopia and Motor Boat Cruise were also themed to Disney Afternoon.

Q While waiting to ride Radiator Springs Racers, I was told by a Cast Member that the license plates on the ride vehicles represented some sort of background information on the Imagineers who worked on the ride. Is this true, and if so what is the relationship? Marc, Broken Arrow, OK

A —They are initials and birthdays of the Imagineers and Pixar animators who worked on the attraction. This is true also of the baby tractors in Mater's Junkyard Jamboree.

Q I have always loved Walt Disney's Enchanted Tiki Room at Disneyland, partly because of its history and the fact that it was the first full Audio-Animatronics show. At the time of the Tiki Room's opening in 1963, there was a full control room for the show located right underneath it (as seen on the *Disneyland 10th Anniversary* show). This control room looked to be very complex for its time. Since Audio-Animatronics technology has certainly advanced by leaps and bounds since the Tiki Room's opening, what is this control room used for today, if anything? Fred, Placentia, CA

A —The room is still used for its original purpose, which is to run the show, though the technology has indeed changed through the years.

Q Dave, Hank Jones told me I could reach you here, and that if anyone knew about these photos, you would. I am a twin who played Little Ricky on the *I Love Lucy* show (*www.mayermoos.org/LUCYSHOW.html*) from the third through fifth seasons. We were doing the part of Little Ricky during the grand opening of Disneyland, so my mom took us down, and I am told that there were some pictures and/or footage of one of us with Lucy and Desi taken in the Tea Cups. Joe, Portland, OR

A —Lucy and Desi are not on our list of celebrities who were at Disneyland on opening day, July 17, 1955. We know that Lucille Ball visited Disneyland on July 1-2, 1957; July 17, 1958 (Desi Arnaz was with her at least that time); August 12-13, 1959; April 12, 1960; and August 6-7, 1961. It would not be easy to look for a photograph without knowing which date.

Q I recently bought a pack of matches that says MEET ME AT DISNEYLAND for Casa de Fritos. Do you know what year it was made? Tricia, Hacienda Heights, CA

A —We do not have a specific date for that matchbook, though Frito Lay sponsored the Mexican restaurant at Disneyland from 1955 to 1982. I know the matchbook was available in the early 1960s.

Q In what year were E tickets last issued? My sister, who was born in 1973, says that she remembers them. Were they still around when she was a kid? Tiffany, Moreno Valley, CA

A —We stopped using the ticket books in 1982.

Q I purchased an Autopia poster, which I was told was handed out and signed by the artist the day Autopia reopened, I believe on June 25, 2000. I am unable to read the artist's signature. Can you help me with any history/background of who the artist was? The poster is huge and has pastel colors (lavenders) with a large orange/pink car in the lead. It has AUTOPIA across the top of the poster, TOMORROWLAND toward the bottom, with DISNEYLAND beneath TOMORROWLAND. Can you shed any light on who the artist is? I was at Disneyland yesterday and was told it was sold in the Gallery. Thank You! Beverly, Ramona, CA

A —Was the poster perhaps signed by Bob Gurr, the Imagineer who designed the Autopia cars? He usually signed his name "R. H. Gurr."

Q On a recent trip to Sedona, Arizona, many references were made about Walt Disney. Please clarify the stories. Walt had a house there and that is where Big Thunder Mountain came into being. Dave, Riverside, CA

A —Despite urban legends repeated in Sedona, Arizona, Walt Disney never owned a house there. Several Disney artists retired to Sedona, so that may have been the origin of the rumor. Many years after Walt Disney died, Big Thunder Mountain at Disneyland was conceived by Imagineer Tony Baxter, based on unique rock formations at Bryce Canyon National Park.

Q Unless I'm crazy, I remember Disneyland being closed on Mondays and Tuesdays in the 1970s. If this is true, when did Disneyland start staying open seven days a week? Michael, Cottage Grove, OR

A —Disneyland was closed on Mondays during the off-season from 1955 to 1957 and on Mondays and Tuesdays from 1958 to 1985.

The Park was on a seven-day schedule during the busiest parts of the year up to 1985, and regularly thereafter. Mondays and Tuesdays were the Park's slowest days, and having it closed then enabled maintenance workers to do their chores without intruding on the guest experience.

Q **Was the Alice in Wonderland ride found at Disneyland ever also at Magic Kingdom, at Walt Disney World, in the mid-1970s? If not, then I have a fanciful childhood memory! Lauraine, Woodbridge, VA**

A —Alice in Wonderland was an attraction that was unique to Disneyland. It never appeared in any of the other Disney Parks.

Q **Where can I find historic information on J. S. Hamel, Consulting Engineer, whose name is on one of the Windows (#62) on Main Street, U.S.A. in Disneyland? I understand he was a combination civil, electrical, and mechanical engineer, all rolled into one. Andrew, San Bernardino, CA**

A —Hamel was an engineer who did consulting work for Disneyland in the 1950s. He was a graduate of the University of Michigan, and worked with civic planner Robert Moses in New York for seven years. He started his own firm in New York in 1936, and among other projects was a consultant to the 1939 New York World's Fair on the layout of illumination, the electrical system, and various other facilities before starting a consulting firm in Burbank, California, in 1947. Hamel held a number of patents in connection with the development of certain lighting equipment and illumination systems. He wrote several articles in professional journals about his Disneyland work.

Q **Is it true there is a basketball court inside the Matterhorn? And if so, why? Cameron, St. George, UT**

A —There is no basketball court in the Matterhorn, though a basketball hoop was placed there so that the mountain climbers who used to appear on the mountain would have something to do during their breaks.

Q I'm doing a research project on the design, construction, and structure of Disneyland (in Anaheim). I was wondering if you knew how Main Street, U.S.A. and Sleeping Beauty Castle are constructed and what materials were used (wood, concrete, etc.). Are all of the castle blocks concrete blocks, or are they stone? And are the towers made of some sort of plaster or wood? Thank you! Kait, Goleta, CA

A —Sleeping Beauty Castle was built of lath and plaster, and sculptured concrete. The "stones" were sculpted, with larger ones at the bottom rising to smaller ones at the top, with the forced perspective making the castle seem taller than it really is. The Main Street, U.S.A. buildings were also wood-framed.

Q I know that Walt Disney asked Richard and Robert Sherman to write a song describing the Tiki Room. What I was wondering is, was the attraction already named the Tiki Room, or was it named that after the Sherman brothers' song? Janine, Garden Grove, CA

A —From checking the materials in the Walt Disney Archives, it appears that the name of the attraction came first—memos in the file use it at least as early as the fall of 1962. The name of the song is actually "The Tiki Tiki Tiki Room," copyrighted in 1963. The attraction opened in June 1963.

Q In the movie *Saving Mr. Banks*, when Walt and P. L. Travers were on the King Arthur Carrousel in Disneyland Park, I noticed the carousel was playing "Zip-A-Dee-Doo-Dah" (*Song of the South*)

and "A Dream Is a Wish Your Heart Makes" (*Cinderella*). I've been frequently visiting Disneyland since 2002, and the King Arthur Carrousel has always played "Once Upon a Dream" (*Sleeping Beauty*) until about a few years ago, when many different songs (including "Zip-A-Dee-Doo-Dah" and "A Dream Is a Wish Your Heart Makes") were added. When Walt was around, did the King Arthur Carrousel ever play other songs besides "Once Upon a Dream," or did the sound track for the carousel ever change since it officially opened, besides a few years ago? Stephie, Las Vegas, NV

A —In a 1955 Disneyland press release, the King Arthur Carrousel was described as featuring "gay calliope tunes." A 1969 issue of *Disney News* suggested that "The Skater's Waltz" was played on the calliope. At some point later, Disney music was added.

Q How many weeks and days did it take the construction workers or "Imagineers" to build Disneyland Park in Anaheim, California, from 1954 to 1955? Michael, Monterey Park, CA

A —There was no groundbreaking ceremony for Disneyland. Construction began on July 21, 1954, when the first trees were removed, and progressed right up until the opening of the Park on July 17, 1955. So, a few days less than a year.

Q Is there any significance to the people "buried" in the cemetery on Tom Sawyer Island in Disneyland Park? Sacajawea is obvious, but what of the others? Are there any credits to Disney colleagues? Jenny, Chaska, MN

A —I believe that most are made-up names, though I did notice W. PIERRE FEIGNOUX. Wally Feignoux was a Disney Legend who handled Disney film releases in Europe from 1936 until his death in 1981.

Q I was wondering at what time Disneyland closed to the public on the press preview day (July 17, 1955), because, as far as I know, the Park only opened its doors at 2:30 p.m. And that was for the people who had the silver tickets; but some people received green tickets to enter the Park only after the telecast at 5:30 p.m., and others with white tickets could only enter the Park at 6:00 p.m.! So if some people were invited to enter the Park as late as 6:00 p.m., to a brand-new park that they had never seen before, I guess that it had to stay open until late in the evening, because even if it did not have many attractions open on that day, people still needed many hours to explore it, especially on such a crowded day. So, do you know until what time the guests were allowed to stay in the Park on that day? Also, besides the silver, white, and green tickets that I've mentioned, were there press preview tickets in other colors? Thanks a lot for all the great information about Disney that you share with us! Marco, São Paulo, Brazil

A —On July 17, 1955, Disneyland announced to its invited guests a closing time of 8:00 p.m., so they could get the Park ready for the public opening the next day. Of course, they may have been unable to adhere to that. To prepare for the live TV special, all attractions closed at 4:00 p.m.; they would then reopen as each land was dedicated. For the remainder of the summer, Disneyland would be open from 10:00 a.m. to 10:00 p.m. The Walt Disney Archives has only the silver Invitational Press Preview ticket, but I have also seen the green and white ones.

Q Early photos of Disneyland's Main Street, U.S.A. show a shop along the east side called Ellen's Gifts. Who was Ellen? What did she sell? Was this her only location, or did Ellen have stores outside of Disneyland? Thank you in advance for your always-fascinating information. Kit, Santa Cruz, CA

A —Ellen's Gifts, also known as Ellen's Metal Gifts, opened with Disneyland in 1955, and closed in May 1957. Ellen was Ellen Wynegar, of South Laguna Beach, California, whose company, Wynegar Enterprises, operated the shop. We are unaware of any other businesses they ran. After the shop closed, Wonderland Music Co. used the space as an art gallery for a few years; then it was incorporated into the Hallmark shop in 1960.

Q **I was wondering what you could tell me about the Court of Angels [sic] inside New Orleans Square in Disneyland Park. Was it built to represent anything in particular? It's a rare place in the Parks, as not many people seem to know about it. Was this done on purpose? Dean, Orem, UT**

A —The Court des Anges, also known earlier as Le Grand Court, with its attractive staircase, balconies, and potted plants, was described by Walt Disney Imagineering in 1966 as a quiet place to get away from the hustle and bustle of New Orleans Square. They noted that the "intimate courtyards were lazy counterpoints to crowded markets." A plaque was mounted on the wall in the courtyard honoring Sally McWhirter, director of store operations at Disneyland, after her untimely death in 1997. The plaque reads MUSIQUE DES ANGES/MUSIC LESSONS/VOCAL INSTRUCTIONS/MME. SALLY MCWHIRTER/ INSTRUCTOR. (*Musique des Anges* means "Music of the Angels.") This was the equivalent of a window on Main Street, U.S.A.; Sally had been active in her church choir.

Q **In Great Moments with Mr. Lincoln, Walt says they did an exhausting research into Lincoln to get things such as his mannerisms. Obviously there's no film footage of Lincoln anywhere, so where did they get information on what Lincoln's mannerisms were? Avi, Irvine, CA**

A —Disney's Imagineers spent five months researching Lincoln's exact measurements and physical appearance. There was intensive study of many photos, paintings, and written descriptions, including passages from Mary Lincoln's diary.

Q I have few questions about Star Tours—The Adventures Continue at Disneyland. During the visit to Hoth, a rebel pilot appears on the TV monitor and (as a reference to the original attraction) says, "Star Tours, this is a restricted area. What are you doing here?" I am sure that the actor is Bill Rogers, better known as the voice of Disneyland. Is this correct? If so, how did he happen to get cast in the role? Also, during the visit to Naboo, a female pilot appears on the TV monitor and says, "Star Tours, follow us to the rebel hangar. You will be safe there." Who is this actress? Is she an employee of Walt Disney Imagineering or Industrial Light & Magic [ILM]? Thanks! Fred, Placentia, CA

A —I checked with Walt Disney Imagineering to get your answer. The rebel pilot is not Bill Rogers, but Rob Howe, and the Naboo squad leader is April Royster; neither of them works for Imagineering or ILM. Also, I'm told that Darren Criss, also of *Glee*, provided some miscellaneous voices.

Q Thank you for sharing the Disney Archives with us during the D23 tour. I was wondering why Billy Hill and the Hillbillies, who do the show in the Disneyland Golden Horseshoe, are not included in your *Disney A to Z* book. And how many shows have they done? Anonymous, Hanford, CA

A —I am pleased that you enjoyed visiting the Archives. For space reasons, I have been unable to include all musical groups in *Disney A to Z* over the years (though I included Billy Hill and the Hillbillies in the Golden Horseshoe Revue entry in the book's fourth edition, 2015). Billy Hill and the Hillbillies began appearing as atmosphere performers in Critter Country and Frontierland in May 1989. They then moved to the Golden Horseshoe on June 8, 1993, where they proudly noted their ten thousandth show in February 2003. After performing at the Big Thunder Ranch Jamboree, according to the Disney Parks Blog, they had their final show on January 6, 2014.

Q

Hi, Dave. Just something I was hoping to clarify. I was reading some of Wally Boag's writings, and it seems that he describes Walt's box at Disneyland's Golden Horseshoe as being on the lower level at stage left—so the lower-right box from the audience's point of view. On *disneyland.com*, they say that Walt's box was upstairs on the right. Which box was actually Walt's? Kenny, Vancouver, WA

A

—Since Wally Boag worked for decades in the Golden Horseshoe Revue, I would tend to agree with his recollections, that it was the lower box, stage left.

Q

Hey, Dave. Who are the paintings of at the Hollywood Tower Hotel? They sort of look like Sisi and Franz Jozef of Austria, but I couldn't figure out why those two would be in there. Thanks for the knowledge. Shad, Salt Lake City, UT

A

—The paintings are of Napoleon III and Princess Eugenia, and are attributed to German court painter Franz Winterhalter.

Q

My aunt played in a big band that traveled around the world in college. She had the opportunity to play at the WESTCOT idea unveiling ceremony. She has maps of what WESTCOT was supposed to look like, plus pins and pennants that say WESTCOT. I was just curious if you knew more about WESTCOT and how rare the items are. Also, I would like to say thank you, because I visited the Walt Disney Studios and met you. You signed a copy

of your amazing book for me; I was just too much in shock, so I forgot to ask you my question. ☺ Thanks. Sidney, Temecula, CA

A —WESTCOT Center was to be a West Coast version of EPCOT Center, with Spacestation Earth as its centerpiece, and a World Showcase. It was initially announced in March 1991, to be built where Disney California Adventure was eventually situated. Items related to WESTCOT would be curiosities, but probably would not have a lot of monetary value, since today few people remember the proposed park. The Park's announcement brochure recently sold on eBay for about $30.

Q I am trying to find out information on the hand-drawn watches they sold in the Parks. Do they still offer them? The time I was at Disney in 2005, they put a new band on and cleaned it for me. I was told that was one of the extras for buying the watch. The last two times I went, I could find no information on them. I was unable to even buy a new band that matched the one that came with it. Any help would be a big help. Thank you. Eric, Somerset, PA

A —I checked with former Imagineer Eddie Sotto, who proposed the artisan watch program at Disneyland; it began in 1994. The watches and related services are no longer offered, as the program ended in 2013. Many different artists were involved. A large batch of original artwork for the watches was recently acquired by the Walt Disney Archives.

Q What year did walk-around characters get introduced at Disneyland? Josh, Las Vegas, NV

A —The first costumed characters appeared in Disneyland on opening day in 1955. The costumes were borrowed from the Ice Capades, which used them in their show. Later, Disney animator Bill Justice would help the Park design its own costumes.

Q **Who wrote and composed the Space Mountain song "Here's to the Future and You"? Jason, Anaheim Hills, CA**

A —RCA's song, "Here's to the Future and You," from 1974, had words by X. Atencio and music by Buddy Baker. Atencio and Baker also partnered on songs for other memorable attractions, including Haunted Mansion and World of Motion.

Q **Hi, Dave. Since the remodeling of Club 33, there are many rumors and myths being circulated again. I was hoping you could help clear some of them up regarding the harpsichord (and artist who painted the top), phone booth (*The Happiest Millionaire?*), vulture, French lift, and any others that you feel could use clarification. Thank you! Karen, Mesa, AZ**

A —The Club 33 harpsichord is not an antique. The painting on the underside of the lid is by Disney Imagineer Collin Campbell. The phone booth was indeed a prop in *The Happiest Millionaire*, but the open elevator was simply a reconstruction based on early elevators. The vulture and other figures that were in the trophy room were Audio-Animatronics figures, and were meant to converse with the guests; the process was planned but never implemented.

Q **True or false: is there a Disney gold pass/golden pass/VIP pass? What is it really called and do you know the total of those given out? Thanks so much! P.S. You are awesome! Deborah, Santa Barbara, CA**

A —True. There is a Disney gold pass. It is given on an annual basis by Disney executives to Disney board members, leaders of companies that are Disney participants, and other VIPs. The number of gold passes, which began during Walt Disney's lifetime, has not been released, but there are not many of them.

Q Does Disneyland keep a record of how many trips the *Mark Twain* Riverboat has sailed around the Rivers of America since the Park first opened? Kevin, Tarzana, CA

A —It would be very difficult to make a count, because many factors would have to be taken into consideration: the number of trips per day, the fact that Disneyland was closed on Mondays off-season from 1955 to 1957 (and on Mondays and Tuesdays from 1958 to 1985), the various rehabs of the attraction, the days on which the *Mark Twain* was cycled with the *Columbia*, and weather closings of the Park and of the attraction. Perhaps someone will attempt an estimate someday.

Q I'm a staunch believer that Disney and railroading go together; there's no other way of putting it. It's a match made in heaven, you might say. So my question is, is it true that for the opening of the Grand Canyon Diorama in 1958, Walt had guests transported to Anaheim on an Atchison, Topeka & Santa Fe Railroad business car? And if so, which business car was used? David, Downey, CA

A —For the grand opening of the diorama on March 31, 1958, Disneyland made arrangements for media guests to be transported in "special railway cars" (no description given) from Union Station in downtown Los Angeles to Anaheim Station, and hence by Disneyland Main Street buses to the Park. The cars, attached to the *San Diegan*, left L.A. at 11:05 a.m. and the guests arrived at the Park by 11:25.

Q Robert Jerome Washo, aka Bud Washo, is a distant relative of mine. At one time his window on Main Street, U.S.A. was mistakenly changed to Robert Wisky. It has since been restored to the proper name at both Parks: Disneyland and Walt Disney World. I have been growing more curious about his involvement with the early formation of the two Parks. What information may you have in the Archives about him? I understand he was involved in a lot of the concrete and masonry work, the dinosaurs and animals at Disneyland, and maybe even as a buyer agent for much of the land assembled in Florida. Jason, Gilbert, AZ

A —Bud Washo (1923–1999) originally served in the staff (manufacture of interior and exterior ornamentation in fiberglass, etc.) and plaster shops at Fox, Columbia, Universal, and Paramount Studios. He joined Disneyland in 1954 as supervisor of the staff-and-plaster shop, and later moved to Walt Disney World to hold the same position. He was not involved in the purchase of the land in Florida.

Q Is it true that Walt Disney denied Alfred Hitchcock permission to film a movie in Disneyland because he was "disgusted" by *Psycho* (1960)? Or is that just a myth? Joseph, Nevada City, CA

A —I have never heard that story, and doubt that it is true. There were no motion pictures that used Disneyland as a setting until *40 Pounds of Trouble*, starring Tony Curtis, in 1962.

Q My grandma gave me an Autopia license that was my grandpa's from when he went as a kid. The license is yellow and is from when Richfield sponsored the ride. There is a partially stamped date on it, which appears to have said AUG 15, 1955 but isn't completely legible. If this is the correct date, it would have only been a month after Disneyland had opened that he would have visited there. There is also a staple mark in it. Would it have been stapled to something when passed out? Could you tell me more about this? How much is it worth? Were these passed out before the ride like they are now? Thank you for your time. Justin, Modesto, CA

A —I also still have my Autopia driver's license from my first visit to Disneyland in 1956. The license was blank; it was up to me to fill in the information on it (and include my thumb print). There was also another later version, which just had space for a signature. Since I cannot remember clearly back almost sixty years, I do not recall whether they were passed out before or after the ride. The stamped date or staple holes on your grandfather's probably indicate they were in a scrapbook or attached to other memories of that day at Disneyland. There have been some of the licenses up for sale on eBay, so you can check there on values.

Q **Is it true that most of the Matterhorn has chicken wire? Kyle, Upland, CA**

A —The Matterhorn Bobsleds does not really use chicken wire. The structure was framed in wood, then covered with metal lath, a mesh that will hold plaster, which was then sprayed on.

Q **When was the decision made to turn the Museum of the Weird into the classic attraction, the Haunted Mansion? Did Walt make the final choice before his passing? Paul, Apopka, FL**

A —Imagineer Rolly Crump worked on the Museum of the Weird around 1964 and 1965, when the Haunted Mansion was going to be a walk-through attraction. After Walt Disney's death in 1966, Crump's plans were shelved.

Q **I am interested in the evolution of the Disney Park tickets. From the basic one-Park, one-day tickets, all the way to the multiple-day, Park Hopper-plus, non-expiring tickets that you can purchase these days. Mara, Medway, MA**

A —The original tickets sold at the front gate of Disneyland in 1955 were simply admission tickets; there were separate ticket booths at each attraction where you had to purchase a ticket. Ticket books were introduced in the fall of 1955, with coupons for the different attractions. The ticket books were phased out at both Disneyland and Walt Disney World in 1982. The original admission tickets did not have an expiration date; they could still be used today. Park-hopping options were added to three-, four-, and six-day World passes at Walt Disney World in 1982 after Epcot opened, though the term *Park Hopper* was not used until 1994. The "Magic Your Way" ticket plan, which began in 2005, first included the Park-Hopper option for one-day tickets if the guest paid an additional fee.

LIVE-ACTION FILMS

Q Hi, Dave. Do you know what happened to the star box from the movie *Escape to Witch Mountain*, 1975? Hunter, McKinleyville, CA

A —Its present whereabouts is unknown. It never came to the Archives.

Q Hi, Dave. I am writing to enquire about the movie *Pollyanna*. My husband and I have just finished a complete renovation of the home where *Pollyanna* was filmed. We have been searching for any interesting information which Disney may have in the Archives on the film or house. I realize you are retired, so I would understand if you can't help, but perhaps you could refer me to someone who could help. Should you ever be in the Santa Rosa area and would like a tour of the home please e-mail and we can show you around. Jennifer, Santa Rosa, CA

A —Congratulations on owning such an impressive landmark in Santa Rosa. Mableton, as the house is known, was built in 1877 and was the residence of Mrs. Juilliard MacDonald when Disney used its exteriors for the filming of *Pollyanna*. The actual filming took place at the house from August 1 to August 7, 1959.

Q I'm researching my family history and remember my mother talking about a movie being filmed in and around Porterville, California, when I was a child. I recently found information that leads me to believe the movie my mother was talking about was *So Dear to My Heart*. It was filmed in 1948 and released in January 1949. I would like to find out more about the exact dates of filming and the exact locations in and around Porterville where filming took place. Or, if there is a book or any other sources I might look into, I would appreciate any and all information. Thank you for your time and kind response. Burt, Rancho Cordova, CA

A —*So Dear to My Heart* filmed at its Porterville location from June 4 to July 11, 1946. Scenes filmed there included the exteriors of the fictional Fulton Corners, with Hiram's shop, Grundy's store, and railroad station, plus a bee tree, swamp, meadows, and a road to Granny's farm. While in Porterville, the cast and crew stayed at the Mt. Whitney Hotel (Walt Disney as producer was one of those who stayed there), the Hotel Porterville, and the Crescent Auto Court. Additional filming was done on location in Indiana.

Q **My family and I used to *love* the movie *So Dear to my Heart*. We would really love to have it on DVD. Was it released on DVD? If so, where can we find it? Deena, Boulder, CO**

A —It was released on DVD as a Disney Movie Club Exclusive; there were also earlier VHS and laser disc releases. As of 2015, it is available on iTunes and Disney Movies Anywhere.

Q **I read that the live-action *Popeye* movie from 1980 was made by Paramount and Disney. What was Disney's involvement with the movie? Justin, Appling, GA**

A —Disney made an investment in the film's production costs, and handled foreign and nontheatrical 16 mm distribution. Another film, *Dragonslayer*, was produced the next year with the same arrangements.

Q **While watching *Mary Poppins* the other night, I had a question about the carousel horses. Were the four horses created for the scene, or were they real horses from a carousel? Also, were they kept and reused somewhere else? Thanks. Richard, Toronto, ON, Canada**

A —The horses were created for the film. Mary Poppins's horse is part of the collection of the Walt Disney Archives, and for years was on display in the lobby of The Great Movie Ride at Disney's Hollywood Studios at Walt Disney World, until it was removed for an Archives exhibit commemorating the film's fiftieth anniversary. Bert's horse was exhibited at a Planet Hollywood location for many years before being reacquired by Disney and displayed in the same Archives exhibit. We do not know the current whereabouts of the other horses.

Q **What *Mary Poppins* props/sets do you have in the Archives? Steven, Concord, NH**

A —The Walt Disney Archives has a collection of items, including Mary Poppins's hat and traveling costume, Jane's orange coat, alphabet blocks, the jack-in-the-box from the Banks' nursery, an Audio-Animatronics robin, and the carousel horse that was on display at The Great Movie Ride at Disney's Hollywood Studios in Walt Disney World for many years.

Q **I was wondering if you know what happened to the Tin Man costume and the house that was in Oz from *Return to Oz*. Thanks. Zach, Antioch, CA**

A —I do not know about the house, but we do have the Tin Man costume, along with Tik Tok and Jack Pumpkinhead, in the Walt Disney Archives, along with many costumes and hand props from the film.

Q **Do you have any idea how the Sherman brothers came up with the word *supercalifragilisticexpialidocious*? Melanie, Northfield, OH**

A —Richard Sherman said in an interview that it was "a word we sort of concocted from our childhood when we used to make up double-talk words." He also recalled that he and his brother brainstormed some words that could be part of it—"supercolossal" and "atrocious" helped lead the way.

Q **The 1982 Disney movie *Tron* is said to have been filmed in part at Lawrence Livermore National Laboratory in Livermore, California. Can you be more specific about the role the lab played, such as what scenes it appears in? Christopher, San Francisco, CA**

A —There were four days of filming at the Lawrence Livermore National Lab, three of the days the company was filming in an area described as "interior laser lab"; the other day was for "interior hallway, interior computer control room, and exterior ENCOM door."

Q **My earliest moviegoing memory is *Bedknobs and Broomsticks*. On the beautiful remastered DVD of the film, notation is made of the missing "Step in the Right Direction" scene. I believe they said that was only seen in the premiere of the film, and then it was cut. Although I was quite young, I have a rather clear memory of seeing that song performed in the film here in my Illinois hometown. Could that at all be possible, and lastly, have they had any success in finding that scene subsequent to the DVD release? Scott, Springfield, IL**

A —The song was cut from the film before release. It was in an early print I saw at the Disney Studio Theater in a screening for distribution executives when the decision was made that the film was too long. Unfortunately when cuts are made in a musical, songs are the first things to go. The song was on the sound track record album, so people often think they remember seeing it in the film when actually they only heard it on the record. The film of the missing song has never been found.

Q **Have there been any non-Disney movies filmed at the Walt Disney Studio in Burbank, California? Justin, Appling, GA**

A —I recall that some scenes from the 1992 *Chaplin* were shot at the Disney Studio. It was one of the last films to shoot on the Disney Studio's old business street.

Q There was a film short always shown with the Disney movie *Blackbeard's Ghost* in theaters in the 1970s. (My daughter and I saw the movies three times.) The short was about a girl named Suzy [*sic*] and a Saint Bernard and, if I remember correctly, about ski-rescue services. Please tell me the name of the short and if it's available anywhere. You'd make my daughter (and me) very happy. Fred, Chicago, IL

A —You are referring to the 1975 reissue of *Blackbeard's Ghost*. Disney also released that year a twenty-eight-minute featurette entitled *Fantasy on Skis*, which indeed featured Susie and a Saint Bernard. The film was a shortened version of a 1962 TV show. Neither version has been released on DVD.

Q What is Walt Disney's highest grossing film? Ethan, Agawam, MA

A —As of 2015, the Disney film that is currently highest on the list of movies from all studios, in fourth place, is Marvel's *The Avengers*. Next come *Avengers: Age of Ultron* in eighth and *Pirates of the Caribbean: Dead Man's Chest* in thirteenth place, followed by *The Lion King*, *Toy Story 3*, and *Iron Man 3*. If you adjust for inflation, *Snow White and the Seven Dwarfs* joins the top ten.

Q I am a high school International Baccalaureate (IB) student hoping to go into archiving and with a passion for Disney history. Recently I was asked to write a four-thousand-word essay on a topic of my choice and chose Disney film propaganda in World War II. While researching, I found a rumor that Winston Churchill arranged a private screening of *Victory Through Air*

Power for President Roosevelt at the Quebec Conference. Is this rumor true? This question has really been bothering me, as I cannot find any solid data about it. Kaitlyn, Phoenix, AZ

A —This story is supposedly true, as reported by Albert Lasker who was an advertising executive and big supporter and colleague of Major Alexander de Seversky, who wrote the book *Victory Through Air Power*.

Q I'm starting a collection on anything that has to do with *The Black Hole*. As a kid, I remember a *Black Hole* record that told the story of the movie. It's not the See, Hear, and Read storybook and record. This had the actual dialogue, sounds, and music from the movie. It was edited, obviously, and did not run nearly as long as the film, but it came right from the movie sound track. Thanks, Dave. Jason, Greenville, SC

A —*The Black Hole* sound track album was released as Buena Vista STER 5008 record in 1979—the first digitally recorded sound track.

Q A lot of people claim, without any sources, that the lemming section of *White Wilderness* was staged. Is there any evidence for this claim? David, St. Louis, MO

A —When the producer of *White Wilderness*, Jim Algar, was asked about this, he said the scene was a reenactment in a controlled situation. No lemmings were killed; they just fell a short distance.

Q I am a student researcher studying depictions of Chief Sitting Bull in film, and I'm very interested in any information the Disney Archives could provide about the Disney production *Tonka* (1958). Are there any production notes or other information that might help me to analyze this production? I would love to try to set up a research appointment if that's possible. Michael, Valencia, CA

A —The Walt Disney Archives is not open to researchers from outside the company. It has no story research files for *Tonka* (1958). The film had a screenplay by Lewis R. Foster and Lillie Hayward (who must have kept their own research files), based on the book *Comanche* by David Appel.

Q I am a huge fan and truly enjoy reading anything about Disney's history. I actually have a question regarding the filming of *The Absent-Minded Professor*. I have read a few things stating that the University of Nevada, Reno (or an area nearby) was used as a filming location. I was wondering if you had many specific details about this, I have not been able to find much. Thank you! Veronica, Reno, NV

A —The only college-related filming, other than interiors done at the Disney Studio, that I could find in the production materials was at Pomona College in California.

Q My family and I watched *The Ugly Dachshund*, and we all thought the set looked similar to that used for *The Brady Bunch* (both the house itself and the turf grass). Were the same sets used for both? Andrew, Nissequogue, NY

A —No, these were completely different sets. *The Ugly Dachshund* was filmed at the Disney Studio in Burbank, California, in 1965, with the back of the house and swimming pool on Stage 3. In fact the swimming pool was built in the same tank that had held the Nautilus in 20,000 *Leagues Under the Sea*. *The Brady Bunch* TV series, which had no connection to Disney, didn't begin airing until 1969. (For the exterior of the *Brady Bunch* house, the producers of that show used a home on Dilling Street in North Hollywood.)

Q Do you have any filming information on the *Snowball Express* movie? We are going to visit Crested Butte, Colorado, and would like to stop and see some buildings and areas they filmed at. Via the Internet, we see some of the buildings are still there. As for the hotel—did they actually build one or part of one, and do you know where they filmed the hotel and ski scenes? Any help would really make the trip fun. Thank you. Paul, Rochester, MN

A —The Archives' production records for *Snowball Express* do not give much detail of the filming in Crested Butte—just notations such as "bank," "garage," "gas station," etc. The hotel exterior was indeed a set built at the location. It included rooms built behind the false front where the crew could warm up between takes in the frigid weather. The ski area was about two miles from town, and filming was done at Washington Gulch, Keystone Slope, and "ski slope near fish hatchery." Most of the interiors were filmed at the Disney Studio in Burbank, California. One item of interest: during production, the name of the film was *Chateau Bon Vivant*.

Q Is *Johnny Tremain* star Hal Stalmaster still alive? I loved Johnny Tremain as a school boy. Thank you. Gerard, Rockland, MA

A —Hal Stalmaster, seventeen years old when *Johnny Tremain* was released in 1957, retired from acting in 1966. He is the younger brother of the actor and casting director Lynn Stalmaster. Hal, born in 1940, currently lives with his wife in Sherman Oaks, California.

Q I am a fan of the Disney films from the 1960s and 1970s. After watching The Love Bug series, I noticed that Dean Jones starred in *The Love Bug* and *Herbie Goes to Monte Carlo*, the third film in the series, but not in *Herbie Rides Again*. Was there any specific reason why Helen Hayes starred in *Herbie Rides Again* instead of Jones? Andrew, St. James, NY

A —Dean Jones once said in an interview that he didn't think the script was up to the quality of that of the first film. It is explained in the film, which starred Helen Hayes as Herbie's new owner, that Herbie's former owner, Jim Douglas (Dean Jones), had gone to Europe.

Q I'm really excited about the movie *Saving Mr. Banks*. Were there any people who worked with Disney during the production of *Mary Poppins* that contributed to making the movie as accurate as possible? Was Tom Hanks the first choice to play Walt Disney? Avi, Irvine, CA

A —Composer Richard Sherman consulted with the filmmakers. Director John Lee Hancock has said that they wanted an actor who could "become Walt Disney. Who would that be? There was only one person that all of us could think of—Tom."

Q I went to D23's 50 and Fabulous: *Babes in Toyland* screening and it was so neat and wonderful to see that movie again after many years. My question is, does the Archives have the costumes of the trees from the "Forest of No Return" scene, the toy-making machine that Grumio invented, and any of the toy soldiers? If not, where have they gone? Avi, Irvine, CA

A —I did rescue a collection of the toy soldiers from the film in searching through a Studio building attic over forty years ago. The Treasures of the Walt Disney Archives exhibit at the Ronald Reagan Presidential Library & Museum in 2012 included Tommy Sands/Tom Piper's wedding costume and Annette Funicello/ Mary Contrary's red velvet cape. The other items probably did not survive.

Q Where can you find the Muppets movie *The Rainbow Connection*? I have looked all over for it, but cannot find the movie. Patrick Marlton, NJ

A —If you are referring to the 1979 *Muppet Movie*, which introduced the song "The Rainbow Connection," it is available from Amazon and elsewhere.

Q I have been searching for the titles of the movies featuring wild animals and narrated as a story for each one. I can't seem to recall the titles, nor the narrator's name. They were often shown on *The Wonderful World of Disney* as I was growing up and they each followed one or more animals' adventures as they were growing up. To further clarify, they were not cartoon animals. I hope you can help me. Stan, West Haven, UT

A —You are thinking of Walt Disney's True-Life Adventure series. There were thirteen films made between 1948 and 1960, and eight of them won Oscars for Best Documentary. Some were featurettes and some were full-length features. Among the best-known titles were *The Living Desert, Beaver Valley, Seal Island, Water Birds,* and *The Vanishing Prairie.* The films were narrated by Disney producer Winston Hibler.

Q I was watching the sci-fi classic *Forbidden Planet* and was surprised to see in the opening credits The Walt Disney Company listed as a contributor to the making of the film. As *Forbidden Planet* was released in 1956, what branch of the Disney Studios worked on that classic film and what did they contribute? Leo, Santa Maria, CA

A —Since the Disney special effects department was top-notch and had won an Oscar for 20,000 *Leagues Under the Sea,* MGM requested the loan of Disney's special effects wizard, Joshua Meador, for their production. Meador created the animated Id monster and the process used to combine it with the live actors, as well as other visual effects for the film.

Q I was curious to know if any props or artifacts from my favorite Disney film *Something Wicked This Way Comes* survive in the Archives. Also, does anything remain from the former 20,000 Leagues Under the Sea attraction at Walt Disney World? Thank you so much for your patience and I look forward to a reply from you. Jordan, Salt Lake City, UT

A —The Archives does not have any props from the 20,000 Leagues Under the Sea attraction in Florida, but one of the Nautilus ride vehicles is submerged at Castaway Cay's Snorkeling Lagoon and Disney Cruise Line passengers can see it when they visit the island. We do have a carousel horse and a couple of casts of Jason Robards's face from *Something Wicked This Way Comes*. There are also matte paintings, carnival flyers, and lightning rods from the film.

Q A long time ago on *Vault Disney* I saw a movie about an old man trying to find some kids in a magical land. I'm not sure if they were his grandchildren or not, but I remember that everyone was little. I think the kids had been turned into little people as well. I remember seeing a lot of trees and grass and maybe flowers. I can't remember as much as I would like. I know it was in black and white, and I think I remember the old man in a car singing with his grandchildren. I would really like to know the name of this movie. I can't seem to find out anything anywhere. Shae, Texas City, TX

A —You may be thinking of *The Gnome-Mobile* (1967). Walter Brennan was the grandfather, and the two kids from *Mary Poppins*, Karen Dotrice and Matthew Garber, played his grandchildren. In the redwood forests of California, while riding in an old Rolls-Royce, they encountered a colony of gnomes that was living there. The movie was in color, but perhaps you saw it in black and white on TV.

Q Hello, Dave. With the newest Oz feature out, I'm interested in an older feature. I think it was *Return to Oz* (but my memory may be hazy) starring Annette Funicello. Was this film ever completed? I'm guessing it would have been around the time she made *Babes in Toyland*. Thank you. Barbara, Mountain Home, ID

A —*Return to Oz*, made by Disney in 1985, starred Fairuza Balk as Dorothy. When she was on the *Mickey Mouse Club*, three decades earlier, Annette Funicello performed in a segment on *The Fourth Anniversary Show*, one of the Disney TV shows from 1957, introducing an upcoming film to be called *The Rainbow Road to Oz*. That film was never made.

Q Why is *Trenchcoat* still not branded as a Disney film when it is tame in comparison to current Disney films like *The Avengers*, *Pirates of the Caribbean*, or *John Carter*, and has it ever seen DVD release? Andrew, Smyrna, GA

A —The film was released on VHS in 1983 and on DVD in 2012. It was released originally without the Disney name during a period before Disney had come up with its Touchstone label for more adult-themed fare. Normally, for later releases, changes are not made in how a film is labeled.

Q What was the first Disney movie, either live-action or animated, to be sold on DVD? Avi, Irvine, CA

A —The first day of release of a Disney movie on DVD was December 2, 1997, but there were eight films released that day, so it is impossible to designate one as being the first. The titles included *George of the Jungle*, *Phenomenon*, *Homeward Bound: The Incredible Journey*, *The Rock*, and *Tim Burton's The Nightmare Before Christmas*.

Q Is there a copy of the song "It Won't Be Long 'Til Christmas," from the movie *The Happiest Millionaire*, sung by Greer Garson and Fred MacMurray? The sound track, as well as *The Sherman Brothers Songbook*, have others singing this song. I just want the original song by the original actors. The song has so much heart; I hope there is a way to find the original. Rebecca, Chesapeake, VA

A —Greer Garson and Fred MacMurray sang the song on the sound track, but it was cut from the film before release. Neither Garson nor MacMurray were known as singers, but their rendition was charming. The footage was saved, and it is on the Restored Roadshow version, put out by Disney on DVD in 2003.

Q My husband and I are planning a trip to Vermont next year. We love the movie *Those Calloways*. We know that the movie was filmed in Vermont, and we would like to know where. We want to go during the changing of the leaves and would love to go to the same area where the movie was shot. Please let me know where and what month the movie was shot. Thank you. Jill, Cheyenne, WY

A —Disney sent a film crew to the Green Mountains range in Vermont from February 23, 1963, through March 10, 1963, to photograph the spectacular beauty of the winter snows. Studio technicians then re-created the area back in Burbank, California, building a small city with a town hall, school, library, shops and homes, a half-acre lake, a marsh with duck blind, and the Calloways' log cabin. To obtain exterior footage of the Vermont locations in fall foliage, the crew and cast returned to Vermont and filmed from September 29, 1963, to October 4, 1963. Many of the locations were near Jeffersonville and Cambridge. To match the Vermont footage back in Burbank, thousands of leaves had to be painted by hand.

Q In the middle 1980s, Walt Disney Productions partnered with Paramount Pictures to do a film. Some teasers prior to the film's release included bumper stickers with a black dragon displayed on a purple background with the words *Dragons Are Real.* I have not been able to find out what film this is for or any other information pertaining to this bumper sticker. Can you help? Thank you. Stephani, Rancho Cordova, CA

A —The film was called *Dragonslayer*. Paramount released it domestically in June 1981; Disney handled the international release. I always loved the dragon's distinctive name—Vermithrax Pejorative.

Q One of my favorite movies is *The Parent Trap* with Hayley Mills. In the movie as the twin Sharon, she switches places to go live as her twin sister, Susan, on their father's California ranch. Were the house and ranch real? I always thought they were so beautiful! It has to be real! Thank you for your time. Dina, Boise, ID

A —No, it was not a real house. The exterior was built at the Disney Golden Oak Ranch, and the interior utilized soundstages at the Disney Studio.

Q I just saw *Saving Mr. Banks*, and loved it. But one thing plagued my mind during the whole movie. How could there have been a Pooh stuffed bear in Ms. Travers's room when the rights to Pooh were only signed over in 1961? The Disney version of Pooh isn't released until after *Mary Poppins*. I have searched the Internet and cannot find a date when licensed Winnie the Pooh items were released for sale. Lori, Rochester, MI

A —Disney's first Winnie the Pooh film was *Winnie the Pooh and the Honey Tree* in 1966. There would not have been

Disney Pooh merchandise before that year. Our earliest Pooh merchandise was sold as an exclusive through Sears for several years.

Q **Who did the *Mary Poppins* concept art that was seen in *Saving Mr. Banks*, and did the Archives show the production team the originals? Did the Disney Archives have the tapes that were recording the creative sessions with P. L. Travers? Which parts of the Disney Studios were used and filmed for the movie? Avi, Irvine, CA**

A —The concept artwork reproduced for *Saving Mr. Banks* was originally created between 1960 and 1963. Included were costume sketches and set drawings done by Tony Walton in 1963, along with storyboard sketches and artwork done by a variety of artists throughout the film's development. The filmmakers did indeed check out the artwork. Some artwork was made especially for the 2013 film, including a drawing of the parrot-head umbrella. And, yes, those fascinating tapes, covering about six and half hours of the story meetings, are in the Walt Disney Archives. The filmmakers used the Studio's main entrance on Buena Vista Street, the door into Stage A, and made various shots around the exterior of the original Animation Building on Mickey Avenue, Dopey Drive, and Minnie Avenue.

Q **Whatever happened to the *Hyperion* airship models made by Peter Ellenshaw for the movie *Island at the Top of the World*? Darby, Torrance, CA**

A —The small model of the *Hyperion* (about five feet in length), used in some of the flying scenes, is part of the collection of the Walt Disney Archives. The gondola was built full-sized so the actors could be filmed in it; it was not retained.

Q I recently found out that an edited version of *The Three Caballeros* was paired up as a double-feature rerelease with the 1968 Dick Van Dyke vehicle *Never a Dull Moment* in the 1970s. I believe that there was also a double-feature rerelease of *One Hundred and One Dalmatians* and *Swiss Family Robinson* in the late 1960s, or at least one of those with another film from around that period. Do you know of many other double-feature rereleases Disney has done besides these and the 3-D screenings of the first two Toy Story movies before the third film came out? Bobo, Melbourne, FL

A —There have been a number of double-feature rereleases, such as *Dumbo/Saludos Amigos* (1949), *The Shaggy Dog/The Absent-Minded Professor* (1967), *The Living Desert/The Vanishing Prairie* (1971), *Dumbo/The Legend of Lobo* (1972), *One Hundred and One Dalmatians/Swiss Family Robinson* (1972) *Old Yeller/The Incredible Journey* (1974), *Treasure Island/Dr. Syn, Alias the Scarecrow* (1975), *Never a Dull Moment/The Three Caballeros* (1977), and *The Jungle Book/The Sign of Zorro* (1978). As you will notice, many of these were released in the 1970s, when the company was not making a lot of new movies. During the days when theaters regularly showed double features, Disney would often release a reissue as a companion to a new feature.

Q I recently saw *Saving Mr. Banks* in theaters, and I was wondering if there were any actual artifacts in the movie. Or were they based off of the artifacts? When I saw the movie, I noticed posters, pictures of his daughters, and models of characters. Aden, Leawood, KS

A —Almost everything was duplicated for the film; there were no original artifacts loaned from the Archives. New prints were made of posters and photographs. Some Oscars, however, were borrowed from a display at Disney's Hollywood Studios in Walt Disney World.

Q Hello, Dave. I've watched *Saving Mr. Banks* recently (it took a long time for this movie to be released in Brazil), and I was wondering if Walt ever took P. L. Travers to Disneyland and, if not, if she went to the Park at all. I've searched the Internet, but could not find a definite answer. Kind Regards. Marco, São Paulo, Brazil

A —Walt Disney did not take P. L. Travers to Disneyland, but Bill Dover, head of the Story Department at Disney, did, on Easter Sunday in 1961. They had access to Walt's electric car and his apartment over the Fire Station, and Ms. Travers reported that she enjoyed her visit very much. Dover was in charge of most of the arrangements for Ms. Travers when she visited the Disney Studio that year. He started with the Story Department in 1957, retired in 1973, and passed away in 1982.

Q I know that the 2012 version of *Frankenweenie* was made and filmed in Three Mills Studios in London, but I was wondering about the 1984 version of the Tim Burton film. I noticed it was filmed somewhere in California, but I don't know exactly where it was. Do you know where it was filmed? Amelia, Santa Monica, CA

A —The original *Frankenweenie* film had its residential location on Stratford Street in South Pasadena, California, but the remainder of the film was shot at the Disney Studio in Burbank.

Q Hi, Dave. Maybe this will not ring a bell at all . . . but when I was a child (1986–1988 sort of time line) I remember Disney Channel often repeating two movies that I don't have names for: 1) a girl that travels with her wolf . . . the setting was probably around 1920 to 1930 . . . the wolf "defends" her through her travels. . . . 2) I have a more murky memory of this one, but it's a girl that I believe moves to a town . . . once in her walks through the forest she finds an old cottage, and a lady is living there, who the people of the town think is a witch. The girl and the lady become close. The backdrop is more like a forest/ woods setting. Grateful if you have any idea as I'd love to watch them with my kids now. Lissa, Houston, TX

A —The first film you recall is *The Journey of Natty Gann* (1985), starring Meredith Salenger and John Cusack. The other film may be *The Watcher in the Woods* (1981) with Bette Davis playing the old woman/witch and Carroll Baker the girl.

MERCHANDISE
AND
COLLECTIBLES

Q My grandmother recently found some small Disney charms that her dad, a salesman, used to sell when she was a kid. Some of these still have the paper backing, saying that they were made by Delta (some of them say Delta and Clem). It also says that these are silver, but some of them are gold/gold-tone. Characters featured are Mickey, Minnie, Goofy, Daisy, Pluto, Donald (along with his nephews and the other two of the three caballeros), as well as many of the characters from *Pinocchio, Bambi*, and *Snow White and the Seven Dwarfs*. Also, some of these charms are on bracelets, have pins on the bottom, or are presented as earrings. What can you tell me about these? Additionally, can you convince my grandmother that they are actually worth something so she won't throw them out because they're "clutter"? Tori, Los Angeles, CA

A —Delta Jewelry and Casting Co. was licensed to make Disney charms from 1945 to 1948. They are uncommon and would no doubt be of interest to collectors.

Q I am a fan of Annette Funicello. I read that there was a doll made of Mary Contrary (Annette) when the Disney 1961 movie *Babes in Toyland* was released. Do you know anything about the doll? Who made this doll, and did it come with outfits from the movie? Donna, Rochester Hills, MI

A —There was a nineteen-inch Mary, Mary Quite Contrary doll made by Gund to tie in with the movie, but the doll bore no likeness to Annette Funicello. It was cotton stuffed, with black yarn hair, a red blouse, red gingham check skirt, white felt collar, white felt apron, and black felt shoes. It sold for $4.

Q I am searching for information concerning a spring-windup doll named Oswald, after the cartoon character of the 1920s. I understand he was before Mickey. Any information and possible value would be appreciated. Phillip, Des Moines, IA

A —There were only three Oswald the Lucky Rabbit merchandise items made during the period that Walt Disney was making the Oswald cartoons—a stencil set, a pin-back button, and a candy bar. We have only an example of the stencil set in the Walt Disney Archives. Other items would have been made later, during the period when Walter Lantz produced the Oswald cartoons. We do not have any information on them.

Q **I have acquired through an estate auction a Mickey Mouse Club Wrist-Ray. Is there any written info on this and any value? Jerry, Beaufort, SC**

A —The Mickey Mouse Club Wrist-Ray was a small plastic flashlight that you wore on your wrist like a wristwatch. It was made by Bantam-Lite of Hempstead, New York, between 1955 and 1959 and sold for 89¢. A color dial let you select a red, green, or white beam, and you could blink out codes or have a steady beam. We do not know current values.

Q **I have an old picture of "lily babies." I believe it is from the late 1930s or early 1940s. It actually glows in the dark and is in an eight-by-ten-inch frame. Does it have any value? Can you tell me anything about it? Stephanie, Lapeer, MI**

A —This sounds like one of a series of luminous pictures of Disney scenes produced by the Henry A. Citroen Company in New York City from 1944 to 1946. They are relatively common and do not have great collectible value.

Q **My boss has a tiny Mickey Mouse figure he displays in his office. He doesn't know anything about its origins. The words MICKEY MOUSE are clearly imprinted on the front; on the back it says MADE IN JAPAN. Mickey has a baseball mitt on one hand and holds a baseball in the other. Andrew, Canyon Country, CA**

A —The figurine your boss has is made of bisque, an unglazed ceramic. Many different versions of Mickey, Minnie, and other Disney characters were made of bisque in Japan in the 1930s and then imported into the United States by George Borgfeldt & Company of New York City. They were popular trinkets during the period.

Q Do you know what happened to the old "sets" used for the Disney View-Master reels? Films like *The Jungle Book*, *Peter Pan*, *Winnie the Pooh*, and *Robin Hood* all used something called "table art." They were actual miniature sets created for the shots as opposed to stills from the films. Any ideas? Kevin, Harper Woods, MI

A —The makers of the View-Master reels retained the sets; we do not know where they are now. The Walt Disney Archives does have one: View-Master presented the company with one featuring Mickey Mouse for Mickey's fiftieth birthday.

Q I'm curious about two items from the 1950s Davy Crockett craze. One is the Alamo, a fort made of tin, I think, with rubber soldiers; the other is a set of Davy Crockett, King of the Wild Frontier movie cards. There are two series of cards: one with orange backs and the other with green backs. On the faces of the cards are stills from the movie. Rich, Port Richey, FL

A —The Davy Crockett stockade and figures were made by Louis Marx and Co. from 1955 to 1956. There are two sets of Davy Crockett cards, produced at the same time, which came with Topps chewing gum. There are eighty in each set. The cards with green backs are a bit scarcer than those with orange ones.

Q I recently purchased two posters at an auction. Both posters were signed by the same person, but I can't fully read the signature. I can only tell that the first name is Milt. I was told that the individual was an artist for Disney. Is this information correct? **Tom, Greenwood, IN**

A —The man who signed your posters was Milt Neil, a Disney animator whose credits include *Fantasia, Dumbo, Saludos Amigos,* and *The Three Caballeros.* After World War II, Neil opened his own commercial studio. He is perhaps best known for creating the cartoon logo for Andersen's Pea Soup, familiar to anyone who travels Highway 101 through Buellton, California. Neil died in October 1997.

Q I have several charming old Mickey Mouse gum cards made by Gum, Inc., but I don't know anything about them. Do you have any information on these cards? **E.J., Delray Beach, FL**

A —Gum, Inc. issued a series of Mickey Mouse gum cards between 1933 and 1937. Two albums were produced for the first ninety-six cards; the cards could be arranged and pasted inside these albums, which were made of thick paper.

Q My husband was born in 1934. On his fourth or fifth birthday, he received a complete set of *Snow White and the Seven Dwarfs* dolls, which we still have. Do you know anything about the history of such a set? **Rosemary, Sarasota, FL**

A —*Snow White and the Seven Dwarfs* was released in December 1937. Several different companies made sets of plush dolls in 1937 and 1938 based on the film's main characters. Ideal Novelty and Toy Co., for example, made a set that retailed for $2. The Snow White doll had her name printed on her dress, and the Dwarfs could actually whistle. The Knickerbocker Toy Co. made a set in three sizes (retailing from $1 up). Richard G. Krueger, Inc. made sets in both velvet and a washable sharkskin material.

Q My wife's grandmother found an old *Sword in the Stone* game piece. The piece includes a "sword" that you pull out of the card to reveal a word. What can you tell me about this piece of Disneyana? David, Charlotte, NC

A —Famous Character Promotions, Inc. was licensed by Disney in 1963-1964 to promote the original release of *The Sword in the Stone* with this game. The promotion, held in supermarket chains all across the country, ran for ten weeks, beginning in early 1964. If you collected all four words in the movie's title, you won $100; some cards also had ONE DOLLAR on the blade, for a $1 prize. After collecting any five cards, you could redeem them for one of ten *Sword in the Stone* picture rings.

Q I have a $1 million bill from *The Happiest Millionaire*. The date printed on it is October 25, 1967. Was this a ticket for the premiere of the film? Brian, Red Lion, PA

A —This item was called a "special promotional herald." The Buena Vista Distribution Company made several versions of this bill to help theaters promote the release of the movie. One version is from the official premiere, which was in Hollywood on June 23, 1967. Yours was probably issued for a premiere elsewhere.

Q When did the first Disney pins make their debut, and how many pins have been made to date? I'm assuming the Walt Disney Archives has all of them. Laurel, Riverbank, CA

A —The very first known Disney cloisonné pin was made for the Mickey Mouse Club in 1930. In that year, Mickey Mouse Clubs operated out of movie theaters nationwide. While a few more pins were made in the 1930s and the ensuing decades, it was not until more than fifty years later that pin trading became popular, sparked by fans' interest in pins during the 1984 Olympic Games in Los Angeles. For the next two and a half decades, more and more Disney pins were released. Pin-trading stations were opened at Walt Disney World in October 1999 and at Disneyland in April 2000. The earliest cloisonné pin in the Walt Disney Archives is a Mickey Mouse Chums pin from 1936. Though we cannot claim that our collection is complete, I would estimate that we have more than fifteen thousand pins.

Q **I have a late-1920s Mickey Mouse hand puppet that belonged to my father. The little mouse has four fingers, and the ears and facial features are the same as those in early drawings of Mickey Mouse. Have you ever seen this puppet or a similar one? John, Ventura, CA**

A —You have a Steiff Mickey Mouse puppet; it was made in 1932. The German firm Margarete Steiff & Co. was first licensed by Disney in 1931 to make its popular Mickey Mouse plush dolls, which were imported into the United States for sale.

Q **I'd appreciate any information about two limited-edition lithographs with a unique history. I think they were produced for Mickey Mouse's twenty-fifth and fiftieth birthdays and are lithographs based on paintings by John Hench. I believe these paintings are housed in the Walt Disney Archives. The first one shows a large Mickey in what appears to be Walt's office, and the second depicts Mickey showing off what is obviously a concept sketch of EPCOT Center. Both lithographs are numbered and signed in pencil by John Hench. They hang in my office. Wayne, Orlando, FL**

A —Your John Hench prints were made in a limited edition of 750 around the time of Mickey Mouse's fiftieth anniversary in 1978. The back of each print was stamped with the Walt Disney Archives seal and initialed by me for purposes of authentication.

The two original paintings, as well as Hench paintings for Mickey's sixtieth, seventieth, and seventy-fifth anniversaries, along with one for the millennium, are part of the Walt Disney Archives' collection.

Q

When I was a kid in the early 1960s, I remember seeing a motorized toy Disney Monorail at FAO Schwarz. I really wanted one! Can you tell me anything about this toy? Dennis, Franklin, TN

A

—The Schuco Toy Company, Inc. of Germany produced a 1:90 scale model electric toy Disneyland Monorail that was sold widely in the United States beginning in 1962. The sets are quite scarce and expensive today, but occasionally they turn up at Disney fan conventions or antique toy sales, and on Internet auction sites.

Q

I have a vase that depicts two fairies making flowers bloom. On the bottom it says DESIGNED BY WALT DISNEY, COPYRIGHT 1940, VERNON KILNS, **and there is the number 123. Please tell me about it. John, Mount Nebo, PA**

A

—Vernon Kilns, a Southern California pottery company, made a series of vases based on scenes and characters from *Fantasia*. There were also hand-painted examples created, which are rarer. The same company made a total of thirty-six different figurines of characters from the film, and there were also a number of dinnerware patterns.

Q

I acquired a porcelain *Dumbo* figurine dated 1941, made by Vernon Kilns, at an estate sale a year ago, and I have always wondered how many figures were in the set. Also, what is it worth? And why was it made? Mario, Albuquerque, NM

A

—Vernon Kilns made several *Dumbo*-themed figurines—there were two poses of Dumbo, along with Timothy, a stork, and a crow.

The last two are especially rare. We have seen Dumbos selling around the $50 to $150 range. The Vernon Kilns company was primarily known for a set of thirty-six *Fantasia* figurines, along with *Fantasia*-themed vases and dinnerware, all eagerly sought by collectors today.

Q **I have a certificate that reads "United States Treasury, War Finance Committee: This is to certify that Maureen Meagher is the owner of a war bond. . . ." Disney characters border the document. Could you tell me if this certificate has any monetary value to Disney collectors? Maureen, Moriches, NY**

A —Certificates such as yours were presented to purchasers of war bonds for their kids during World War II. They have no cash value per se, though collectors often pay $50 to $150 for them.

Q **I found a black, oval-shaped box that has the words DISNEY HATS around the rim of the lid. The box has titled pictures going all around the outside. The titles are: *A Home on the Mississippi*, *Trotting Cracks on the Snow*, *Peytona and Fashion*, and *American Forest Scene*. Can you tell me more about this box? Jessica, Montara, CA**

A —There was a Disney Hat Company in New York City back in the 1800s. It is very likely that the company was started by a distant relative of Walt Disney's. We know that in 1847 Edward Wolfington Disney, a cousin of Walt Disney's grandfather, moved as a child from Ireland to New York, where he eventually became a hat manufacturer and importer.

Q **I recently purchased a postcard at an antique store. The card looks like a framed oil painting of Mickey, who is dressed in a blue suit and holding a hat with a feather in his right hand down at his side and what appears to be a coat in his left**

hand. The postcard is titled "Old Masters" and was published by Classico San Francisco, Inc. What can you tell me about this? Marcus, Anderson, IN

A —Classico was a Disney licensee for postcards in the 1990s. Through the years, various Disney artists have had fun portraying the Disney characters as if some of the old masters had painted them. Yours sounds like a depiction of Mickey as Thomas Gainsborough's *Blue Boy*. The original Gainsborough painting, probably the most famous portrait in the country, hangs in the art gallery of the Huntington Library here in Southern California, so it would have been well known to the Disney artists.

Q I have come into possession of a number of white paper cups with a circle design with Mickey in the middle and a platter of hamburgers and a shake. It also has the words MICKEY'S KITCHEN. What can you tell me about this? Loren, Topeka, KS

A —Mickey's Kitchen was The Walt Disney Company's first venture into operating restaurants outside its Parks. It began in 1990 with one next door to The Disney Store in Montclair, California; later, a second restaurant was opened in Schaumburg, Illinois. The fast-food restaurants, which emphasized healthy fare, did not catch on, and the two were eventually closed.

Q I got a stuffed bear for my seventh birthday. I am almost forty-eight years old [in 1998]. The tag says that it is a Disney product, made by the Andover Toy Company in New York. His name is Bongo Bear. Was he from an early film or story? Donna, Morton, PA

A —Bongo the circus bear is the star of half of our animated feature film *Fun and Fancy Free* (1947). In the movie, Bongo escapes from the circus on a unicycle. In the forest, he meets and falls in love with a girl bear named Lulubelle, but he has to confront a hulking bear rival, Lumpjaw, before he can win her. He ultimately wins the fight using skills he learned at the circus. The film was released on DVD in 2000.

Q **Back in the 1960s, I remember lots of plastic one-inch-tall Disney figures, which I think were called Disneykins. Do they have any value? Karen, Colonia, NJ**

A —The Louis Marx Company, one of the most prominent toy companies of the time, made Disneykins from 1955 to 1980. They made more than a hundred different figures, and some are scarcer than others. An old price guide lists them as ranging from $2 to $100.

Q **I've heard that there is a Goofy wristwatch with the numbers going counterclockwise. Is that true? T.T., North Hollywood, CA**

A —Yes. In 1972, Helbros released a Goofy wristwatch that actually has the numbers placed in backward order on the dial, and Goofy's hands moving backward as well. It takes some effort to learn how to tell time backward, which is probably the reason for there being so few of these watches. The watch originally sold for $19.95, but some years after production stopped, it became popular with collectors and prices escalated to around $700 to $900. Years later, however, The Disney Store produced a reproduction of the original watch, and various versions were available for some years after that. With the reproductions of the watch available, the value of the original ones has stabilized or even diminished somewhat.

Q **I have a Disney picture disc of Walt Disney's *Snow White and the Seven Dwarfs*. Can you tell me what year they came out**

with these and if they made other picture discs besides this one? Edward, LaPlace, LA

A —The phonograph record picture disc of *Snow White*, with an illustration printed on the vinyl of the record, was released in 1981; there were ten others from that and the following year: *Pinocchio, Lady and the Tramp, Mary Poppins, The Jungle Book, The Fox and the Hound, Cinderella, Bambi, Mickey's Christmas Carol, Peter Pan,* and *Mickey Mouse Disco.*

Q I have an early Donald Duck figurine. It is either a chalk holder or a pencil holder. It is approximately 2 ¾ inches wide and about 5 inches high. On the back it says c (which is in a circle) WALT E. DISNY (note spelling), and on the bottom it says MADE IN JAPAN. As I look at it, Donald is looking to the left, and his right hand is touching the brim of his hat (United States Navy) as if saluting. His bow tie is red, and his hat and sleeves have a black ring around them. Do you have any information on this? Thank you! Linda, Rochester, NY

A —That item is actually a toothbrush holder, made of bisque (a chalky ceramic) in Japan around 1935 and distributed in the United States by George Borgfeldt & Company. There were a number of similar toothbrush holders, also featuring Mickey Mouse, Minnie Mouse, Pluto, and the Three Little Pigs.

Q In 1959, at the time of the release of the Disney *Sleeping Beauty* film, a coffee company advertising on the Disney TV show offered as a premium a castle (complete with drawbridge) that must have been about two feet tall, along with small figures of the various characters from the movie, the tallest of which might have been six inches tall. The castle and the characters were all printed on sturdy paper. Do you have any information on it? John, Hazlet, NJ

A —In 1959, Hills Bros. Coffee offered a Walt Disney's Sleeping Beauty Castle with a working drawbridge that you could assemble. It came with sixteen *Sleeping Beauty* figures, and "a catapult that really works." You could get order blanks at your neighborhood grocery store; the castle cost $1.25.

Q **Could you tell us about the first Mickey Mouse doll? Cindy, Burlington, VT**

A —The first Mickey Mouse dolls were made by an enterprising housewife named Charlotte Clark after seeing her first Mickey Mouse cartoon. She obtained a license from Disney and made the dolls for several years. Since she was unable to satisfy the demand, Disney licensed McCall's to create a pattern so seamstresses could make their own Mickey dolls.

Q **How did there come to be Donald Duck orange juice? Are there other Disney foods? A.P., Wayne, NJ**

A —Back in the late 1940s, Disney began licensing Donald Duck to food companies, and the character was used prominently on labels for a variety of food products besides orange juice, including bread, canned vegetables, frozen fish, and soft drinks. Donald Duck orange juice is the only product from those early days that is still around. Today you can find new food products featuring Mickey Mouse, Winnie the Pooh, and Buzz Lightyear, among others.

Q **When I was a child, I had a record that helped me work on math facts such as addition, subtraction, multiplication, and division. I seem to recall a bird with a pencil-shaped nose on the cover. I believe it was a Disney recording. Am I correct? Patti, Broadview Heights, OH**

A —There were actually two separate albums, *Addition and Subtraction* and *Multiplication and Division*, starring Jiminy Cricket and Rica Moore. The records were first released as Disney recordings in 1963. And you're right, the first album does indeed feature the pencil bird on the cover.

Q **I recently found a box of Donald paper straws for 50¢. The box is orange, with Mickey and other characters on the back explaining how straws are a more hygienic way to drink! I would like to know when this product was released? Javier, Temecula, CA**

A —Herz Manufacturing Company of New York City began making boxes of straws featuring Donald Duck as well as Mickey Mouse in 1948. They continued to sell in stores for the next two decades.

Q **Can you tell me any history about a set of rubber figures of the Seven Dwarfs, which I own? F.V., Depew, NY**

A —Seiberling Latex Products Co. made the set of hard-rubber Dwarfs at the time of the release of *Snow White and the Seven Dwarfs* in 1937. There was also a figure of Snow White to go with the set, but she was made of hollow soft rubber, so few have survived in good condition.

Q **I have some small figurines of *Sleeping Beauty* characters. Are they worth anything? V.W., Miami, FL**

A —The *Sleeping Beauty* figures you have were made by a California firm, Hagen-Renaker, at the time of the film's original release. They are very scarce today and sell for high prices.

Q **Was there much collectible merchandise made at the time of the original release of *Fantasia*? M.S., Allentown, PA**

A —When the film came out in 1940, merchandisers must have felt that it did not lend itself to merchandise, and you find almost none of it today. There were a number of different books, a theater program and, notably, a collection of ceramic pieces made by Vernon Kilns.

Q **How can I tell if Mickey Mouse toys are old and valuable? J.L., New Orleans, LA**

A —The most collectible Mickey Mouse items date from the 1930s, and they can be identified by the copyright notice. If it says © WALT DISNEY ENTERPRISES it is from the 1930s; the © WALT DISNEY PRODUCTIONS dates it as later. The early version of Mickey usually had black oval eyes, with a pie-slice shape cut out of one side (but watch out for recent items reproducing the old-style Mickey).

Q **Dave, recently on the D23 "Ask Dave," you addressed some individuals' questions regarding the time frames of products. Can you please provide a time line of company changes to the copyright names? Thanks. Keith, Port Orchard, WA**

A —There is no exact answer to this question, because licensees overlapped the wording of copyright notices, especially when a particular product was sold for many years. Generally, the earliest Disney merchandise was copyrighted W.E.D. or W.E.Disney, or Walt Disney. Soon that changed to Walt Disney Enterprises, or W.D.Ent., or W.D.E., which was used throughout the 1930s. Walt Disney Productions, or WDP, was used until the mid-1980s; then it became The Walt Disney Company or Disney.

Q **Was the Flubber that Fred MacMurray invented in *The Absent-Minded Professor* ever merchandised? O.F., Grand Rapids, MI**

A —Obviously Flubber was a fictional substance, but at the time of the film's release, in 1961, there was some pliable plastic-like material merchandised for children as Flubber by Hassenfeld Brothers (Hasbro) for $1. It was advertised as "Every bubble a bounce."

Q **What can you tell me about a Mickey Mouse spoon that I have from my childhood? It has WM. ROGERS MFG. CO. on the back. E.B., Portland, OR**

A —The spoon you have is probably one of the most common items of Disney memorabilia from the 1930s. It was available as a premium from Post cereals in 1937. You sent in 10¢ and a box top, and you would get a spoon. It is amazing how many families still have one of these Mickey Mouse spoons in the back of their silverware drawers.

Q **My son was a devoted fan of the *Zorro* series. He has asked for a Zorro wristwatch. Is there now or has there been such a thing? L.E.M., Northfield, OH**

A —There was indeed a Zorro wristwatch, but it was made a long time ago, in 1958, and there are no more available. Occasionally the watches turn up at antique shows, but they are usually fairly high priced.

Q **I recently took a tour of the amazing Franz Bakery here in Portland, Oregon. The tour guide said that the building across the street—which they now own—once housed the Vogan Candy Company. She further explained that, when a young Walt Disney was once in Portland (as his parents apparently lived here for a brief period), he designed a bunny mascot for Vogan that they used on their wrappers—his first commercial exposure, and one of the first uses of a product mascot, ever. Put simply: is any of this story true? Cabel, Portland, OR**

A —The Vogan Candy Company in Portland was the manufacturer of one of only three merchandise items featuring Disney's Oswald the Lucky Rabbit in 1927. Universal was the distributor of the cartoons, and their merchandising man in the Pacific Northwest, F. F. Vincent, had convinced Vogan that they should do an Oswald candy bar to tie in with the cartoons. According to one report, it was a "very tasty confection" called a Milk Chocolate Frappe Bar, featuring Oswald's picture and selling for 5¢. The candy bar was very popular, becoming the best-selling one that Vogan had produced. They had an extensive merchandising campaign, with newspaper advertising, counter cards, window cards, and even a banner on their trucks. While it was one of the very first Disney merchandise items, it did not include the Disney name on it. It is true that Walt Disney's parents lived for a time in Portland, but that probably had nothing to do with the candy bar campaign. Walt's sister, Ruth, spent most of her life there.

Q I have a Wyland bronze of Ariel getting a ride on a dolphin that may have been made for the Disneyana, circa 1990. The people at Wyland have never seen this bronze and have no record of it. (I sent them photos.) The Wyland Gallery at Boardwalk suggested I contact you. I can send you photos if it will help get information about this piece and where it was made. Hope to hear from you and get some answers for this mysterious piece of art. Robert, Toledo, OH

A —This bronze was produced for Walt Disney World, and was an immediate sellout. Examples today sell for over $5,000.

Q Disney used to sponsor Disneyana about every year at Disneyland or Walt Disney World. Several years ago, Disney stopped doing this. Is there a chance that they will reinstate this event? Are there any places to buy and sell Disney memorabilia without doing it online? I am a touchy-feely type person and I want to see the item, not look at a picture online. I have things like matchbooks, stationery from the Disney Inn, and lots of watches. Periodically I want other things and would love to see other people's collections, or would like to offer some of my collections for sale. Thanks so much. Marcia, Murphysboro, IL

A —The last Disney company-sponsored Disneyana Convention was in 2002 at Epcot. Today, instead, we have D23, our community of Disney fans, and its biannual D23 Expo. There is also a non-Disney organization, the Disneyana Fan Club (formerly National Fantasy Fan Club), which has annual conventions and Disneyana sales (*www.disneyanafanclub.org*).

Q I'm a pin trader who likes to find and trade unique Disney pins! Last year I traded for this small, unpainted metal circular pin that has the symbols E, 4, and A and Mickey's head all in the spaces between the arms of an X (kind of like a symbol in each slice of a pie). Around the bottom rim of the pin it says EARS FOR THE ARTS. It doesn't have the official pin-trading symbol on the back, but it does say DISNEY, with the copyright symbol. Can you tell me what this pin is? When was it released? Where did it come from? Or, if you don't have any records, do you know of anyone who might have information on it? Thank you! Stephie, Las Vegas, NV

A —Ears for the Arts began in 2011 for students participating in the Disney Performing Arts programs at the Disney resorts, and the pin you have was their "badge of honor." The first pins were presented on February 11, 2011. The *E 4 A* stands for Ears for the Arts.

Q When our boys were little, we acquired a Donald Duck ride-on bouncy ball at a garage sale. The ball is blue and has Donald's head on it. It has held up for twenty-five years so, obviously, it was made well. Was this released by Disney or another toy company? Sheryl, Sacramento, CA

A —The Donald Duck bouncing toy, called a Hoppity Hop, was made by Sun Products Company, under license from Disney, in the 1970s. There was also a Mickey Mouse version.

Q I have a metal music box, for lack of a better term, that was "vintage" when I received it as a wedding gift thirty-five years ago. I've never seen another like it. It has a metal crank with a small wooden peg on the end on the right side. It has Mickey and Donald parading on the front, and DISNEYLAND printed on the lid's edge. The lid lifts up to reveal a paper roll, which you can roll back to its original starting point. When you turn the crank, it plays "The Star-Spangled Banner" and sounds like an accordion. I haven't played it in many years, because I'm afraid to break it. The box is probably ten inches square, and is decorated on all four sides. I would guess it was produced around the time Disneyland first opened. Can you tell me anything more about it? Diane, Bishop, CA

A —Your music box was made by J. Chein and Co. of New York City beginning in 1953. It originally sold for $4.98, and you could buy extra music rolls at four for $1.

Q What is the story about the Vinylmation figures? Tracy, Mount Dora, FL

A —The first Vinylmation (the name a combination of its medium, *vinyl*, plus *animation*) figures were introduced in 2008 as collectible yet affordable designer toys created by Disney Theme Park Merchandise. While the figure form is shaped like Mickey Mouse, the philosophy behind it is not that Mickey

Mouse is simply being dressed up to look like someone or something else; instead, Disney artists begin with that basic Vinylmation shape and can design features, outfits, accessories, and other details to express creativity from many angles.

Q **I am interested in researching the relationship between the Disney Company and the Hamilton Vending Company of Kansas City, Missouri. In about 1938, Hamilton Vending marketed/ distributed two gum ball vending machines that carried a decal of Mickey Mouse and his pals circling the glass globe. All indications are that this was a licensed use of the images. Any information you can provide or suggestions about appropriate sources of information would be greatly appreciated. Roger, Indianapolis, IN**

A —Disney had a licensee contract with Hamilton Enterprises, Inc. of Kansas City, from 1938 to 1941 to make the gum ball machines. We have one in the Archives, which I found at an antique store in 1975 for $185.

Q **I have an original Mickey Mouse cartoon book called *Mickey Mouse Runs His Own Newspaper* from 1937. Do you know how rare these books are or how much it would be worth? Melanie, San Diego, CA**

A —This was a book in the Big Little Book series, from Whitman Publishing Co. of Racine, Wisconsin; it is relatively scarce, as are all Disney books from the 1930s. For the values of the books, you can check Internet used-book sources such as *Bookfinder.com*, *alibris.com*, or *AbeBooks.com*.

Q **I purchased a fire extinguisher at an antique fair about fifteen years ago. It has a Mickey Mouse plaque on the front with Walt's words from opening day at Disneyland. It's always been part of**

our Disney collection, and I'm hoping it is not a fake. What information do you know about this item? Darryl, Steger, IL

A —Sorry: as you guessed, this is a fake. It was created for sale to collectors, without the permission of the Disney Company, in the early 1970s. The brass plaque on the fire extinguisher can also be found separately.

Q I have a map of the Indiana Jones attraction that came in a little folder that said INDIANA JONES TEMPLE OF THE FORBIDDEN EYE FIELD MAP, and I was wondering if the map was a piece of merchandise or something else that was given away as a promotional item. Marco, Phoenix, AZ

A —The Indiana Jones and the Temple of the Forbidden Eye Field Map was a merchandise item from 1995; it sold for $5.95.

Q I recently was given a gift to add to my Donald Duck collection. It's a bubble bath bottle and only has coloring on the front side of it. On the bottom it says WALT DISNEY PRODUCTIONS COLGATE PALMOLIVE CO. NEW YORK, NY. Is this an authentic Donald Duck piece of memorabilia or just a wannabe? Barbara, DeWitt, MI

A —It is authentic. The bubble bath, called Soaky, in the Donald Duck bottle, was made by Colgate-Palmolive in 1961. There were other Disney-character Soaky bubble bath bottles through the years, such as Mickey Mouse, Snow White, Dopey, King Louie, Baloo, Thumper, Bambi, Pinocchio, Jiminy Cricket, Goofy, and Pluto.

Q Several years ago, while vacationing in Germany, I came across a sign being sold at a flea market. The metal sign is approximately eight inches by eighteen inches and includes a color drawing of Mickey in a car with a road sign nearby that says 350 M. [i.e., miles] TO followed by a logo with NU-BLUE SUNOCO on it, with the dominating words UNSURPASSED IN MILEAGE. At the bottom is the phrase IN TESTS AGAINST 14 EXTRA PRICED FUELS—MARCH, 1940. Of course I purchased it. I would imagine that it was originally an American sign, but I know nothing else about it. Can you help? James, Pittsburgh, PA

A —Sun Oil Company of Philadelphia was a Disney licensee from 1938 to 1946, using the Disney characters to promote their Sunoco products on signs, postcards, blotters, etc.

Q I have a large collection of Disney-character alphabet blocks in different sizes and colors, with two colors on a block. Is there any record of what sizes and type of characters/letters and colors were produced together on a block? Some characters/letters seem to come in only two colors, and others are in four colors. Thanks for all the great info. Bill, Mission Viejo, CA

A —The primary Disney licensee for alphabet blocks was Halsam Products of Chicago, which was first licensed in 1934; they were purchased by Playskool in 1962, and Playskool continued doing the blocks at least through the 1970s (when they were sold in large cans). The Disney blocks were sold throughout these decades, with the packaging changing from time to time, but the blocks remaining pretty much the same (other than new characters being added). They were advertised as "safety blocks," with smoothly finished sides, rounded corners and edges, and harmless lacquers. The pictures I have seen of them all show two-color blocks.

Q I found a "Snow White's Last Call for Dinner" picture published by the New York Graphic Society Fine Art Publishers and was wondering if you could give me any information about it. James, Seattle, WA

A —The New York Graphic Society was licensed from 1945 to 1949 to make full-color lithographic prints of scenes from *Snow White and the Seven Dwarfs* and *Bambi,* and they did several from each picture. Purchasers could buy a twenty-inch-by-twenty-four-inch one for $4; a fifteen-inch-by-eighteen-inch one for $2; or a ten-inch-by-twelve-inch one for $1.

Q **I have an unusual lithograph that I received when I purchased the *Cinderella* DVD. It is a picture of Cinderella in her torn gown, but when you tilt it at a certain angle it transforms into her ball gown. Is this what they used to call a sericel? And is it worth anything? I am a Disney collector, and a D23 member. Pat, Doraville, GA**

A —The process is called lenticular printing. Several of the *Cinderella* lenticular prints from 2005 have sold on eBay for $25 each. A sericel, on the other hand, is a cel made with a silk-screen process (that is, not painted by hand).

Q **My parents used to buy ceramic art pieces each Christmas time, with each year depicting a specific Disney scene. I think these pieces were approved (and licensed) by Disney each year. When did these pieces stop being produced? I would like to buy my parents whatever version they don't have (they have most between 1981 and 1995) but cannot find any information about these pieces (what they are called, who made them, etc.). Any guidance would be great. Each piece would stand about eight inches to ten inches tall. Erik, Alexandria, VA**

A —Grolier produced Disney Christmas figurines made of bisque, a chalky ceramic, for each year from 1979 to 2007. Perhaps these are the ones to which you are referring. They were all limited editions, with the edition size (and price) going up as the years went on. The 1979 figurine sold for $29.95; and the 1988 went for $50.

Q A friend bought me a cookie jar at an auction. It has Mickey on one side and Minnie on the other. The bottom of the jar states that it is a patented Walt Disney Productions item. There is no date on the jar, and I was wondering if you would research the age and let me know. It doesn't look like the Mickey and Minnie Mouse that I know. It looks like it is from an earlier time. Thank you. Kay, Southport, NC

A —This Mickey and Minnie cookie jar is known as a Turnabout, and it was made by Leeds China Co. of Chicago. They were licensed by Disney from 1944 to 1954, so the cookie jar would have been made during that period. On most of these cookie jars that I have seen, most of the paint has worn off through the years.

Q Growing up, I had a Mickey Mouse alarm clock. I can't remember what it looked like, but can recall parts of what Mickey would say for the alarm: ". . . time to get up, brush your teeth, and have a good breakfast. Bye now, and don't forget to wind the clock." Then a train horn would sound. I'd love any additional details about this alarm clock if you have any. I would really like to find one to add to my Disney collection; not sure what happened to the one I had back then. This was in the mid-1980s, if that helps. James, Boise, ID

A —The Mickey Mouse Talking Alarm Clock Choo-Choo was first made by Bradley in the 1970s or early 1980s. Bradley was first licensed by Disney in 1972. Examples of the clock often turn up for sale on eBay.

Q I'm *obsessed* with Disney pins; I have over three hundred pins, and I'm only eleven! Could you describe what the first pin made looked like and when it was made? Also, is it in the Archives? When did pin trading start? Kobe, Delaware, OH

A —One of the earliest Disney pins I have seen is a Mickey Mouse Chums pin made in England in the 1930s; there is an example of it on display in the Archives. But actual pin trading at the Parks began at Walt Disney World in 1999, and at Disneyland the following year.

Q Hello, Dave. I am looking for information on the history of Disney sewing buttons and rivets. For example, when were the first Disney buttons/rivets made, where were they made, what characters were on them, were the buttons sold in sets, what material were they made of, etc.? Terri, West Branch, MI

A —The earliest known Disney licensee making buttons was the Leo F. Phillips Co., Inc., of New York. They were licensed in 1937 to produce "novelty dress buttons made of Catalin and/or other plastic materials." Their license was canceled in 1939. We have one card of three Mickey Mouse buttons in the Walt Disney Archives.

Q You've mentioned that the merchandise from the 1930s had a copyright notice of Walt Disney Enterprises. Was that like a written notice or a sort of stamp? Kris, Miami, FL

A —It was not a stamp, simply a written copyright notice. Depending on the size of the object, and thus the space available to write it, it could have been © Walt Disney Enterprises, Walt Disney Ent., W.D. Ent., or WDE.

Q Where can I find the 1960s version of the Carousel of Progress? Are there any sound tracks for it or DVDs on it available anymore? Ethan, Agawam, MA

A —There was a souvenir record released in 1968 as Disneyland record DL-599, *General Electric Carousel of Progress: "Great Big Beautiful Tomorrow,"* including a medley of Disney tunes, but no sound track album. There are also the CD sets *Walt Disney and the 1964 World's Fair* and *A Musical History of Disneyland*, which feature materials from the show, including the sound track.

Q

I have a Walt Disney Davy Crockett pocketknife that was given to me by my father. It is yellow, has a picture of Fess Parker with his legendary coonskin hat on, and there is musket and hatchet crossed behind his picture. . . . It also has the following written on it: WALT DISNEY'S DAVY CROCKETT, FESS PARKER AS DAVY CROCKETT, and at the bottom it has a registered trademark next to WALT DISNEY PROD., INC. On the can opener is serial number: P 2391732. Do you have any history to share about this knife? Fred, Canton, MI

A

—The knife was made by the Imperial Knife Company, which was licensed for Davy Crockett items from 1955 to 1959. There were three versions of the Davy Crockett knife, with original retail prices ranging from 59¢ to 98¢. Examples have sold on eBay in recent years for prices up to a hundred times the original cost.

Q

I have a wooden box I got at an antique shop in Quebec, Canada. It is on wheels, has different Disney characters on the side, and has lettering on it that says WALT DISNEY'S MICKEY MOUSE PUSH 'EM CAR. I use it as a toy box in my grandkid's playroom, along with other vintage Disney items. Any idea of value or history? Thanks and *love* your column. Actually got to meet you at the Studio one day and am looking forward to seeing you at the Expo this summer. Terri, El Cajon, CA

A

—If it is the one I am thinking of, it has a Mickey Mouse Club logo on it, so that would date it to the last half of the 1950s. There are several for sale on eBay as I write this.

Q Knowing my love of all things Disney and especially the little Orange Bird (my first souvenir being the drink container when I was five), my nine-year-old daughter happened upon a two-inch-tall figurine of him here locally [in Florida]. She was with her grandmother at the time and insisted on being allowed to purchase him for me. Is there anything you can tell me about this figurine, as I have not been able to find anything online about merchandise of him such as this. It has the WALT DISNEY PROD. stamp on the bottom of his feet. It's invaluable to me because of it being given with so much love from my daughter, but I thought it would be neat to tell her what she found. Thanks for any help! Mary, Havana, FL

A —Your particular figurine is not familiar to me, but with that particular copyright notice, it would date between 1971 and 1987, the years that the Florida Citrus Growers sponsored the Sunshine Pavilion at Walt Disney World's Magic Kingdom. During that period, Orange Bird merchandise could be found at various citrus stands off the Florida highways. Since the Orange Bird returned to Walt Disney World in 2012, new products have been produced by Disney Theme Park Merchandise.

Q Are Disney Dollars still in use? I discovered a few of them at my parents' house while I was home over the holidays. They are still in a bank envelope that says DISNEY DOLLARS, CURRENCY WITH CHARACTER. Anonymous

A —Yes, Disney Dollars are still in use. In fact, there were some new ones released for 2014.

Q My husband has inherited Mickey and Minnie figurines. They have a WALT DISNEY and MADE IN JAPAN mark on the back of them. They look like the 1930s Mickey and Minnie and are made of porcelain bisque. My question, however, centers around what they are holding. Minnie has a brown book with a cross on it that gives the appearance of a bible and Mickey is holding what seems to be an old bayonet-style gun. Did Walt Disney produce these figurines? Thank you for your help. Shelley, Butler, GA

A —Disney did not produce them. They were produced in Japan during the 1930s under a license granted by Disney to George Borgfeldt & Company of New York City. There were several hundred different figurines of Disney characters, primarily Mickey, Minnie, and Donald. The Minnie you have is actually holding a nurse's kit, with Mickey holding a rifle with bayonet attached.

Q I recently came across a drawing that was tucked away in my baby book. It is a drawing of Mickey's head. It appears to have been drawn with a black marker or charcoal pen. Above Mickey's head is printed HI LAURIE and the letter *i* in Hi is dotted with a heart. Below his head, it is signed "Roy." My mother told me it was drawn for me by Roy when I was about four years old. I am fifty-eight now. I was wondering if you could tell me where I might get this appraised. Laura, Mundelein, IL

A —These Disneyland drawings by Roy Williams have little collectible value, other than its sentimental value to the person who obtained it.

Q Hello! I found an unopened videotape of *Snow White and the Seven Dwarfs* from 1998, I believe, with my movies. It says it was the first time it was ever on video! Is this true and, if so, is it worth anything other than coolness? Eliza, Orlando, FL

A —It was actually first released on videocassette in 1994. The early videos have little collectible value.

Q I have a little ceramic Mickey Mouse sitting in a canoe. There is no Donald Duck, just M.M. It was given to me in the 1930s. Where can I get full information on it? Thanks. William, El Cajon, CA

A —This is a bisque figure, made in Japan, and distributed in the United States in the 1930s by George Borgfeldt & Company. There was also a canoe with Donald Duck in it. There have been examples offered on eBay recently.

Q What was the first Disney-based merchandise on the market? Daniel, Pevely, MO

A —There was an Oswald stencil set, candy bar, and pin-back button, all licensed through Universal, which owned and distributed the Disney Oswald cartoons. The first Mickey Mouse item was a writing tablet. Supposedly Walt was walking through a hotel lobby in New York City, and a man offered him $300 if he would allow Mickey to be used on the tablets. Walt needed the $300, so he said okay.

Q I saw a *Steamboat Willie* ear hat on D23's *Armchair Archivist*, but I can't find any information about it. I was wondering if this is a rare hat and what year it came out. Elizabeth, Vancouver, WA

A —These were sold in the Disney Parks. A friend of mine, Gary, recalls purchasing one for his son, Matthew, about four years ago at the Mad Hatter on Main Street, U.S.A. in the Magic Kingdom at Walt Disney World. Matthew says it cost $15. I don't believe that it is especially rare.

Q I have a unique Disneyland serving tray that was made by the California Metalware Corporation, of El Segundo, California.

My reason for believing it is unique is that the depiction of Disneyland reveals that it (Disneyland) is quite unfinished, and there is the big top tent to the right of Main Street, U.S.A. in behind the buildings. I have read that the tent was in the early plans for the Park. I would be so pleased to know what information you have on this tray. I really appreciate the work you have put into developing your *Disney A to Z* encyclopedia. I have all three volumes. Bill, Hebron, IN

A —California Metalware was licensed to produce and sell those trays from 1955 to 1958. The tray was designed before Disneyland was built, so it features an early concept of the Park. Rather than redesigning the tray, the company continued selling the original design for the three years of its license. The tray could be purchased separately for $1, or as a TV tray with aluminum-finish tubular steel folding legs for $2.95.

Q A few years ago we were cleaning out the attic and came across a rolled-up map of the United States. Once we unrolled it, we saw its title: STANDARD OIL COMPANY OF CALIFORNIA PRESENTS MICKEY'S AND DONALD'S RACE TO TREASURE ISLAND GOLDEN GATE INTERNATIONAL EXPOSITION ON SAN FRANCISCO BAY. Both sides of the map are very legible, but the game pieces that were to be placed around its edge are nowhere to be found. What can you tell us about this game? Are any of the pieces in the Archives? Dwight, Pasadena, CA

A —The game was a promotion by Standard Oil, under license from Disney; the maps were available at Standard gas stations. Also available at the stations was a periodic publication called *Travel Tykes Weekly*. There were twenty issues during 1939, and each one included two of the game pieces to be placed on the map. We have in the Archives a map and a complete set of the weekly newspapers.

Q **Hi, Dave. My sister in New York purchased a picture of Jiminy Cricket in a thrift store. On the picture there is a gold sticker that says** THIS IS AN ORIGINAL HAND PAINTED CELLULOID DRAWING ACTUALLY USED IN A WALT DISNEY PRODUCTION. RELEASED EXCLUSIVELY BY DISNEYLAND 1313 HARBOR BLVD. ANAHEIM, CA. COPYRIGHT WALT DISNEY PRODUCTIONS. **There is some damage. I was wondering if it is worth anything, in case it should be insured. If you would like, I could send a picture of it. Helen, Port St. Lucie, FL**

A —These cels of Jiminy Cricket that were sold at Disneyland in the 1950s and 1960s were from Jiminy's TV appearances, primarily on the *Mickey Mouse Club*, not from his original appearance in *Pinocchio*. You can check eBay to see what similar Jiminy cels are selling for. Of course, any damage greatly affects the value.

Q **I have two boxed board games with the Disney titles *Treasure Island* and *20,000 Leagues Under the Sea* by Gardner Games Co., but I can't find any information about them. I have searched all of my Disney reference books and guides, but find almost no information on Disney board games by Gardner Games, except that they did business with Disney from 1955 to 1960. So far the Internet has not yielded any tangible information either. Can the Walt Disney Archives offer any further information? Thanks! Gredo, St. Cloud, MN**

A —Gardner Games Co. of Chicago was indeed a Disney licensee for those six years. The *20,000 Leagues* game from 1955 had a list price of $1. The *Treasure Island* game listed at $3. Other Disney games Gardner produced included a basketball game, a beanbag bucket game, a Casey Jr. game, and a Davy Crockett Adventure play set.

Q **We are trying to get information about the storybook-with-records collection, approximate time line 1960s. The records are 45 rpm. Cynthia, Davis, CA**

A —Disney had a Storyteller (ST) series of twelve-inch LP records, including booklets, beginning in 1957 and lasting into the 1980s. Another series, the Little Long Playing (LLP) seven-inch records, began in the 1960s. Most were labeled SEE THE PICTURES, HEAR THE RECORD, READ THE BOOK.

Q **I am hoping you can help me with finding out the history of a Disney record I recently acquired. The record is titled *Disney's Family Reunion* and includes a twelve-page, illustrated lyric book. According to the sleeve, the record is "presented by Kraft in celebration of . . . Disneyland's twenty-fifth anniversary." Was this record released by Disney, or was it simply licensed to Kraft? David, Fairfield, CA**

A —This LP record album was released in 1979, and it is indeed a Disney product, created for Kraft Foods to use as a promotion. The catalog number is DL-3518.

Q **I was wondering if Disney ever licensed Mickey Mouse to a high-end watch company like Rolex? Andrew, Northville, MI**

A —There was a 1984 fourteen-karat gold men's wristwatch made by Baume and Mercier, a prominent watch firm from Geneva that was founded in 1830; that watch sold for $3,500, with a women's version at $1,800. But perhaps the highest price was for a handmade eighteen-karat gold watch with mother-of-pearl dials, by Gerald Genta, in 1991. Its asking price was $15,500.

Q **We have a charcoal sketch of Donald Duck that was signed by Clarence Nash on November 8, 1946, to my brother-in-law. He**

must have been in Atlanta at the time. It says "Dickey is my pal." We are trying to find out the value of this sketch and decided to go to the source to find out if you could be of help. **Aileen, Rome, GA**

A —Sorry, we have no information on values; such items are worth only what someone is willing to pay. Clarence Nash, the voice of Donald Duck, would have been in Atlanta for the premiere of *Song of the South*, held on November 12 at the Loew's Grand Theater.

Q On our last trip to Disneyland, we noticed all the new Mouse ear hats that are available that can be custom-made—super idea! And we started asking around as to who was the first person to suggest the Mouse ears, and what year they started. I have a small collection from way back, but was just wondering. . . . We came to Disneyland the first year it opened when I was a child and visited very often over the years. We even got to meet Walt Disney on the River Belle [*sic*] one afternoon . . . what a superb treat. We have had season passes for a number of years, and never tire of visiting whenever we can, for our birthdays, anniversaries, and any number of excuses we can make up to celebrate our lives just by being there . . . it truly is a magical place . . . keep sharing the joy! **Jeanne, Banning, CA**

A —The Mouse ear hats were originally the idea of Roy Williams, who was a Disney story man and the Big Mooseketeer on the *Mickey Mouse Club* TV show. The original licensee, the Benay-Albee Novelty Co., began producing and selling the hats, after they became popular because of the show, at Disneyland and in stores everywhere.

Q I am trying to locate a listing of the individual die-cast *Cars* from the movie. My grandson, Dalton, has been collecting them and currently has around two hundred of them. I want to order some of the ones that we are unable to buy locally but need a listing to see what we are missing. If you are unable to help me, please let me know who could. I really appreciate any assistance that you can give me. Thank you very much for your time. Norma, North Liberty, IA

A —The die-cast cars were made by Mattel; you can find some listings on the Internet.

Q I have a limited-edition cel of "Two Mexican Girls" from *The Three Caballeros*. There are the initials *WD* with *P* underneath. Can you tell me whose initials they are? Cindy, Rockville, MD

A —The cel was produced in a limited edition of 250. WDP would stand for "Walt Disney Productions," which was the name of our company up until 1986.

Q A number of years ago, our friend Tom Kettering suggested I contact you with this question: Is it possible to determine if an animation cel is an original production cel without taking it out of its frame? Also, what I have is signed by Walt Disney. Any suggestions would be appreciated. Thank you so much. Angelica, Oceanside, CA

A —One can make an educated guess whether a cel is a production cel if it is framed, but if there is any question about it, you would probably have to unframe it. Walt Disney occasionally signed matted cels for friends, but he also signed similar matted dye-transfer prints.

Q I have an *Empress Lilly* coin with the *EL* monogram on one side and the boat on the other side. It came in a gold foil box with red flocking on the inside. Any information would be appreciated. Linda, Kissimmee, FL

A —Your bronze *Empress Lilly* coin was produced in 1979 for sale at Walt Disney World. The *Empress Lilly* riverboat was once moored at Pleasure Island; it is now Fulton's Crab House.

Q My mom, who was born in 1925 and passed last summer, was given a Kodatoy projector and reel/s of Mickey Mouse cartoon film when she was young. The projector seems to be in very good shape, although I haven't plugged it in. The films have been kept in an old tobacco tin. Some time ago, Mom played the films for my sister who remembers it/them as being "Tugboat Willie," but I don't want to possibly damage them by trying to run the projector on my own. I hope you can guide us to additional information of value or safekeeping or who might be able to help. Thanks! Rebecca, St. Joseph, MI

A —According to an article in the March 1931 issue of *Modern Mechanix*, the 16 mm Kodatoy projector, made by Eastman Kodak, was "recently introduced." It was during this same period that Disney licensed Hollywood Film Enterprises to release shortened versions of its cartoons for home-movie use. The projector itself is unrelated to Disney. The projector is, of course, an antique; the films have little or no value because all have been released on DVD in recent years.

Q I am trying to find out more information on a plush Pluto doll that was given to me. I can't find any information on it. It looks old; my guess is it is from the 1970s or 1980s. It is a very simple-looking Pluto with a single-string smile and a red plastic collar. The tag is kind of faded, but I can see that it says WALT DISNEY PRODUCTIONS MADE BY CALIFORNIA STUFFED TOYS LOS ANGELES, CA MADE IN THE USA. Who is California Stuffed Toys? What was their relation to Disney? Thank you. John, Riverside, CA

A —California Stuffed Toys was a Disney licensee from 1972 to 1974, and again from 1987 to 1988, so your Pluto would have been made during one of those two periods.

Q I have recently acquired a Mickey plush toy from the 1930s. I have not been able to find another example of this plush. Mickey is wearing a leather apron and has leather boots. Does Disney maintain a collection of original toys? Dan, Alexandria, VA

A —The Mickey you have was sold by the Knickerbocker Toy Company in 1935. Missing from yours are a hat, lariat, and pistols. That is not an apron, but rather chaps. The Archives does have a large sample collection of original toys, but it is not meant to be complete.

Q For my birthday, my sister gave me a Disneyland Park map that looks like an antique. The front says YOUR GUIDE TO DISNEYLAND and COMPLIMENTS OF BANK OF AMERICA. The copyright reads COPYRIGHT, 1955, BY DISNEYLAND, INCORPORATED. When you first unfold it, there is an ad for the Disneyland branch of Bank of America advertising money orders, and when it is fully unfolded, there is a full-color map with COPYRIGHT, 1956, WALT DISNEY PRODUCTIONS. It's an amazing gift, but I'm wondering if there is anything to look for so I can tell whether this is an original map or a reproduction. Thank you! Robyn, Modesto, CA

A —I am unaware that those Bank of America guides have ever been reproduced. They predate the large-size Disneyland souvenir maps by a couple of years, and are a nice collectible.

MISCELLANEOUS

Q

Dave, my question is regarding the Disney Studio Theater in Burbank, California. I had the pleasure of visiting the Studio in 2006 and remember there being cement slabs in front of the theater with the handprints and signatures of Disney Legends such as Julie Andrews, Annette Funicello, and Ward Kimball. I noticed at the event that the slabs were gone. I understand the theater recently underwent a significant renovation, but what happened to the signed slabs? Tim, Henderson, NV

A

—The steps in front of the theater were the original location for the handprints and signatures of the Disney Legends. Because the concrete was weathering, we instead made brass plaques from the handprints and they are now displayed, along with all the more recent ones, in Legends Plaza at the Disney Studio. The original concrete slabs are saved in one of the Archives' warehouses.

Q

I run the World Carrot Museum, online at *www.carrotmuseum. com*, and am researching the role of the carrot during World War II. I have found that Hank Porter, on behalf of Disney, created several "carroty" characters for use in the British publicity campaign to eat more vegetables. Can you throw any light on these original cartoon characters via any archives/books you have? John, Skipton, North Yorkshire, England

A

—According to David Lesjak's book *Toons at War*, "Disney artists helped the British government promote food products by designing a family of carrots for England's Food Minister. The January 11, 1942, issue of the *New York Times Magazine* announced, 'England has a goodly store of carrots. But carrots are not the staple items of the average English diet. The problem is to sell carrots to [the English public].' The Disney-designed carrots included Carroty George, Dr. Carrot, and Clara Carrot. The vegetable characters were reproduced on a poster and recipe booklet, and the carrot images were used extensively in a newspaper ad campaign."

Before *Disney on Ice*, there was *Disney on Parade*, which ran from 1969 to the mid-1970s. There were many segments through the years and some Disney Legends like Ward Kimball and Bill Justice worked on it. Can you please provide a little history and some facts about *Disney on Parade*? Richard, New York, NY

—*Disney on Parade* was affectionately known around the company as *Disney on Wood*, to differentiate it from the later *Disney on Ice*. I recall attending a preview performance in Long Beach, California, in 1969, shortly before I turned in my proposal for the Walt Disney Archives. The show, with lavish production numbers reminiscent of an ice show, was presented in sports arenas all around the country, beginning in Chicago on December 19, 1969. There were four versions of the show, with the last in 1973.

Dave, are there specific requirements in order to become nominated as a Disney Legend? I am very curious as to how the process works and if any (or many) people are nominated but not selected. Thanks! Jeffery, Pflugerville, TX

—There is a Legends committee at Disney made up of representatives from the various areas of the company—Parks and Resorts, Imagineering, animation, film production, corporate, etc. They compile lists of candidates, and they receive suggestions from people inside and outside the company. They are looking for people who have made a significant contribution to The Walt Disney Company. There is a Web site if you want to see who has been selected as a Disney Legend in the past.

Q Dave, my mother worked for Walt Disney in the 1940s. Her name was Janey Blackburn Bryan. She may have been working there when she passed away in December of 1946. I've spent most of my life trying to find out more info on a mother I never knew. I was five months old. Any information would be greatly appreciated. Anything. Robin, San Jose, CA

A —We have only a little information on Janey Bryan. We know that she started at the Disney Studio as an assistant animator on May 15, 1944, and left three months later on August 15. The World War II era brought new opportunities for women at the Disney Studio, because so many men had gone off to war. Before the war, almost all the animators had been men, with the inkers and painters being all women. Why your mother was only at Disney for three months we do not know.

Q Hi, Dave. I had the great pleasure of meeting you on a Disney Studios tour a couple of weeks back. There was a watch that I saw in one of the cabinets that I'm really interested in learning more about. It has an orange background with what I could only figure out was a goat on the front. It also had a dark-brown band. I am not familiar with this character or watch. Can you let me know more about this? Thanks. Jesse, West Hollywood, CA

A —That was Danny, the little black lamb from the 1948 feature film, *So Dear to My Heart*, starring Bobby Driscoll and Beulah Bondi. Since Danny did not appear on much merchandise, and as he was not a well-known character, the watch is quite scarce.

Q I don't have a question, Dave, but I thought this would be the only medium to reach you at this time. I was able through a lottery to get a chance to come to the Studio for a tour with D23 members in the first week of November, and the biggest thrill was to meet you and shake your hand. What an honor.

My heart raced when I came through the door and you were there. How awesome. *You are* a Disney Legend. My wife and I were celebrating our thirtieth anniversary and that was a gift unexpected. Take care; be well. Ed, Weymouth, MA

A —Thank you. Even though I have retired, I still like to come visit the Archives to lead the D23 tours there; it is a pleasure for me to meet the groups of D23 members, because they are some of Disney's biggest fans.

Q I recently read *The Hand Behind the Mouse*, the biography of Ub Iwerks. I know his surname is pronounced "eye-works," but does his first name rhyme with "tub," or is it more like "you-bee?" Tom, Oakland, CA

A —It rhymes with "tub." Ub was short for Ubbe (pronounced like "tubby"). Ubbe Ert Iwwerks was Walt Disney's chief animator in the 1920s, but he later shortened both his first and last names. His father was a Dutch immigrant (Ub was born and raised in Missouri).

Q I know that the 2003 Disney annual stockholders' meeting was held in Denver, Colorado, during a blizzard. Where have most of the other annual meetings been held? J.M., Walnut Creek, CA

A —The location holding the record is The Walt Disney Studio in Burbank, California, where all annual meetings through 1969 were held. Because of increased attendance, a move had to be made in 1970; the first non-Studio site was the Pantages Theatre in Hollywood. Later, six consecutive meetings were held at the Dorothy Chandler Pavilion of the Los Angeles Music Center. The site that comes in second, with ten meetings, is the Anaheim Convention Center. The first meeting outside California was in

Lakeland, Florida, in 1979, and six have been at the Walt Disney World Resort. Other than cities in California and Florida, only one city has hosted an annual meeting more than once: Kansas City, Missouri, in 1988, 1998, and 2012.

Q   **I just watched a documentary about MGM Studios that has a segment about the 1945 movie *Anchors Aweigh*, including the scene where Gene Kelly does a dance routine with Jerry, the mouse from Tom and Jerry. According to Kelly, William Hanna, and Joseph Barbera, the original idea was that Kelly should dance with Mickey Mouse, but Walt Disney said that Mickey would never appear in an MGM film. Any idea why? Ken, London, England**

A   —It was not Mickey Mouse but Donald Duck who was suggested for the *Anchors Aweigh* dance sequence. In that scene, Kelly wears a sailor suit, just as Donald does, so it would have been a good match. Jerry, however, was an MGM-owned character, so it is likely that economics rather than a refusal from Disney led to the use of Jerry. As for the idea that Mickey would never appear in an MGM film, Mickey Mouse was in the 1934 MGM film *The Hollywood Party*, introducing a Disney-made color Silly Symphony-type sequence called "The Hot Choc-late Soldiers."

Q   **I recently saw an old movie called *The Hollywood Party*. Near the end of the film I was surprised to see Mickey appear in the film. There was also a short cartoon about chocolate soldiers. What do you know about this film? Also did Walt do the voice of Mickey in this picture? Matt, Thousand Oaks, CA**

A   —*The Hollywood Party* is an MGM movie from 1934. It was rare for Walt Disney to agree to prepare animation for another company's picture, but he did so in this case. It was a black-and-white film, but Mickey Mouse, in black and white, introduced a color segment, similar to films in the Disney Silly Symphony series, that was inserted in the film—it was titled "The Hot Choc-late Soldiers." It is likely that Walt did Mickey's voice, because he was regularly doing it at that time.

Q **Traveling down U.S. Route 27 in Florida, I passed Florida's Natural citrus-producing plant. Along with this brand were the names and logos of other juice brands printed on buildings— among them Donald Duck, with his picture. There is even a statue of Donald on one building. Is this brand associated with Disney? Kim, Gainesville, FL**

A —Donald Duck Orange Juice is a licensed product of Florida's Natural Growers in Lake Wales, Florida. Their Disney license dates from 1941, so in 2011 they celebrated their seventieth anniversary.

Q **When was the first Mickey Mouse Club started? J.E., Santa Fe, NM**

A —The first Mickey Mouse Club was begun at the Fox Dome Theater in Ocean Park, California, in 1929. Within a year, there were hundreds of Mickey Mouse Clubs associated with movie theaters throughout the country. These were real clubs that kids joined. The children attended Saturday meetings where Mickey Mouse cartoons were shown, a Chief Mickey Mouse and a Chief Minnie Mouse were elected, Mickey Mouse credos were recited, and Mickey Mouse Club bands entertained. At the height of their popularity, in 1932, these clubs had more than a million members. TV's *Mickey Mouse Club* with the Mouseketeers did not come along until twenty-three years later.

Q **I got the biggest kick out of the caricature of Dave Smith. Having met Dave at the Archives and many Disneyana**

Conventions, I can say the artist did a great job of capturing the man. Who did the cartoon? J.C., Santa Clara, CA

A —Peter Emslie did the caricature of me years ago, before he had ever met me; he had seen me on a TV interview. He is a Canadian who has been interested in Disney since childhood. As a teen, he supplied caricatures to the local newspapers in Toronto. Eventually he served a stint as an artist for our merchandise art departments in New York and Canada. Later, he was invited to become part of the art department at Walt Disney World, where he did marketing designs, usually with Disney characters, for many projects. These days, he is back in Canada, where he does freelance artwork.

Q **How did you get your job? Were you a Disney expert before you worked there? Laurel, Lexington, KY**

A —I was a librarian at UCLA (the University of California, Los Angeles) when I was selected as the Disney archivist, though I had earlier worked at the Library of Congress in Washington, D.C. While I wouldn't have called myself a Disney expert at the time, I had grown up with Disney films, TV, and Disneyland; and had compiled a Disney bibliography. Generally, I was in the right place at the right time when Disney needed someone with my talents.

Q **What's your favorite Disney Park, and why? Rene, Lanao del Norte, Philippines**

A —My favorite park for a day visit is Disneyland, since I grew up with it. For a multiday vacation, I prefer Walt Disney World, and at that resort my favorite park is Epcot.

Q **My friend told me that Disney "dresses up" the Seven Dwarfs on the Team Disney Building at different times of the year or**

at special events. Is that true? What kind of ways are they outfitted? Louise, Brooklyn, NY

A —Only one of the Dwarfs seemingly holding up the roof of the building at the Disney Studio in Burbank, California, has been dressed up. Each holiday season, a huge Santa cap is placed on Dopey. At the time of the release of *Lilo & Stitch*, a cutout of Stitch covered Dopey.

Q I heard there are tunnels that run under the Disney Burbank studio. Is that true, and what are they for? Shannon, Tarzana, CA

A —There is only a single tunnel at the Disney Studio, and it runs from the old Animation Building to the Ink and Paint Building. Its purpose was for moving cels and artwork from one location to the other during inclement weather.

Q What is your favorite piece in the Walt Disney Archives, and why do you cherish it so much? Ryan, Romeo, MI

A —I think my favorite piece is a drawing by Walt Disney on a postcard written to his mother when he was fifteen years old. He was home in Kansas City and she was in St. Louis taking care of her brother, who was ill. Such things are rarely owned by collectors; we are lucky to have it in our collection.

Q My dad served on the USS *Sea Cat* (SS 399) during World War II. I was wondering if out of the 1,200 insignias or patch art from Disney, did they create one for this submarine? Gary, Pleasant Hill, CA

A —Yes, Disney designed an insignia for the USS *Sea Cat* in April 1944 at the request of the submarine's commander, R. R. McGregor. It featured a caricature of an angry-looking catfish.

Q Is there any specific information on the history of the partnership between Coca-Cola and Disney? When did it start? How did it start? It seems that the two are synonymous with each other, but I wonder how it all started. Crystal, Seattle, WA

A —Coca-Cola sponsored the first Disney TV show, *One Hour in Wonderland*, which aired as a special on December 25, 1950. When Disneyland opened in 1955, Coke became a participant with the Refreshment Corner on Main Street, U.S.A. and remains a participant there today. Coca-Cola is now the global beverage provider for all of Disney's eleven Parks in the United States, Hong Kong, France, and Japan.

Q Do you happen to know the current location of James Baskett's historic statuette? He played Uncle Remus in *Song of the South*. I know that Walt Disney had a huge hand in getting the Academy to recognize Mr. Baskett's work. Unfortunately, Mr. Baskett passed away shortly after the award was presented to him, and I am curious to know if the statue is back with the Academy or even in the Disney "vault"? Shaun, Indianapolis, IN

A —The Oscar went to James Baskett personally in 1948, so I would assume that it is owned by his heirs. The Disney company has never had possession of it.

Q Disney revolutionized theme park entertainment with Audio-Animatronics figures. What are the oldest Audio-Animatronics figures still being used at the Disney Parks? Which is the most complex? What is the largest? Ryan-Philippe, North Hills, CA

A —While they have been upgraded through the years, the first Disneyland show with Audio-Animatronics figures was the Enchanted Tiki Room in 1963. Human figures were first created for the 1964–1965 New York World's Fair; the humans in the

Carousel of Progress and Great Moments with Mr. Lincoln were later added to Disneyland. The largest figures were the dinosaurs in Universe of Energy at Epcot and the mammoth Yeti in Expedition Everest, but the tallest one currently is the new Maleficent in Fantasmic! at Disneyland. The most complex early figure was probably Abraham Lincoln for the Fair; he was later simplified because he had possibly been made too elaborate, which caused maintenance issues. But the new Lincoln figure that was inaugurated in 2009 at Disneyland is again very sophisticated, with twenty functions in the head and face, as opposed to seven in the preceding figure. Today some other Audio-Animatronics figures have very realistic movements, such as the auctioneer in Pirates of the Caribbean and the Wicked Witch of the West in the *Wizard of Oz* scene in The Great Movie Ride, or can even walk around, such as Lucky the Dinosaur. Other complex figures today are Mr. Potato Head in Toy Story Midway Mania! and Stitch in Stitch's Great Escape.

Q **I know that Ear Force One is the name of Mickey's hot-air balloon. What was the name of Donald Duck's balloon? Thanks! Melanie, Dedham, MA**

A —It was known as Zip-A-Dee-Doo-Duck. It made its inaugural flight on November 20, 1987.

Q **Dave, I was talking with a World War II vet, and he recalls Disney characters being used as insignia for squadrons. He wondered if this was something the Disney Studio did for the service or was something done independently of Disney. He fondly recalled some of the training films that were produced by the Studio. Thanks. Michele, Pocasset, MA**

A —In the early 1940s, as the turmoil of World War II was beginning in Europe, Walt Disney began receiving requests from military units to design insignias featuring the Disney characters. Walt was pleased to have his artists prepare these insignias as part of his contribution to the war effort. During the war years, the Disney Studio would create about 1,200 insignias for American and allied units. The units would request the insignia, and Disney artists would prepare the artwork free of charge to the unit. These insignias were then featured on the noses of airplanes, and on ships, tanks, and the jackets of servicemen. Donald Duck appeared on many designs—his temper fit him for such a role— but Mickey Mouse was rarely used, except perhaps for a chaplain's group of the Signal Corps. A unit such as the Flying Tigers might have a flying tiger created just for it. These Disney insignias did much to foster good morale during a dark and distressing period.

Q **Are any of Walt Disney's early studio locations marked? What is in those locations now? Larry, Boise, ID**

A —The first Disney Studio site, on Kingswell Avenue in Los Angeles, does not have any official markings, but the building is now a copy shop, and the owner has put his own sign in the window. There is a Gelson's supermarket currently on the site of Disney's Hyperion Studio, where Oswald and Mickey were created. There is a small commemorative sign on a lamppost on Hyperion in front of the market. Even though Disney moved to Burbank, California, in 1940, most of the Hyperion Studio buildings remained until 1966.

Q **Are there any Disney roller coasters with loops? Tanya, Waukegan, MI**

A —The first Disney roller coaster to have a loop was Indiana Jones and the Temple of Peril at Disneyland Paris (1993). Riders there were also inverted on Space Mountain (1995), and later in other Parks on Rock 'n' Roller Coaster and California Screamin'.

Q **When was the first Disney video game released? Was it tied to a movie? Renee, Cheyenne, WY**

A —The first Disney video games were Tron games for Mattel Electronics' Intellivision and Atari in 1982.

Q **Were there any Disney live-stage ventures outside the Parks before Disney came to Broadway? Sheila, Detroit, MI**

A —There were actually quite a few, including licensed Mickey Mouse stage shows (by Fanchon and Marco) in the 1930s. In the 1970s, there were stage versions of *Snow White and the Seven Dwarfs* in St. Louis and at New York's Radio City Music Hall. Arena shows began with *Disney on Parade* in 1969, followed by the ice shows in 1981.

Q **How involved are the people at Disney with the game *Kingdom Hearts*? I have been wondering for some time how that got started. Alyssa, Broken Bow, OK**

A —*Kingdom Hearts* was conceived in 2000 by Tetsuya Nomura and Shinji Hashimoto for the Japanese company Square Enix, which was collaborating with Disney Interactive Studios. Disney gave Nomura much latitude in the use of the Disney characters, but he tried to keep to their established roles. Nomura also added in Final Fantasy characters that had been created by Square Enix.

Q **I was thinking about all the cool innovative stuff Disney has made for shows, movies, theme park rides, and attractions. I was wondering if Disney holds any patents? Aaron, Raleigh, NC**

A —Yes, through the years Disney has obtained many patents, including such innovations as the multiplane camera, which first gave depth to animation; Audio-Animatronics figures, the robotic figures in our Parks; and various versions of ride vehicles.

Q **My family and I went on a Disney Cruise last fall. All of the characters on the ship autographed my daughter's pillowcase. There was one we couldn't place. His name was Max. Can you please help identify this character? Jennifer, DeKalb, IL**

A —Max is Goofy's son, starring with his father in the 1990s animated TV series *Goof Troop*.

Q **Is the voice of the Grinch in the animated version of *How the Grinch Stole Christmas* the same voice that narrates the Haunted Mansion ride? Laurel, Long Beach, CA**

A —No, they are not the same person. Paul Frees narrates the Haunted Mansion attraction. The Grinch TV film, which was not made by Disney, featured a different actor, Boris Karloff, most famous for starring in the original Frankenstein movie.

Q **I have a friend whose father, Perry Russ, used to work with Imagineer sculptor Blaine Gibson. As I understand it, Mr. Russ worked here in Florida on Epcot projects and then later on other projects around Walt Disney World (including the Magic Kingdom). Can you tell me anything about Mr. Russ and the projects that he worked on? Brian, Kissimmee, FL**

A —I remember Perry well. He was a well-liked master sculptor at Walt Disney World and Walt Disney Imagineering for twenty years, beginning in 1972. Besides working on Emporium window displays and sculpting figures for merchandise, he created the cast of talking fruits and vegetables for the Kitchen Kabaret in The Land at Epcot, the Mickey atop the world on the Crossroads of the World pylon at Disney's Hollywood Studios, and the original bronze Tinker Bell figure I among others received as a twenty-five-year Disney employee service award. Perry was noted for his tremendous talent and artistic judgment.

Q **I am always amazed that Dave answers some very tough questions about Disney history. Is there something that has stumped him? Barry, Grand Forks, ND**

A —Good question, Barry. Indeed every month there are a number of questions for which no answers are readily available. Sometimes, for example, we are asked about a remembered TV show, but the requester is unable to provide us with enough information for us to be able to identify the title. At times, it isn't a Disney show at all which they remember. One type of question that is often difficult or impossible to answer is one starting with the word *why*. The reasons why Walt Disney or his staff made certain decisions, selected a particular character name, or decided to build a particular attraction were often never recorded.

Q **Can you identify a movie I recall seeing about fifteen years ago? It was about a man who found a caterpillar that could talk, sing, and dance, and who signed up his find with Walt Disney. I cannot find anyone who has ever heard of this movie. C.H., Torrance, CA**

A —You aren't imagining things. The film you saw was *Once Upon a Time* (Columbia Pictures, 1944), starring Cary Grant (as a freewheeling promoter) and Janet Blair. The caterpillar's name in the film was Curly. Curly was a child's pet—and the child did not want to give Curly up so he could go to work for Walt Disney and become famous.

Q **What is the origin of the Buena Vista name, which has been used on many of the Disney enterprises? J.M., Pleasant Hill, CA**

A —The Buena Vista name comes from the street on which the Disney Studio is located. The company moved to the Buena Vista site in 1940. When Disney set up its own film distribution company in 1953, Buena Vista Distribution Company was a logical choice for the company's title.

Q **What is the most unusual item in the Archives? C.M.G., Orleans, MA**

A —I think it may be a Mickey Mouse gas mask that was produced by the Sun Rubber Co. for use in England during World War II. The feeling was that kids might be more willing to carry their gas masks if they featured Mickey Mouse.

Q **What set locales were located on the back lot of the Disney Studio in Burbank, California? J.S., Agoura, CA**

A —There were four primary areas of outdoor sets at the Disney Studio: the Zorro street, originally built for *Zorro* but later used for many European settings; the Western street, constructed for *Elfego Baca*, *Texas John Slaughter*, and other Disney Western miniseries of the late 1950s; the residential street, first used for *The Absent-Minded Professor*; and the business street, completely rebuilt for *Something Wicked This Way Comes*. None of the buildings were permanent, and they could be moved, or removed, when necessary. All of these sets are now gone, as the Disney Studio has needed more space for offices and support facilities.

Q **Is the covered bridge, observed in several Disney movies, located at the Disney Studio? J.R., Washington, D.C.**

A —No, that often-photographed bridge is at Disney's Golden Oak Ranch, in Placerita Canyon, about twenty-five miles north of Burbank, California. Purchased in 1959, the 691-acre ranch has served as an ideal setting for such films as *Follow Me, Boys, The Parent Trap, The Apple Dumpling Gang*, and *The Horse in the Gray Flannel Suit*. Other studios use the ranch also, and it has been featured in *Mame, Roots, The Waltons*, and *Little House on the Prairie*. With Twentieth Century Fox and Paramount having sold their large ranches, the Golden Oak Ranch has become practically the only surviving movie ranch.

Q **Before Radio Disney, was there ever a Disney radio series? R.T.B., Peabody, MA**

A —Yes, there was. It was called the *Mickey Mouse Theater of the Air*, and it was heard on NBC in 1938. Walt Disney did the voice of Mickey Mouse.

Q **What ever happened to the shows that Disney created for the 1964–1965 New York World's Fair? H.W., Las Vegas, NV**

A —At the close of the fair all four shows were transported to Disneyland, where they became these popular attractions: Great Moments with Mr. Lincoln, General Electric's Carousel of Progress (later moved to Walt Disney World), It's a Small World, and Primeval World.

Q **Does Tokyo Disneyland have a castle and, if so, is it based on the castles at Disneyland or Walt Disney World? B.L., Lebanon, PA**

A —There is a Cinderella Castle in Tokyo Disneyland and it is based on the castle at Walt Disney World. (Disneyland's castle is the Sleeping Beauty Castle.) Tokyo's Cinderella Castle differs from the one in Florida, however, as it at one time featured an exciting Mystery Tour that highlighted some of the famed Disney villains.

Q When did Disney make its first educational films? I recall Disney films when I was in school twenty years ago. K.R., Malibu, CA

A —Actually, Walt Disney made his first educational film in Kansas City in 1922. It was a dental training film, made for local dentists, entitled *Tommy Tucker's Tooth*. Not until World War II did the Disney Studio get really involved with educational films, producing training films for the military. Out of that evolved a group of postwar educational films for schools, with one of the most popular being *How to Catch a Cold* (1951).

Q How big is the Disney Studio? M.M., New Orleans, LA

A —Built in 1940, the Studio covers forty-four acres. There is a theater, a commissary, a Studio store, and buildings for animation, camera, ink and paint, sound recording, editing, costume and music, marketing, administration, etc. And, finally, there are seven soundstages for live-action filming. The last large one was built specifically to house the fantastic leprechauns' throne room for *Darby O'Gill and the Little People*, with three built later for TV filming. Formerly there was also a large back lot of outdoor sets.

Q I just wrapped up my playing of the new Wii game *Epic Mickey*, which was fantastic; also a great tribute to the classic Disney characters, places, and collectibles by the way. In the ending of the game, a calendar is seen on the wall beside our lovable mouse with the date November 18 showing. Does this date have a significance in Disney lore, to be featured so prominently in the game? I would likely not have noticed the calendar and date, but after following your column for a while now, it seems these dates are typically not an accident! Jay, Bainbridge, OH

A —You are right; this was no accident. November 18, 1928, was the date that Mickey Mouse made his debut in *Steamboat Willie* at the Colony Theater in New York City. We are pleased that you are enjoying our game.

Q

I'm trying to find information concerning an Army helicopter unit patch that was rumored to have been designed by the Disney Studios. The patch is a smiling tiger inside a diamond with rockets on the border of the diamond. The unit was D Company, 229th Assault Helicopter Battalion, which served in Vietnam. A group I'm a member of has acquired one of this unit's helicopters and we are researching her history with the Army with the goal of restoration in mind. Thank you. Tom, East Moline, IL

A

—Disney designed the insignia you described for the 229th Assault Helicopter Battalion, known as the "Smiling Tigers," in January 1967. Separate insignias were created two years later for Company A and Company B of the 229th. The first showed a raccoon in a triangle; the second showed a Native American warrior shooting an arrow, with a heart as the arrowhead.

Q

Could you please tell me which attraction in the Disney Parks would have been the first to take photos of guests as they rode, and then were available for purchase? Maxime, Bruges, Belgium

A

—The first was Splash Mountain at Disneyland Park, where Professor Barnaby Owl's Photographic Art Studio opened at the end of the attraction on January 31, 1992. It was actually the idea of then Disney CEO Michael Eisner, who had been impressed by press photos taken of himself at the debut of the attraction in 1989. Since then the photo system has been added to Disney Parks worldwide, for such attractions as Space Mountain, Tower of Terror, Expedition Everest, Dinosaur, Test Track, and Rock 'n' Roller Coaster. But there was an earlier attraction that took photos not available for purchase: Journey into Imagination at Epcot. That attraction opened in 1983, the year following the attraction's opening.

Q **Has Disney ever made any animated shorts with an Irish or Saint Patrick's Day theme? Megan, Columbus, OH**

A —Live-action films, yes, such as *The Fighting Prince of Donegal, The Secret of Boyne Castle,* and *Darby O'Gill and the Little People,* but I cannot think of any animated shorts. There was a Little Golden Book entitled *Little Man of Disneyland* about a leprechaun.

Q **How many employees did Disney have in 1923? Armenthia, Detroit, MI**

A —The company did not get started until October 16, 1923; by the end of the year there were only four employees, two of whom were Walt and Roy O. Disney. Five more employees were hired in 1924, and seven were added in 1925. Only a couple employees were added in 1926, then thirteen in 1927, five in 1928, and thirty-one in 1929. Some only worked for a short time, such as Walt's future wife, Lillian Bounds, and his sister, Ruth.

Q **When I was in grade school in the 1960s, we saw some great Disney educational films on the blood system and such—with a live spectacled professor host and a cartoon imp that helped him. Maybe one on atoms also? I make educational films now and would love to see these again—any clues? Anonymous**

A —You may be thinking of educational films in a Bell science series, produced for TV, that included *Hemo the Magnificent* (about the blood system) and *Our Mr. Sun.* Frank C. Baxter was the professor-narrator. These were not Disney films.

Q I have been to The Walt Disney Family Museum many times and absolutely love it. My question is, what was the determining factor to put the museum in San Francisco? Also I saw once on a TV show about the museum (they did not address my previous question) that there was some sort of warehouse in the Presidio that has Disney artifacts. Why were they there, in San Francisco and at the Presidio? Anonymous

A —The key reason for the San Francisco location is that Diane Disney Miller, Walt's daughter, who was spearheading plans for the museum and providing its funding, lived in the San Francisco area. Thus, she could keep an eye on the progress of construction, and later the actual running of the museum. It had been for years her desire to create a museum that would honor Walt Disney as an individual, not as the head of a huge company. The beautiful museum does just that. If the museum had been built in Burbank, Anaheim, or Orlando, it would have been too closely associated with the company. The warehouse you mention was a temporary storehouse for the museum objects before the building was finished.

Q I am doing a project on Disney for school. I was wondering if you have any information on the relationship between Premier Cruise Line and Disney before Disney Cruise Line was created. Many thanks. Katy, Stamps, FL

A —Before Disney Cruise Line, Disney licensed Premier Cruise Line of Cape Canaveral, Florida, to be the official cruise line of Walt Disney World, and to operate cruises featuring the Disney characters on ships dubbed *The Big Red Boat*. This arrangement lasted from 1985 to 1993. Disney's first ship, the *Disney Magic*, sailed in 1998. Premier Cruise Line shut down in 2000 after filing for bankruptcy.

Q **Has Disney ever allowed other studios to use Disney songs in their movies? Steven Spielberg said in an interview that Disney allowed him to use "When You Wish Upon a Star" in** *Close Encounters of the Third Kind.* **Robert, Middletown, NY**

A —Disney does not have licensing rights to all of the songs that have appeared in the Disney films. For example, the songs from *Snow White and the Seven Dwarfs* and *Pinocchio* are retained by Bourne Co. Music Publishers, so Spielberg would have obtained his license from them.

Q **Please let me know what the "23" in D23 stands for. I'm new to the fan club and I didn't see where they stated what the "23" stood for. I probably just missed it. Thanks. Jimmy, Townsend, MA**

A —"23" stands for 1923, which is the year in which Walt Disney founded his company. On October 16, 1923, he signed his first contract, to produce the Alice Comedies.

Q DISNEY ON ICE IS CELEBRATING 100 YEARS **is the teaser we are seeing here in Colorado. I discovered that Disney was founded in 1928. How can that be a hundred years? Thanks. Ernie, Thornton, CO**

A —You are correct that the number does not apply to Disney company history. *Disney on Ice: 100 Years of Magic* started in 2001, when we were celebrating the hundredth anniversary of Walt Disney's birth. The first Disney ice show, *Walt Disney's World on Ice*, debuted in 1981, though there were earlier ice shows, more than sixty years ago, starting with the Ice Capades, which had segments featuring Disney characters. The Disney company was founded in 1923 (hence D23).

Q **I was wondering if you could help me find the narrator to Disney's film** *The Story of Menstruation.* **I tried searching on**

the Internet, but the most I could find is that people wrote that the narrator was uncredited. Her voice kind of sounds like Betty Gerson's (the voice actress who narrated Disney's *Cinderella*), but I don't want to make any assumptions. Amanda, Durham, NC

A —The narrator of this well-known educational film was Gloria Blondell. Ms. Blondell came to the Disney Studio on July 25, 1945, to record the narration. She also occasionally did the voice of Daisy Duck, and is known for appearing on TV series such as *Thriller*, *Wanted: Dead or Alive*, *The Life of Riley*, and *I Love Lucy*.

Q Mr. Smith, are any members of the Disney company who worked on designing unit insignia during World War II still alive? Also, are there any books that you could recommend on the subject? Wayne, Las Vegas, NV

A —None of them are still around. I suggest *Disney Dons Dogtags: The Best of Disney Military Insignia from World War II*, by Walton Rawls (Abbeville, 1992) and *Disney During World War II: How the Walt Disney Studio Contributed to Victory in the War*, by John Baxter (Disney Editions, 2014).

Q I have long heard that Disney provides gifts or Cast Member exclusives to its employees for certain events or anniversaries, whether that be personal or company. When does this program date to, and do you have an item that you received that is a personal favorite? Dan, Edwardsville, IL

A —Disneyland began honoring its Cast Members with service awards beginning with its Tencennial in 1965, but the Disney Studio did not follow suit until 1981. But besides these service awards, there were indeed occasional gifts to Cast Members throughout the company, starting also around the 1980s. Often it would be a button or pin. I fondly remember an ornate metal key given to us at the opening of New Fantasyland at Disneyland in 1983, and special commemorative bronze coins for the grand openings of Epcot and Tokyo Disneyland. Cast Members were also given the opportunity to purchase limited-edition lithographs created for Mickey Mouse's fiftieth birthday and other events, and there have been occasional cast-exclusive cels.

Q **I recently found that in the early 1960s Mr. Disney had considered the St. Louis riverfront as a possible site for Disney World before settling on central Florida. Was this a serious consideration? Does the Disney Archives have any plans or sketches of what he was considering? Thank you. Tracy, Lexington, KY**

A —There was indeed serious consideration of Disney's doing a project in St. Louis, but not on the scale of Walt Disney World. For more details, I suggest that you find the book *Walt Disney's Missouri*, by Brian Burnes, et al., published in 2002. There is a chapter on the St. Louis project, including copies of plans.

Q **In Golden, Colorado, there is a place called Heritage Square. It is rumored that Walt Disney had something to do with this place. There's also a place that has now closed in Denver called Celebrity Sports Center, with a bowling alley and indoor pool, which it was said Walt was an investor in, along with Art Linkletter. Do you know anything about either one? Carissa, San Jose, CA**

A —Disney had nothing do so with Heritage Square, but several former Disney employees (including early Disneyland vice president C. V. Wood) were involved in its inception. It was originally created as an amusement park called Magic Mountain in 1959, but it closed because of financial difficulties the following year. A decade later, the park was reborn and opened as Heritage Square. The Celebrity Sports Center was indeed a Disney facility. It was opened in 1960, having been built by a group of celebrity investors that included Walt Disney and Art Linkletter, but in 1962 it was purchased from the original investors by Walt Disney Productions. Disney kept the center until 1979, when it was sold. It had been used by Disney to train personnel who would be involved in similar occupations at Walt Disney World. The center was demolished in 1995, and a Home Depot store is now on the site.

Q **Out of all of the actors and actresses who have graced Disney films—both live-action and in voice-over character roles—do you know who has appeared in the most, and what they are? Barbara, DeWitt, MI**

A —That answer would be difficult to determine, because there are actors who have played many minor roles in Disney films. So, we can guess at a few. As a leading actor, Dean Jones appeared in more than twenty-five films and TV shows; John Ratzenberger has done voice roles in all the Pixar features along with other Disney work; Clarence Nash, as Donald Duck, provided a voice in more Disney theatrical cartoons than any other voice artist.

Q **I know that having a window on Main Street is the highest honor in the company. I was just wondering, as there are now quite a few Main Streets, is any one of them more "honorable" than the other? (For example, is a window on Main Street in Disneyland a higher honor than one on Main Street in the Magic Kingdom?) Or are they all equal and one is put in wherever there's room? Jonathan, Woodmere, NY**

A —I would say that they are all equal. Of course, one could argue that the original windows at Disneyland Park might be more significant because Walt Disney himself selected the people to be honored. But I would deem it a tremendous honor to be commemorated on a Main Street window in any of the Disney Parks.

Q

I was wondering, is there anyone still left at The Walt Disney Company who Walt Disney hired, or anyone who remembers working with Walt Disney still working for The Walt Disney Company? Larry, Tampa, FL

A

—Sadly, with the passage of the years (forty-five-plus), there is only one person left at the Disney Studio who was hired during Walt Disney's lifetime: animation director Burny Mattinson. There are still several people at Disneyland who were hired prior to 1966.

Q

When your career as Disney's first archivist began, did you ever expect to someday be an author and be in such demand by Disney fans, guest-speaking at so many events? Or did you think an archivist position would be one of solitude? If the direction your job went in was not expected, was it a welcome surprise? When did you first realize fans wanted a piece of Dave Smith? Thank you for continuing "Ask Dave" even during your retirement. Scott, Regina, SK, Canada

A

—Thanks for your kind comments. I don't think I expected to become an author when I started the Archives in 1970, but eventually it became obvious that Disney fans wanted access to some of the information in the Archives. I started what became my "Ask Dave" column in 1983, and then the books began with four trivia books, collections of Walt Disney quotations, and the *Disney A to Z* encyclopedia; the latest is the current *Disney Trivia From the Vault*, compiling my "Ask Dave" questions. There will be a fifth edition of *Disney A to Z* in 2016. It has indeed been gratifying to have my books so well received.

Q Why was Regis Philbin honored as a Disney Legend? I don't recall him ever contributing anything to the Disney legacy. Mike, Laguna Beach, CA

A —ABC is part of The Walt Disney Company, and several ABC personalities have been honored in recent years for their contributions to the network. Besides, Regis hosted the *Walt Disney World Christmas* parade on TV for many years.

Q Prior to the establishment of the Walt Disney Archives in 1970, what did the Studio do to preserve the props, artifacts, and Disney-related historical items? Is there any indication that Walt thought about preserving his studio's history? Thanks! Kevin, Mount Washington, KY

A —Before the Walt Disney Archives, individual company departments took care of their own history. The Legal Department, Animation Department, and Imagineering already had extensive collections, and they have kept them. Other collections, from such departments as Consumer Products, Music, Film Production, Publicity and Public Relations, Personnel, Still Photography, Corporate Administration, Buena Vista Distribution, Publications, and various departments at Disneyland formed the basis of the Archives.

Q Is there any connection between the America Sings attraction and its Sam the Eagle character and the eagle character designed for the 1984 Summer Olympics? Larry, Thousand Oaks, CA

A —There is no connection, other than that they were both created by Disney artists. Eagle Sam in America Sings was designed by Imagineer Marc Davis for the Disneyland attraction. A decade later Bob Moore, an artist at the Disney Studio, designed Sam the Olympic Eagle for the 1984 Olympics.

Q How does one become a Disney historian? You watch documentaries, and these random people show up, and alongside their name it says "Disney historian." Sounds like my kinda dream job. Michael, Livermore, CA

A —"Disney historian," as usually cited, simply refers to someone who has researched and published in the field of Disney history.

Q Arizona State University has a myth about its mascot, the sun devil Sparky, that it is a caricature of Walt Disney done by a disgruntled employee. Is there any fact to this? Juliet, Phoenix, AZ

A —The mascot, Sparky, was designed by former Disney artist Berkeley "Berk" Anthony. Anthony worked at the Disney Studio from 1935 until he was drafted for World War II in 1941. Some people have speculated that Sparky looks somewhat like Walt Disney, but Anthony never confirmed that.

Q What was the first question you got? When did you get your first question? Have you got a question you could not answer? If so, what was it? How long have you worked for Disney? When you were hired, was Walt Disney around? What is your favorite Disney ride? Kobe, Delaware, OH

A —When I first started my column, in the *Disney Channel Magazine* in 1983, nobody knew about it yet, so I had to make up the first questions myself. Once the columns began being published, then the questions started coming in. We've received many questions that could not be answered; often I would have to ask a person who worked on a particular film or project, but as time goes on, some of those people are no longer with us. I worked for Disney for more than forty years but did not start until a couple of years after Walt Disney died. My favorite Disney attraction is Pirates of the Caribbean at Disneyland. I also enjoy Soarin' Over California at Disney California Adventure.

Q **Who was the Disney vice president of personnel in 1961? Laura, Dallas, TX**

A —There was no one with that title. Ken Sieling was personnel manager, a position he had held since 1953.

Q **What is the difference between the Disney Archives and libraries? How many libraries and archives does Disney have? Patrick, Savannah, GA**

A —Archives and libraries have some similarities, but the collections of libraries are primarily books and magazines, while archival collections are much broader in scope. Archives are usually related to a single entity, be it a company, church, school, or local, state, or national government. Besides the primary Walt Disney Archives, Disney probably has more than a dozen departmental and divisional libraries and archives.

Q **At a recent Destination D, Roy Patrick Disney was given a Mousecar award, I believe for his father, Roy E. I can't seem to find info online as to what the Mousecar is about and how or why it is awarded. Could you enlighten us, please? Walt, San Jose, CA**

A —The Mousecar is the Disney version of the Oscar. The award was created by Walt Disney in the 1940s to honor those who had performed a service to the Disney company. Over the past seven decades, many have been presented.

Q I understand that both Walt Kelly and Chuck Jones worked for Disney before becoming famous for their work elsewhere. Did any other artists become famous after working for Walt Disney? Michael, Lindale, TX

A —There have been many famous artists who worked for Walt Disney early in their careers. Besides the two you cite, others have included comic artist Virgil Partch, book illustrator Kay Nielsen, *Dennis the Menace* artist Hank Ketchum, and children's book author Holling C. Holling.

Q I recently came across Disney animator Les Clark's grave (and that of his wife, Georgia) in Pleasant Ridge Cemetery in Benton County, Tennessee. There is a portrait of Mickey Mouse engraved on his stone. He was born in Ogden, Utah, and died in Santa Monica, California. I wonder, why is he buried so far from his home and his birthplace? Andy, Nashville, TN

A —This was his wife's family's cemetery. Les was buried in the Pleasant Ridge Cemetery in 1979, followed by his wife, Georgia, in 2000. Georgia was born in Benton County, Tennessee, so she obviously picked the last resting place for herself and her husband. Georgia's parents, James and Ora Vester, are in the same cemetery.

Q Looking for historic prices for Walt Disney stock, symbol DIS. Paul, Schnecksville, PA

A —It is difficult to compare the price of Disney stock through the years because it had stock splits in 1956, 1967, 1971, 1972, 1986, and 1992. The first public sale of Disney stock took place in 1940. When it was first listed on the New York Stock Exchange on November 12, 1957, the opening price was 14⅞. In 1965, the price ranged from 44 to 60¾.

Q Dave, we just returned from the Seattle Fanniversary and the Archives speaker, Justin Arthur, and the D23 speaker, Billy Stanek, got me thinking about the curatorship each of you have! So how many of you are there? Do you search the country (possibly the world) for Disney artifacts? Are there many items that were given away in the early days that are sought after? Does your team do actual restorations? Keith, Port Orchard, WA

A —While the number changes from time to time, there are currently about a dozen people in the Archives and Photo Library. The Archives' staff is constantly on the lookout for materials for the collection—some things come up on regular distribution lists and others are asked for separately. The Archives has been around long enough that it is well known within the company, and many Cast Members remember to call the Archives when they become aware of something that might add to the archival collections. There are indeed some items that were given away in the past that today would be kept for the Archives—one example being the camera and camera stand used to film *Steamboat Willie*. The staff does oversee restoration of fragile items.

Q I recently acquired some photos in northern Michigan, by an artist who supposedly worked at Disney in the 1940s or 1950s. His name is Ferris Parsons. Do you have any record of such a person working there? If so, in what capacity? I may try to write an article about him, if I can find enough information. Thanks! Brian, Brooklyn, NY

A —Ferris Parsons was not an artist at the Disney Studio, but rather a cameraman. He only worked in the Disney Camera Department for a little over three months, from September 21, 1942, to January 4, 1943.

Q **I know you started working at Disney around 1970. Did you ever get to meet Roy O. Disney? Victor, Chicago, IL**

A —Yes, Roy O. Disney was one of the executives who signed off on hiring me, and for that I am most grateful. I enjoyed working with Roy very much during the last couple of years of his life. He was a very modest, grandfatherly gentleman who to me never really seemed comfortable as the head of a large company. One thing he did was ask me to work on my own time on the Disney genealogy— that gave me some one-on-one time with him.

Q **I have a question re: the Snow White Cottages on Griffith Park Boulevard in Los Feliz. Designed by storybook architect Ben Sherwood, and built in 1931 near Disney's Hyperion Studio, no doubt these nearby cottages served as visual references for the Dwarfs' cottage in Disney's *Snow White* (1937). But is it true that Walt Disney (or the Studio) leased these cottages for a time and used them as animator studios? Also, is it true that Claude and Evie Coats lived in one of the cottages? Much speculation and urban legend exist about these questions, but I'd love a definitive answer. Thank you, Dave. Leslie, Los Angeles, CA**

A —There are even untrue rumors that Disney built the cottages. The Studio never leased them for offices, but some of the Disney artists—namely Ham Luske, Dick Lundy, Fred Moore, Herman Schultheis, and Lee Morehouse—rented living space there, since the cottages were so close to the Hyperion Studio.

Q **If the official name of the company is The Walt Disney Company, why do copyright notices from 1996 onward say Disney Enterprises? Richard, Hewlett, NY**

A —Starting in 1996, Disney Enterprises was a new segment of the company that licensed the Disney characters for merchandise, with its name used on merchandise copyright notices. Walt Disney Enterprises had originally been a company division back in the 1930s that had a similar purpose, but the name had not been used for more than five decades.

Q **Hi! I've just gotten three old Disney posters featuring Mickey, Minnie, Donald, and Goofy in World War II–type clothing, and Red Cross emblems and hats. They are loading sandbags, carrying Red Cross Relief boxes, and saluting under a Red Cross Flag. The Walt Disney copyright is at the bottom. Do you know anything about these? Thanks. Cindy, Holly Hill, FL**

A —During World War II, the Disney Studio was asked to help contribute to the war effort by designing propaganda and promotional posters for the military, the Red Cross, government agencies, and other entities. There were many of them. In addition to the posters, Disney artists designed more than 1,200 insignias for military units.

Q **Was Mickey mouse a presenter and copresenter at the fiftieth annual Academy Awards, the sixtieth annual Academy Awards, and the seventy-fifth annual Academy Awards? Matthew, North Hollywood, CA**

A —The Disney Parks' walk-around Mickey helped present an award in 1978 with Jodie Foster and Paul Williams, and an animated Mickey Mouse interacted with Tom Selleck as a presenter at the 1988 Academy Awards ceremony and with Jennifer Garner in 2003. Those were the only times for Mickey, though other Disney characters appeared in the 1990s. Mickey did, however, appear in a short special cartoon, made by Disney for the 1932 ceremony, in which he led a parade of caricatures of that year's award nominees.

Q Wikipedia states that Walt Disney has fifty-nine Academy Award nominations (including twenty-two wins). But according to the list provided, I keep tallying sixty—fifty-nine of them being in the short subject and documentary categories. Is Best Picture nominee *Mary Poppins* not officially counted among the fifty-nine/sixty nominations? Besides those, I know he also has four honorary awards. Michael, Irvine, CA

A —There were actually 115 Academy Award nominations given for Disney films during Walt Disney's lifetime, plus honorary and technical awards. By my count, fifty-nine of those nominations were for Walt Disney personally, including the *Mary Poppins* Best Picture nomination. Walt personally won a total of thirty-two Academy Awards (one of those, for *Winnie the Pooh and the Blustery Day*, being presented posthumously).

Q How many Academy Awards has The Walt Disney Company won? Wen, Shanghai, China

A —As of 2014, Walt Disney, Disney staff members, and actors appearing in Disney films collectively have won 104.

Q How many Disney movies have been nominated for Best Picture at the Oscars? The only ones I can think of are *Mary Poppins*, *Beauty and the Beast*, *Up*, and *Toy Story 3*. Justin, Appling, GA

A —Those were the only ones released under the Disney name to be honored with Best Picture nominations. Other Disney-released films (by Touchstone, Hollywood Pictures, and DreamWorks) nominated were *Dead Poets Society*, *Quiz Show*, *The Insider*, *The Sixth Sense*, *The Help*, *War Horse*, and *Lincoln*.

Q I already know that Walt Disney hated sequels, but did he like making remakes of his films? Paul, Evanston, IL

A —I have not heard that he disliked remakes. *The Ugly Duckling* remake in color won an Academy Award, and *Orphan's Benefit* was also redone for the color era.

Q **Has the Disney company provided copies, or originals, of its films to the Library of Congress, to be stored? If not, does Disney have a secure, fireproof storage facility for its early films? Thank you! Dolores, Peoria, AZ**

A —The original negatives and protection prints of all of the Disney films are stored in a secure location. As do other motion picture companies, Disney supplies a copy of a film to the Library of Congress if it is requested.

Q **I live near the Library of Congress Audio Visual Conservatory in Culpeper, Virginia, and have seen several great Disney movies as part of their public viewing program. Does Disney store all of its films in the Library of Congress, or is it only certain films? Where are original films of TV shows kept for posterity? Are there several storage facilities that Disney uses? Todd, Locust Grove, VA**

A —When I worked at the Library of Congress in 1964, that was part of my job. Two copies of all films were submitted to the Copyright Office at the Library of Congress to gain copyright protection, but then the prints were returned to the production companies so they could use them during the initial release. Each year, the Library would select a number of films for its permanent collection, and request that a print be returned. Today, the Library also manages the National Film Registry, which picks twenty-five films of the past each year, films that it deems "culturally, historically, or aesthetically important." As of 2014, nine Disney films have been added to that list since it began in 1989. Disney also stores in secure locations protection prints and negatives of all of its theatrical and TV films.

Q **Dave, why didn't Disney honor any new Disney Legends last year [2014]? It seems like the first time they haven't announced any new honorees since the program began, isn't it? Shaun, Kissimmee, FL**

A —Beginning in 2009, Disney started naming a new group of Legends every other year, at the D23 Expo. So after 2009 there was a group in 2011, 2013, and 2015. There was no Legend ceremony in 1988, and in 1997 and 2002 the ceremonies were held in France for European Legends. Two Legends were named in Japan in 1998. The 2001 ceremony was held at Walt Disney World; all the rest have been in California.

Q **I've read conflicting accounts about a Disney park being built on the site of the 1964–1965 New York World's Fair grounds after the fair was over. Most accounts say that Robert Moses asked Walt Disney, but Walt said no. A few accounts say that Walt wanted to build there, but Moses said no. Do you know which is correct? Thanks as always. Louis, Rego Park, NY**

A —Walt Disney was well along in planning Walt Disney World when the 1964–1965 New York World's Fair closed in the fall of 1965, so he would have had no interest in building a theme park in New York. Besides, he insisted that sites for Disney Parks have weather conditions that support year-round operation. The two-year-long fair had been closed from October to April in each of its two years primarily because of weather factors.

Q **Hi, Dave. I have a sketch of Mickey on my wall that was given to me around 1979. It was drawn and addressed to me by a Disney artist at the Burlington Mall in Massachusetts on some sort of early mall tour. It is signed "from Mickey and Russell."**

Do you have any idea who this artist was and maybe what the circumstances of the tour may have been? Thanks for all you do! Steven, Brandon, FL

A —This would have been Russell Schroeder, who was a character artist at Walt Disney World. I inquired of him, and he recalls being in Boston doing drawings in the late 1970s, but at a department store downtown, not the Burlington Mall. This was a promotional tour to bring a bit of Disney to people around the country, with as a side effect to encourage them to visit Walt Disney World.

Q **Hi! Do you know the names of every classic Disney movie ever made? I keep trying to find them all but I can't seem to find them! Can you put all the names on Disney somewhere? Please and thank you! Sheyenne, Forsyth, MO**

A —You will find all the Disney feature films listed in my *Disney A to Z* encyclopedia (the book's latest is the fifth edition, fall 2016).

Q **I interviewed Director Charles Jarrott for my next book, *Conversations with Great Britons of Stage and Screen*. He made three films with the Disney organization. He indicated that he had been named a Disney Legend. I cannot locate his name in the list of the Legends. Can you confirm—or not—that he was named a Legend? I also interviewed Richard Todd, Angela Lansbury, and Glynis Johns, all of whom are listed. Thank you in advance for your assistance. Barbara, Encino, CA**

A —Charles Jarrott, who died in March 2011, is not one of the Disney Legends. His Disney films were *The Last Flight of Noah's Ark, Condorman,* and *The Littlest Horse Thieves.*

Q We have a large World War II submarine prop in front of our marina which, after working with the Navy, was traced to the World War II submarine the USS *Drum*, SS228. The *Drum* has quite an impressive service record in the Pacific theater. We decided to recognize this history and the United States Navy's Submarine Service by creating a flag of the *Drum*'s logo (an octopus beating a drum). When we requested our flag vendor to create the flag, they advised us that the *Drum*'s logo had originally been designed by Walt Disney. They provided a picture of the original artwork, which is unmistakably signed by Walt Disney. Did Walt Disney have a connection to the *Drum*? Did he work on the logos for other Navy vessels in World War II? J., Washington, D.C.

A —It was not Walt Disney personally who drew the insignia, but some of his artists were asked to prepare insignias for ships and military units during the war. In total there ended up being around 1,200 of them. Lt. M. H. Rindskoff, executive officer of the USS *Drum*, requested in late 1943 that Disney design an insignia for the ship, and it was completed in March 1944.

Q Do you know if there are any Disney characters that begin with the letter *X* or at least have the letter *X* in their name? If so please tell me. Thanks. Jacob, Richmond, TX

A —(David) Xanatos was a character in the TV series *Gargoyles*. In a Donald Duck comic book there was a villain named Madame Triple-X.

Q This is probably a strange question, but I don't see anywhere else that I can ask it. My wife and I will be celebrating our twenty-fifth wedding anniversary. My wife's only request has been to be remarried by Mickey. Where can I get some info regarding this? Dennis, Somerset, NJ

A —Sorry, but the Disney characters do not participate in wedding ceremonies, though they occasionally make appearances at receptions.

Q **Is George Rowley, one of the original Disney animators, still alive? Mike, San Clemente, CA**

A —George Rowley, an effects animator at Disney from 1938 to 1954, passed away in 1991 at the age of eighty-six. After he retired, he moved to Leisure World in Southern California and was known there for cartoons he drew for the residents' newspaper.

Q **I have inherited from my mother a silk screen print (so I'm told by an art appraiser) of Donald Duck and Pluto in army gear, in a rowboat. There's a sign saying TO TOKYO that is next to them in the water. The rowboat has "P156" on the back of it. My mother always kept a photo of the USS General D. E. Aultman, a ship with the number P156, with this drawing. Mom was in the United States Marine Corps during World War II and was stationed at El Toro air base in California. I would like to know any history about this picture. I have spent hours searching online and have never been able to find anything. Thank you in advance for any insights you may be able to provide. Donna, Shawnee, KS**

A —This is indeed the insignia that Disney designed for the USS General D. E. Aultman, a troop transport ship manned by United States Coast Guard personnel. It is one of the 1,200 insignias Disney designed during World War II. The insignia was requested by the ship's captain, S. P. Swicegood, drawn by Disney artist Roy Williams, and delivered to the ship in July 1945.

Q **When I saw the "This Day in Disney History" for September 13, I was so excited to see a picture of Danny Kaye with**

Minnie on the Dumbo ride! However, there was no mention of him specifically in the write-up. Can you shed a little light on the Disney–Danny connection? I am a huge fan of both! Todd, Locust Grove, VA

A —The inimitable Danny Kaye, a favorite of mine too, was the host of two Disney TV specials, *Kraft Salutes Disneyland's 25th Anniversary* in 1980 and *EPCOT Center: The Opening Celebration* in 1982.

Q **Family lore has it that my mother's uncle, Frederick Williams, was Disney's paymaster for many years. Unfortunately, Uncle Freddie passed away many years ago and we were never able to completely verify this story. I tend to believe it has some merit, as my mother remembers going to the Disney Studios when she was a teenager in the 1950s and getting to watch a film being made. Also, Uncle Freddie sent me an application for Disneyland in 1982. I completed it, went to several interviews, and was hired to work at the Haunted Mansion for the summer! I had a great time and fulfilled my dream of working for Disney! I would appreciate any information you can provide that would shed some light on this family tale! Congratulations on your retirement and enjoy it! Laurie, Gilbert, AZ**

A —Fred R. Williams was payroll supervisor at the Disney company from 1958 to 1973. He passed away ten years later.

Q **When I first went on a Disney cruise, the tram from the ship to the beach had a tape describing the "Proffits." What is the significance of the name? My wife's maiden name is Proffit. Joe, Selden, NY**

A —According to the mythology created for Castaway Cay, Marian Profitt was one of the original castaways who landed on the island in the 1920s, and she was the one who saw the need to educate the children of the island, as the castaways brought nearly a dozen with them. Marian set up Discovery Tents in a sandy cove near a whale dig, a convenient place for the children to study science, nature, music, literature, and the culture of this beautiful region. The children were taught conservation awareness so that they would understand the importance of preserving the natural habitat of the island's flora and fauna. Marian's husband, Dr. Max Profitt, searched the lagoons for sunken treasure. He found a three-hundred-year-old Spanish galleon laden with gold and jewels, but instead of taking the treasure for himself, he set up dive trails so he could share these amazing artifacts with others. The Profitts were simply fictional characters created by the Disney Imagineers.

Q   **I'm trying to compile a list of all the lobby cards and stills released for the Disney animated and live-action movies. I know that for every movie rereleased, Disney would reissue the lobby cards and stills, but I'm looking for specifics: dates of set release and rerelease, number of cards per set, details about the production stills, and press kits. Do you know of any reference material or Web sites that would list or have information regarding the released publicity materials? Or do you know of anyone that could help me further? Thank you for your consideration. Ada, Portsmouth, VA**

A   —I know of no published source for such information. The listings in my *Disney A to Z* encyclopedia indicate the reissue dates for feature films, so you can assume there was a new set of lobby cards for each reissue (they were usually changed, at least in the format and borders, from the previous release). A number of eight-by-ten black-and-white stills was sent out to movie theaters to help them promote the film; Disney studio publicists selected the stills to send out, and the number of stills varied.

Q How does Disney organize its Archives? What database does it use? I'm a new archivist at a small company who's been given the task of digitizing our collection, and I was wondering how the "big" companies do it. Meg, College Station, TX

A —The Walt Disney Archives uses Filemaker Pro as a general database program, though other specialized software has been used for particular areas, such as museum objects and photographs.

Q In the spring 2010 issue of *D23* on page 58 is a photo (#79) of the famous Mickey Avenue–Dopey Drive intersection. In the same issue, on page 23, is a plot plan of the Walt Disney Studio. My question is, on this plot plan, where is this famous intersection located? My guess would be the corner of B Street and Second Avenue. Jeff, Ogden, UT

A —Per that 1975 map, the iconic Mickey Avenue–Dopey Drive sign is located on the northeast corner of A Street and Second Avenue. A Street equates to Mickey Avenue and Second Avenue to Dopey Drive. The sign was originally placed there as a prop for the 1941 film *The Reluctant Dragon*.

Q The Neiman Marcus Christmas catalog of 1985 identified the front cover as "a reproduction of his [Walt Disney's] 1933 Christmas card to his employees—a happy congregation of characters making a dash through the snow, passing a milestone, and headed for better times." Being a fan of Disney since I was four—I am now seventy-three—I framed this cover. Might it be available in any other form? Thank you so much! Floyd, Bella Vista, AR

A —That was actually the cover of the 1981 Neiman Marcus Christmas catalog, and it pictured the 1932 Disney Christmas card. The original card shows the characters riding in their sleigh toward a milestone that reads 1933; that causes many people to assume it is a 1933 card, but actually it is 1932 and they are heading toward the New Year, 1933. The 1932 card is quite rare, and originals rarely turn up for sale. I am not aware that the artwork is available elsewhere.

Q **I was wondering how you got your start working at the Walt Disney Archives. I majored in history in college and will be starting the Disney College Program soon and would love nothing more than to eventually work at the Archives. Any advice? Thanks and have a magical day! Kaitlyn, Blue Bell, PA**

A —I just happened to be in the right place at the right time, and had the qualifications and experience that Disney needed, when I was selected to start the Walt Disney Archives. While the Archives rarely has openings, since you will be on the Disney College Program, you might network with people in the Archives during the time you are working for the company. Your Disney College Program advisers should be able to help facilitate this.

Q **Is there a particular item that you would love to have in the Archives? Jonathan, Pawtucket, RI**

A —The first movie I recall seeing as a child was *Song of the South*, and I identified with the young boy, played by Bobby Driscoll, who was my age. I have always wished that we had the velvet suit that he wore in that film.

Q **How many Disney movies are there in total? Jamison, Jackson, MI**

A —With the release of *Ant-Man* in 2015, there are 700 Disney theatrical features.

Q Hi, Dave! I wonder if you can tell me about Tom Scherman's Iron Man. Why does it exist? Was it built for a specific project? When was it created? Where is it now? I have a photo that shows the Iron Man in the 1980s at Grizzly Flats next to Ward Kimball's locomotives. Was that a specific project, or just for fun? Thanks. Will, Wheat Ridge, CO

A —It was just for fun. Tom Scherman's Iron Man from the early 1980s was nonfunctional, and was used for photo ops that day posing next to Ward Kimball's Chloe locomotive, supposedly to have a race. For more information on the Iron Man, see the Tom Scherman blogspot: *http://tomscherman.blogspot.com/2010/10/tom-schermans-iron-man-and-great-race.html*. Scherman is best known for making intricate models of the *Nautilus* from *20,000 Leagues Under the Sea*, which have been displayed at Disney Parks, and the Iron Man was inspired by concepts for that film.

Q My wife's father was stationed at Fort Riley during World War II and had the opportunity to meet a man who turned out to be a good friend during their service days. It was Fred Rice, who I understand was a Disney artist. We actually have a hand-drawn sketch of Mickey Mouse he gave my father-in-law back in 1943. I was wondering if you could tell me anything about him and what he might have done while at Disney. Any assistance would be greatly appreciated. Robert, Hazleton, PA

A —The only information that the Walt Disney Archives has on Frederick H. Rice is that he was employed in the animation effects department at the Disney Studio from February 1940 to September 1941.

Q Who's your favorite Disney character? Who's your favorite Muppet? And what's your favorite Pixar movie or character? You the man, Dave! Kenny, Lithonia, GA

A —My favorite Disney character is Pluto, and my favorite Muppet is Sam the Eagle. My favorite Pixar film is *Ratatouille*, with my favorite character being Remy.

Q I've been contracted to help the Los Angeles Public Library catalog their menu collection. In a recent donation from Lord Publishing Company, we have two proofs from Walt Disney's Studio Restaurant in Burbank, California. One is for the restaurant as a whole, the other for Counter Service. Since they are only covers with no menu or inner content information, there is no date attached. I was hoping you could help me pin down a date (or range) for our records. Stacy, Los Angeles, CA

A —The two menu covers you have are probably from the 1940s. Unfortunately they cannot be dated more precisely.

Q Dave, I really enjoyed the *Treasures of the Walt Disney Archives* exhibit at the Reagan Library last year. I particularly enjoyed the re-creation of Walt's formal office. Everything in the office was apparently exactly where it was at the time Walt passed away, but I noticed that on the piano stand were several pieces of sheet music—two of those in the front being the Annette Funicello songs "The Monkey's Uncle" and "Strummin' Song." Since "Strummin' Song" was released in 1961 and "The Monkey's Uncle" in 1965, it seems unlikely that those two particular pieces would have been on the piano up in front, considering Walt died in December of 1966. Are those in fact the pieces of sheet music that were there when Walt died, or was there no sheet music, or unknown music, on the piano at the time of Walt's death, and randomly selected ones were thus placed on the piano? Joseph, Manhattan Beach, CA

A —We have to qualify one statement: when Walt died, his secretaries remained in the office about a year, clearing up the files and straightening up the furniture and furnishings. So we do not know exactly how the office looked in December 1966. After that first year, the office was closed up until I arrived in mid-1970. When I first saw the piano, the three items of sheet music visible on the piano were "A Blue Poke Bonnet and a Stove Pipe Hat" (by Eric Correa, Leni Mason, and Carl Lampl), "Babes in Toyland," and "The Strummin' Song." But there were more than fifty song sheets on the piano, almost all of them songs from the Walt Disney or Wonderland Music Co. (the two Disney music labels).

Q Some songs from the Disney album *Music from the Park* are copyrighted "Wonderland Music Company, Inc." What is Wonderland Music Company? Grant, Portland, OR

A —Disney has two in-house music companies, Walt Disney Music Company and Wonderland Music Company, for its classic

Disney-related songs. The first is affiliated with ASCAP and the other with BMI, the two national performance-rights organizations. Some composers are members of one group, and some are with the other.

Q **A few months ago a friend sent me a tape of Disney songs without the song titles. I would love to know the title and the movie one particular song appeared in. Its chorus is, "Tall Paul, tall Paul, he's my all." Andrew, Houma, PA**

A —"Tall Paul" was not a movie song, but rather a popular song sung by Annette Funicello. It was first released on the Disneyland Records label. The booklet from the Annette boxed set has this to say: "The Disney people came across two struggling songwriting brothers, Richard M. and Robert B. Sherman, and a novelty rock 'n' roll song they'd written called 'Tall Paul.' The song, a 90-second dose of cotton candy about a girl in love with the tallest guy on the high school football team, struck [producer Tutti] Camarata as a perfect fit for Annette's unschooled voice." On the charts, "Tall Paul" reached number seven in 1959.

Q **There have been so many fascinating documentaries about the making of the Disney Parks and individual movies, but I do not recall ever seeing a documentary about the musicians who contribute to the Disney experience with their music. Music in the Parks and at their events is such an integral part of the experience. It would not be a true Disney experience without the music! Who are the people who provide these experiences for us? Cheryl, Cedar Rapids, IA**

A —Music has indeed been an exciting part of our Parks, and the contributions of composers have been mentioned in numerous books. At first Walt Disney used his staff composers, such as Oliver Wallace, George Bruns, and the Sherman brothers, to write the music he needed for Disneyland. Perhaps the most prolific of the composers for Disneyland and the later Parks was Buddy Baker; he remained a staff composer until 1983. In more recent years there have been such people as George Wilkins, Bob Moline, Don Dorsey, Russell Brower, Bruce Broughton, Joel McNeely, Edo Guidotti, and Richard Bellis creating the music. There is a documentary film, *The Boys: The Sherman Brothers' Story*, released on DVD in 2010, and a 2014 documentary by Dave Bossert, *The Tunes Behind the Toons*.

Q **How many movies did the Sherman brothers write songs for? Laura, Milwaukee, WI**

A —They wrote more than a hundred songs for about twenty-five Disney feature films, along with many more for TV, recordings, and theme park attractions.

Q **As I child I learned a Christmas song called "Willy Clause." My wife finally found a 45-rpm record of it by Molly Bee from the early 1950s. I put it in iTunes and it popped up as a Disney record. Is it a Disney record or was that a glitch? Stephen, San Bernardino, CA**

A —This was not a Disney song, though it could have been on an early Disney Christmas phonograph record. Molly Bee recorded the song in 1952 on the Capitol label. One fact that might cause confusion: it was written by Mel Leven; Leven worked for Disney on *One Hundred and One Dalmatians* and *Babes in Toyland* in the 1960s.

Q **I have enjoyed collecting music from Disney films and Parks over the years. In regard to the movie sound tracks, is there a single resource that lists all the Disney films and their respective music? By the way, *The Boys: The Sherman***

Brothers' Story is a must for any fan of Disney music. Accolades to the Sherman brothers' sons for their effort in the project! Ned, Newport News, VA

A —I know of no complete listings of Disney songs, though there are many books that have been written about Disney music and would have partial lists.

Q **Do I detect uncanny similarities between the songs "Who's Afraid of the Big Bad Wolf?" and "Laughing Place" (from Song of the South)? A.N., Muscle Shoals, AL**

A —While there are some similarities between the two songs, there was probably no conscious attempt to make them similar. "Who's Afraid of the Big Bad Wolf?" was loosely based on "Happy Birthday"; these songs obviously had a pattern that proved successful.

Q **What Disney songs have won Oscars? J.P., San Diego, CA**

A —There have been fifteen: "When You Wish Upon a Star" from Pinocchio, "Zip-A-Dee-Doo-Dah" from Song of the South, "Chim Chim Cheree" from Mary Poppins, "Under the Sea" from The Little Mermaid, "Sooner or Later (I Always Get My Man)" from Dick Tracy, "Beauty and the Beast" from Beauty and the Beast, "A Whole New World" from Aladdin, "Can You Feel the Love Tonight" from The Lion King, "Colors of the Wind" from Pocahontas, "You Must Love Me" from Evita, "You'll Be in My Heart" from Tarzan, "If I Didn't Have You" from Monsters, Inc., "We Belong Together" from Toy Story 3, "Man or Muppet" from The Muppets, and "Let It Go," from Frozen.

Q **In what Disney film did the song "Mule Train" appear? I noticed it has a Disney copyright. T.P., Norridge, IL**

A —When the Walt Disney Music Co. was originally established in the late 1940s, it bought the rights to a number of songs for its catalog. Some were never used in a Disney film. "Mule Train" was one of the most popular of those songs; the 1951 hit "Shrimp Boats" was another. In recent years, the Disney Music Company has concentrated on Disney songs.

Q When were the first Disney phonograph records released? G.W., Oakland, CA

A —The first Disney records were small picture discs released by RCA Victor in 1933. Disney was involved in two other "firsts" in recording history: the *Snow White and the Seven Dwarfs* album was the first album ever made directly from the sound track of a motion picture (previously, the producers of a film would bring the orchestra and singers back onto a soundstage and rerecord the tracks). The *Pinocchio* album two years later was the first to use the term *sound track* on an album.

Q Did the Sherman brothers ever perform one of their songs in a movie feature? Mark, Spokane, WA

A —They were filmed with Walt Disney in a promo film introducing the song "There's a Great Big Beautiful Tomorrow" to General Electric, which sponsored the Carousel of Progress at the 1964–1965 New York World's Fair. Richard Sherman is also known to have played a kazoo with the orchestra for some sound track recordings.

Q I recently bought a CD made in 1996 that has music from the Parks as performed by famous artists. On the CD is "Grim Grinning Ghosts" as performed by the Barenaked Ladies. It sounds very similar to the version heard in HalloWishes. Are they the ones who performed it? I always thought the same

male vocalist could be heard in Fantasmic! Am I correct? Erica, Antioch, CA

A —According to Steve Davison of Walt Disney Imagineering Creative Entertainment, the Barenaked Ladies recording was not used in HalloWishes. The male vocalist is Tim Davis, who served as the vocal/session director for *Glee.*

Q **What is your fave song in the world? Grace, Palm Springs, CA**

A —Assuming you are referring to the Disney "world," I love "Little April Shower" from *Bambi,* and "Golden Dream" from *The American Adventure* at Epcot.

Q **When I was fourteen, I was a member of a song-and-dance troupe called *The East End Kids.* We traveled to France and performed at what was then called Euro Disney. (This was in 1993.) While I was home for the holidays visiting my parents, I found a certificate and a T-shirt I received from Disney with the title JOURNÉES MUSICALES MAGIQUES [Magical Music Days] on it. Does Disney still sponsor these programs that help send teenagers to perform at their Parks, both national and internationally, who are not technically employed by the Disney company? We were an independent organization located in Pittsburgh, PA, but contracted through Disney to perform abroad. It was an amazing experience for me and I was just curious. Thank you. Liza Marie, Brooklyn, NY**

A —These popular programs are still going on. At the United States Disney Parks, they were known as Magic Music Days for many years. The program is now called Disney Performing Arts OnStage.

Q **Hello, Mr. Smith! I'd love to talk with you about my grandfather, Bob Jackman, who was the head of the music department for**

many years. We just visited the Archives at the Disney Studios and came across an e-mail in his file that mentioned you remembered him and that he was working when you started working at Disney. If it's at all possible, I'd love to ask what you remember of him and his career there! Thanks! Molly, Tiburon, CA

A —I did not know Bob Jackman well, though I met with him several times. Mainly, I worked on musical matters through his knowledgeable assistant, Flo Daniel. I recall Bob as being very friendly and helpful to a young man just getting started with the Archives. It always impressed me that he had been the voice of Goofy in some cartoons in the 1950s when Pinto Colvig was unavailable.

Q Hey, Dave. I was listening to my recently purchased album of *Four Parks: One World*, and I could have sworn that I heard the theme for Fantasmic! playing. I checked the name of the song, and it was the entrance melody to Epcot. I just got back from Disney, so I know that the opening notes of the Epcot theme are extremely similar if not identical to the theme for Fantasmic! Is there any connection between the two songs, or am I just hearing things? Jonathan, Aiken, SC

A —That track, known as "Legacy," is by composer Steve Woods. The Fantasmic! theme is by Bruce Healey. According to Epcot composer Russell Brower, the "Legacy" track introduction is similar to John Williams's *Star Wars* or *Superman* openings (a fanfare technically known as a "brass pyramid"), with a melody harking back to the music composed for *The Rocketeer*, Soarin', and Fantasmic!

Q I was at a Mystic Manor soft opening at Hong Kong Disneyland and I loved it. My question is, what is the name of the theme song Danny Elfman wrote? It certainly isn't "Grim Grinning Ghosts." Joshamee, Los Angeles, CA

A —We checked with Walt Disney Imagineering, and the Elfman song is simply known as "Mystic Manor Theme."

Q Mr. Smith, one of my favorite songs out of the Disney repertoire is "What, No Mickey Mouse?" written by Irving Caesar in, I believe, 1932. I have only heard two recordings, one featuring a male vocal ensemble from the 1930s and another by Phil Harris. Are there any other recordings of this song, and what is the history behind it? Jared, Terre Haute, IN

A —Those are the only two recordings of which I am aware. The 1932 78-rpm recording (Brunswick 6389) featured Ben Bernie & All the Lads; the Phil Harris recording was put out by Buena Vista Records as a 45-rpm record, F-477, in 1970. The song was also published as sheet music.

Q In the early 1990s, Disney released a series of VHS tapes under the name Walt Disney's Studio Film Collection. On each tape, before the movie began, there appeared a trailer for the collection. This trailer had a very catchy sound track. I know there are many people who would like to know more about the song in that trailer. Who is the composer, and does it have a title? Thank you. Jeff, Rock Cove, NS, Canada

A —This is probably what is known in the industry as "needle-drop" music—generic music that filmmakers use for trailers and other short-deadline projects. Cues from these music libraries are inexpensive to use because there are no musicians or singers to pay. It is very possible that the piece does not even have a title.

Q I seem to remember Diana Ross recording a theme song for a Disney film in the early 1980s. I thought it was for *The Last Flight*

of Noah's Ark, but I recently viewed that film, and the theme song is attributed to Alexandra Brown. Am I remembering this incorrectly? Many thanks. Bill, Roselle, NJ

A — You might be thinking of the song Diana Ross recorded for the non-Disney animated film, *The Land Before Time.* It was entitled "If We Hold on Together." Diana Ross and the Supremes recorded a number of Disney songs in 1967, and while the album was unreleased at the time, the songs have since become available.

Q **Does Disney still have what's known as the Disney Choir, a choir that sings in Disney movies? Avi, Irvine, CA**

A —There is no one specific choir for films, but Disney does have a Cast Member choir, which performs for the annual Candlelight Processionals and other events.

Q **We recently came across two 45-rpm records by the Firehouse Five Plus Two. Two of the band members are listed as Ward Kimball and Frank Thomas. Are we right to assume that these are the same men who were Disney animators, or is it just a coincidence? Gino and Gerry, Pacifica, CA**

A —The Firehouse Five Plus Two was a Dixieland jazz band made up of Disney Studio personnel. The group played from the end of World War II until 1971. Led by Ward Kimball, the Firehouse Five Plus Two included Frank Thomas, Eddie Forrest, Harper Goff, and George Probert.

Q **When I was at the D23 Expo I saw a record that I have, *The Scarecrow of Oz,* in the Archives. What can you tell me about this album? How many were made, and was it associated with any other Disney project? Thank you. Marie, Brooklyn, NY**

A —*The Scarecrow of Oz* long-playing record album, narrated by Ray Bolger, who was the Scarecrow in the MGM film, was released by Walt Disney Records in 1965, but we do not know how many were made. It was a Storyteller Album, ST-3930. Years earlier, Disney had purchased the rights to most of the Oz books that were written by L. Frank Baum (but not later ones written by others). Walt had considered making a motion picture entitled *The Rainbow Road to Oz* in the 1950s, but it was never made. The film would have starred some of the Mouseketeers.

Q Dear Dave, as a child in the 1980s, I had a large collection of Disney Records, including *Splashdance, Totally Minnie, Rock Around the Mouse,* and one I believe was called *Cowboy Mickey* (or something to that effect). While the other titles are easily available on CD, I cannot find any evidence that this *Cowboy Mickey* album existed! Nothing on eBay or Amazon; I can't even find it in a Google search. What was the name of that album and is there any availability today? Adam, Providence, RI

A —The album you are thinking of is *Pardners: 14 Great Cowboy Songs,* released in 1980. It featured Larry Groce and the Disneyland Children's Sing-Along Chorus. The same album was released on both the Disneyland and Buena Vista labels.

Q Classic Disney Park songs like "Yo Ho (A Pirate's Life for Me)," the Tiki Room song, and "Grim Grinning Ghosts" have such a warm, characteristic sound. Were those songs recorded in a Disney studio, or was that work done elsewhere? Todd, Locust, VA

A —According to Glenn Barker at Walt Disney Imagineering, all of these were recorded on A Stage, the large orchestra stage, at the Disney Studio in Burbank, California. The organ for "Grim Grinning Ghosts" was recorded on the twenty-four—rank Robert

Morton pipe organ at Whitney Recording Studio in Glendale, California.

Q **Did Walt have a favorite sound track or a favorite song from a movie? Jonathan, Pawtucket, RI**

A —The only song I recall hearing about is "Feed the Birds" from *Mary Poppins*. That film's sound track might have been his favorite also.

Q **I was listening to my *Beauty and the Beast Original Broadway Cast* CD the other day. The song "A Change in Me" was added to the musical a few years after its Broadway debut, so it is not on the original cast CD. Do you know of any CD that has that song on it? Robert, [No city provided], NJ**

A —Susan Egan, the initial Belle on Broadway, recorded the song for her album *So Far*. It had been added to the Broadway show when Toni Braxton was playing Belle.

Q **I recently bought a piece of sheet music titled "Mike Fink's Christmas" from 1955 by George Bruns. While the cover states it's from the Disneyland TV program featuring Davy Crockett and Mike Fink, I can't recall ever hearing or seeing this piece of music before. Can you tell me if this song was ever used in a TV special or anywhere else? Thank you! Kristen, San Jose, CA**

A —The cover should probably say that it was inspired by the Davy Crockett and Mike Fink TV shows. The song wasn't used on any of the shows.

Q **In the early 1970s, Gulf gas stations released a Disney music collection. I remember seeing the advertisement during *The Wonderful World of Disney*. The songs were not performed**

by the original singers but by the pop and jazz singers of the time. Do you recall these recordings, and are they still available anywhere? Sherri, Plainfield, NJ

A —Gulf Oil put out the phonograph record albums *Walt Disney's Happiest Songs* in 1967 and *Walt Disney's Merriest Songs* in 1968. The versions of the songs on those records have not been rereleased. The records themselves can sometimes be found in used record stores, antique stores, flea markets, and on eBay.

Q I bought a Disneyland 45-rpm record at a yard sale. On the cover it reads *Mickey Mouse March*. The songs on it are "Mickey Mouse Club March," "A Cowboy Needs a Horse," "Today Is Tuesday," and "Little Cow." Is this part of a set? Richard, Newark, DE

A —You have Disneyland Record number LG-651. There were five other *Mickey Mouse Club* records issued at the same time, LG-652 through LG-656, but they were not really issued as a set. There is a price guide by R. Michael Murray called *The Golden Age of Walt Disney Records, 1933–1988* (Antique Trader Books). Your record is listed in the book at $15 for near-mint condition.

PUBLICATIONS

Q When I was young, I had a Little Golden Book called *Little Man of Disneyland*, about a leprechaun who lived in an orange tree on the land where Disneyland was to be built. He met up with Donald and Mickey for a preview of the Park, and Disney built him a new home inside Disneyland, where he lived happily. So—I've heard that there was once a tree in Disneyland with a leprechaun-sized door in it, for fans of the book. A) Is this true? B) If so, where was it located? Thanks. Kevin, Papillon, NE

A —This is a story fondly remembered by many readers, but the rumor about an actual tree with a miniature door in it at Disneyland was untrue until 2015 when Disneyland added the leprechaun elements to a tree in Adventureland. The book, published in 1955, was written by Annie North Bedford (a pseudonym of Jane Werner Watson).

Q I was wondering, what was the first book to have Mickey Mouse in color? And would it be valuable if I found one? Jeffrey, St. Petersburg, FL

A The very first Mickey Mouse book, entitled *Mickey Mouse Book* (1930), did not have full color—only green, black, and white. But the second book, *The Adventures of Mickey Mouse* (1931), did feature Mickey in color. Original copies of the book are valuable, though the book was reprinted for its fiftieth anniversary, and those reprints are naturally worth much less.

Q A person who I saw at a book sale had a signed copy of the Walt Disney book *Perri* that has glued-in pictures. I said I would find out for her how much it is worth, as she is not really computer literate; so any pointers where I can find out more would be nice. David, London, England

A —The *Perri* book, produced by Marc Barraud, with the tipped-in photographs, is scarce, but not terribly expensive (Internet book dealers have it for $25 to $40). However, an authentic signature of Walt Disney would greatly increase the value. Barraud also did other Disney nature books, all with beautiful photographs.

Q **I am looking for the *Pigs Is Pigs* poem I used in elementary school for a public-speaking event. It was in a red hardcover Disney book that had many stories in it. Perhaps *Storyland*? It was in poem format, not story. It started out like the clip I saw of the 1954 movie by Disney. The poem goes: "In the Westcote Railway Station / In the year 1950 / The agent there was Flannery / The best there was alive. / Now Flannery ran his station / Exactly by the rules / He tried to learn each one by heart / Just like a kid in school." Is there a copy of that book out there somewhere for purchase, or even just a copy of the poem for my students to use in the same way? Annette, Fond du Lac, WI**

A —This poem was created by the Disney story team for our 1954 cartoon *Pigs Is Pigs*, based on the well-known 1905 story of the same title by Ellis Parker Butler. It was indeed published in the Golden Press book *Walt Disney's Story Land*, first published in 1961 and kept in print into the 1990s.

Q **As a child, I remember a poem published in a magazine around Christmas time that was many pages long, and featured Disneyland. I cut the poem from the magazine and read it all the time to my younger brothers and sisters. After a number of years I went to the place I kept it, only to find it not there; all the younger siblings denied taking it. When I had children, I attempted to find it through contacting various magazines, but no one was able to help. Now, as a grandmother, I would love to have this poem to share again with a new generation. Do you know the title and if it is available? Karen, Clifton Park, NY**

A —You may be thinking of "A Christmas Adventure in Disneyland," published in *Family Circle* magazine in December 1958.

Q I am cataloging the Disney–Golden Book *Supercar* by George Sherman, with pictures by Mel Crawford. I'd like to create a unique authority record for Mr. Sherman, since he shares his name, George R. Sherman, with a geologist and the author of *The Negro as a Soldier*. I understand from a brief article on the Net that Mr. Sherman died in 1974 and that he worked as "head of foreign relations" and in the publications department from the late 1950s until he died. Can you find the man's date of birth and possibly his full middle name? Emilie, Minneapolis, MN

A —His full name was George Ransom Sherman; he was born September 30, 1928, and died August 3, 1974. When I met him in 1967, he was head of the Disney Publications Department. He was one of my first contacts at the Disney Studio.

Q My mother has found in her loft two identical original booklets called *The Art of Animation*. Have you ever heard of it or seen it? I can send over photos of the front cover and the inside cover pictures, which are from *Sleeping Beauty*, I believe. My parents actually met Walt Disney when they worked for the famous store called Selfridges back in the 1960s, when my father was the window dresser. He was given the booklets after having designed and produced a window display about Disney. Unfortunately no photos of the window creation existed, since the cost of a camera in those days was too much for my parents. Any advice or help would be great. Karen, Colchester, England

A —The brochure you have was created for the traveling *Art of Animation* exhibit, which used *Sleeping Beauty* to explain the methods of producing a Disney animated feature. The exhibit, which began in 1958, was shown in the United States, Europe, and East Asia.

Q As the Muppets are now a part of the Disney family, I would love to know when Kermit the Frog spoke/wrote the following quotation, so that I can use it in my wedding ceremony: "I really do believe that all of you are at the beginning of a wonderful journey. As you start traveling down the road of life, remember this: . . . never fly as cargo." Nikki, Edison, NJ

A —The quote is from a book, *It's Not Easy Being Green: And Other Things to Consider* (New York, Hyperion, 2005), p. 132.

Q I recently acquired a copy of *The Disneyland News* newspaper from July 1955. The copy that I have seems to look old enough, but the headline doesn't look right. The newspaper that I have reads, "Vol. 1, No. 1" and "July 1955," along with a headline reading, "The R. L. Purdys Visit Disneyland." Of course, the newspaper that I am familiar with and have seen many times has a headline that reads, "50,000 Attend Gala Park Opening." Were there two different headlines for the same paper, or is the one I have a fake? Thank you. Peter, Monrovia, CA

A —Guests to Disneyland in the mid-1950s could get their own headline printed on *The Disneyland News*.

Q As a Christmas gift, I received the 1995 *Disneyland Nickel Tour* book. It states that the postcards discussed were drawn from the collection of Vernon Orr and then put in chronological order mainly according to the 1979 checklist book. So, is the Orr collection still with us, and where might it be? Does the Walt Disney Archives have as extensive a collection of cards?

Is it available to the public? Thanks for your help! Charles, Williamsburg, VA

A —I do not know what happened to the Orr collection. Both of the authors of the 1995 book—David Mumford and Bruce Gordon—have passed away. The Walt Disney Archives does have a very large collection of Disney Park postcards. The Archives is not open to the public, but if you have specific questions, they can try to answer them for you.

Q **I have a book titled *Lilo & Stitch: Collected Stories from the Film's Creators*. The book's title page is signed by eighteen people who, I believe, are those who worked on the film. Some of the names are Sean Sullivan, Chris Greco, Karrie Michaels, David Yorke, etc. I believe these are original signatures. I am wondering, where is the best place to go to find the book's value? Kathi, Clemson, SC**

A —Yes, those are artists who worked on the film. Sorry, we have no information on values. Most people check eBay for similar items.

Q **I have Walt Disney's Comics no. 60, September 1945, vol. 5, no. 12, the first comic issued after World War II. Were comics made during the war, with metal restrictions in place in the United States? David, Winnipeg, MB, Canada**

A —The Disney comics continued to be published throughout World War II. However, because of metal restrictions, the number of staples holding them together went from two to one from 1943 to 1946.

Q **When I was in my teens, I recall reading comic strip adaptations of forthcoming or current Disney movies in the Sunday newspaper, in color. Could you please tell me when these ran,**

and remind me of some of the movies featured? Thank you very much. Jay, Cumming, GA

A —The first newspaper comic strip adaptation of a Disney movie was for *The Adventures of Robin Hood and His Merrie Men,* beginning on July 13, 1952, and running for five months. These comic strip adaptations continued for well over a hundred Disney films during the next three and a half decades, with the last one being *Tramp's CAT-Astrophe, featuring Lady and the Tramp,* running from November 1986 to February 1987.

Q I recently acquired Disney Editions' *Windows on Main Street* by Chuck Snyder. I was surprised to see that Harper Goff was not included in the book. Was that done because his window is in Adventureland and not on Main Street? Are there other honored Disney employees on windows in places other than Main Street? John, Centennial, CO

A —Unfortunately, the *Windows on Main Street* book could not include every single person who has been honored with a window at the Disney Parks. There are indeed some that are not on Main Street, U.S.A., at Disneyland. Besides Harper Goff in Adventureland, there are Glenn Hicks and Fess Parker in Frontierland and Sally McWhirter in New Orleans Square.

Q I have a book that was my father's. It was given to him in 1956. The book is called *Walt Disney's Vanishing Prairie* by Jane Werner and the staff of the Walt Disney studio. It is a green hardback with pictures of prairie dogs on the front. I have looked on eBay, etc., and all I find are books with the same name but pictures of buffaloes on the covers. The book has a copyright date of 1955, published by Simon and Schuster of New York. I wonder if this book is worth anything or if I should keep it for the great-grandchild. It is in very good shape. Thank you for anything that you can tell me about this book. Lynne, Denver, CO

A —That is the same book; the prairie dogs are on the hardcover, the buffalo are on the dust jacket. The book is not especially valuable; I think your great-grandchild would enjoy it.

Q Is Uncle Scrooge a Disney character, owned by Disney or licensed to them? I ask because Carl Barks seems to have created him after leaving Disney for a comics company, where he created him. Nick, Woodland, CA

A —Uncle Scrooge McDuck is a Disney character. Carl Barks was hired by Western Publishing Co. to write and draw some of the Disney comics they produced under license from Disney. It was while doing Donald Duck comics that he introduced Uncle Scrooge.

Q Hi, Dave! I just purchased a copy of your *Disney: the First 100 Years* on eBay. It says, "To Toby—A Century of Disney history for you!" Signed by Dave Smith. Dated 12/20/99. The seller said you signed it for Toby Bluth. I have been waiting patiently to find a nice copy for a decent price. With your signature (and if this was for Don's brother), this would be a great addition to my autographed Disney book collection. Thomas, Lodi, CA

A —I counted Toby Bluth as a friend when we both worked at the Disney Studio, and in fact I have made a collection of autographed copies of his many books. I am even pleased to have some original Toby Bluth artwork. So it is very likely that I signed the book for Toby in 1999.

Q I would like to read a biography of Walt Disney. Which one do you consider the most accurate and readable biography of him? Rosy, Charlottesville, VA

A —Heavily researched biographies include those by Neil Gabler (*Walt Disney: The Triumph of the American Imagination*) and Steven Watts (*The Magic Kingdom: Walt Disney and the American Way of Life*), but the only one by someone who actually knew Walt Disney is Bob Thomas's *Walt Disney: An American Original*. Diane Disney Miller's early biography of her father, written with Pete Martin, *The Story of Walt Disney*, is long out of print but can be bought from online secondhand book dealers.

Q **Would you consider writing a book to tell the stories of how you came upon some of the Disney treasures that are now in the Archives? For instance, you could tell the story of how you acquired the snow globe used in *Mary Poppins*, along with a photo of that piece. I'm sure fans would love to know how you found treasures in the most unexpected places or through the generosity of others. Carrie, Santa Barbara, CA**

A —Others have also suggested such a book. Perhaps someday. ☺

TELEVISION

Q

I have several of the Walt Disney Treasures DVDs. Who is the voice-over announcer who narrates the previews of "next week's adventure" and introduces Walt Disney at the start of the TV show? Brett, Newport Beach, CA

A

—The announcers used most often on the Disney TV shows were Dick Tufeld and Dick Wesson.

Q

There was a Disney show in the 1990s set in the Parks about the Parks and everything Disney. It was a live-action show. The hosts were a male with red hair and a female with brown hair. My daughter was on one of the shows set in Walt Disney World in February 1996. I would love to see if I can order a copy of the show. How can I do it? Jackie, Broomall, PA

A

—*Walt Disney World Inside-Out* (and its companion show *Disneyland Inside-Out*) aired on Disney Channel in the mid-1990s. J. D. Roth and Brianne Leary are the hosts that you recall. Unfortunately, for copyright reasons, it is not possible to purchase DVDs of individual Disney shows of the past.

Q

On one of the *Walt Disney Presents* episodes, Walt Disney mentioned a 1776-era street to be constructed at Disneyland. What happened to it? E.R., Guthrie, OK

A

—In 1956 Walt Disney announced plans for a Liberty Street at Disneyland, to be located behind the east side of Main Street. Included would have been a Hall of Presidents. But this was long before Audio-Animatronics figures were invented, so the presidential figures would have been mere mannequins. Other projects occupied Walt's time, while eventually the Audio-Animatronics process was perfected and deemed ideal for the planned Hall of Presidents. However, Liberty Street was never built at Disneyland; instead it made its debut as Liberty

Square at Walt Disney World's Magic Kingdom in 1971. The Hall of Presidents show has become one of the most inspiring ever produced by Disney Imagineers.

Q **Hi, Dave. It has been brought to my attention that you did a booklet or article on the old Disney *Mission to Mars/Man in Space* cartoons from the late 1950s. If so, please bring the title and publisher to my attention, as I cannot locate it through the usual means. John, Smithfield, RI**

A —The article was called "They're Following Our Script: Walt Disney's Trip to Tomorrowland," published in the magazine *Future* (May 1978). A shortened version of the same article, titled "Walt Disney's Conquest of Space," with different illustrations, appeared the same month in *Starlog*.

Q **My brother and I have always wondered about Goofy and his son, Max. Goofy seems to be unmarried, and we wonder who Max's mother was. We have tried looking in all the older cartoons, but found nothing. Perhaps you can tell us. Alexandria, Naples, FL**

A —The writers of the stories for *Goof Troop* and *A Goofy Movie* did not create a mother for Max. In some early cartoons, Goofy played a character known as George Geef; there was also a Mrs. Geef and their son, Junior, in those films.

Q **Dave, I just read your Q&A on *Secrets of the Pirates Inn*, and I have a VHS version of the movie in Walt Disney Home Video packaging. In addition to the feature's description, stills, starring cast, producer, book credit, director, etc., it also has a green triangle with a *U* in it and the words UNIVERSAL SUITABLE FOR ALL along with a bar code. The side of the box has "554 PAL VHS" at the bottom. In typical Disney fashion, there is no release date on it**

either. Could it be a really good bootleg, or is it possible that it was actually released? Eric, Orland Park, IL

A —This seems to be a video released in England; sometimes films that don't have video releases in the United States do indeed have them abroad.

Q **Hello. I grew up watching Disney. I have recently searched for the Halloween specials that aired on Disney Channel back in the 1980s. I have found a few; however, I am looking for one in particular. I don't remember the name of it, but it was aired during the mid- and late 1980s and it starred Richard Masur . . . could you possibly help with a name or where I might find it? Thank you. Justin, Bend, OR**

A —You are thinking of *Mr. Boogedy*, which aired on our TV show, in 1986. A sequel, *Bride of Boogedy*, aired the following year. The two films have not been released on videocassette or DVD.

Q **Hi, Dave. Recently a coworker and I were talking about how important Disney was in our childhoods. We recalled stories of sitting around the TV on Sunday nights watching *The Wonderful World of Disney* shows. One show in particular we were discussing was *Moochie of the Little League*, a movie from roughly 1959 that re-aired on Disney Channel in 1985. Researching it on the Internet, it looks like that was an episodic show and not a movie. Can you tell me more about the beloved character Moochie, and if any of those episodes are available today? I believe it would be something my children would get a kick out of. Thanks. Lori, Lebanon, OH**

A —*Moochie of the Little League* was a two-part TV show from 1959. The two parts were combined into feature length and made available for rental on 16 mm film to schools and other organizations with the title *Little League Moochie*, but it has never been released on videocassette or DVD.

Q **I would like to watch the documentary series including the episode *Man in Space*, circa 1950s. Is it available on DVD? As a child it inspired me to pursue a degree in science. Please advise, and sincere thanks for your time. Thomas, Bozeman, MT**

A —The Disney space films were released in the Walt Disney Treasures DVD, volume 11, *Tomorrowland*, in 2004.

Q **I was wondering if Disney Productions will ever run the old *Zorro* series again on TV? Does Disney offer the complete series on DVD or VHS? Great series, although I believe the original series was produced in 1958 and 1959. Thanks. Frank, Lake Havasu City, AZ**

A —The complete set of *Zorro* shows was released on DVD in the Walt Disney Treasures series in 2009. There are no plans to run the series on TV.

Q **Where can I get a list of Disney TV miniseries from the 1980s? I'm looking for one that was about a group of kids who go far into space. I think it was part of the *Disney Sunday Night Movie* series, but I can't think of it. Kyle, Bushnell, IL**

A —You can find information on the Disney TV shows in Bill Cotter's book, *The Wonderful World of Disney Television*. The show you may be thinking of is *Earth*Star Voyager*, a four-hour TV movie that aired in two parts in January 1988. In the film a group of young cadets is sent off in a spaceship in the twenty-first century to find a new home for humanity when Earth is deteriorating.

Q **I remember watching a show when I was little. It had a little spotted animal with a long tail and he was always around a**

monkey in a pink T-shirt. What was the name of this cartoon? Where has it gone? I haven't even seen it anymore. Has it been discontinued? If so when? Austin, Ogden, UT

A —You are thinking of Marsupilami, whose friend was Maurice, a gorilla. Maurice was indeed in a pink T-shirt. The animated shows aired back in 1993-1994—there were only thirteen episodes—and were based on a European comic book character from the 1960s.

Q I worked the scoring stage at the Disney Studio in the late 1970s. I'm trying to recall the composer that wrote much of the music for the new *Mickey Mouse Club*. I seem to recall his first name was Peter. John, Thousand Oaks, CA

A —Peter Martin, with Marc B. Ray, wrote several of the introductory songs for the different days of the week for the 1970s version of the *Mickey Mouse Club*. Composers listed for the complete shows were Buddy Baker, Robert Brunner, and Will Schaefer.

Q Which episode featured a pack of dogs running into Walt's office and leaping into the air from his desk? Michael, Millbrae, CA

A —That was Walt Disney's introduction to *Bristle Face, Part II*, which aired on February 2, 1964.

Q I seem to remember a TV tour of the Disney Studios hosted by Hayley Mills, who at the time was recording dialogue for *The Black Cauldron*. Was she ever involved with that project, or is my memory playing tricks on me? Allen, San Francisco, CA

A —Hayley did a TV show entitled *Disney Animation: The Illusion of Life* in 1981, which was inspired by the book by Frank Thomas and Ollie Johnston of the same title. She appears in a segment showing how the animators pick the right actors for the characters' voices. I remember this episode well, because Hayley filmed part of it in the Walt Disney Archives, relaxing between takes in my office.

Q **When EPCOT Center first opened in 1982, there was a special on TV (I don't remember if it was on Disney Channel or network TV), but it had a short biography on Walt Disney. As the short film was being played, Mac Davis sang a song called "Marceline" in reference to Walt's boyhood hometown. Is there any place I could find that song? Was it ever released on a CD or album? I remember as a kid watching that over and over just because I liked the song "Marceline." Jason, Greer, SC**

A —The song, "Marceline," actually came from the Disney TV show *Walt Disney: One Man's Dream* (1981). It was written by Ken and Mitzie Welch, and the composers were nominated for an Emmy Award for their song. I am not aware of any CD or album releases.

Q **In an episode of *Disneyland* entitled *The Fourth Anniversary Show*, Walt tells the story of a visit to the Studio by Russian composer Sergei Prokofiev, who proceeds to play "Peter and the Wolf" for Walt, inspiring him to make the animated version that appeared in *Make Mine Music*. Is there any truth in this story, or was it just staged for TV? Templeton, Louisville, KY**

A —The TV show version was staged, but the meeting did actually happen. Prokofiev visited the Disney Studio on February 28, 1938, with his lawyer Randolph Polk, to play the piano score of "Peter and the Wolf" for Walt Disney and Disney composer Leigh Harline. Supposedly Prokofiev had written the piece with Walt in mind. It took a while, but a contract was finally signed three years later, and our "Peter and the Wolf" came out in *Make Mine Music* in 1946.

Q There was a lovely young blond actress who appeared with Walt in many of his lead-ins to the *Wonderful World of Color* TV show. She was one of the paint girls in the premiere episode, *An Adventure in Color*; brought Walt blueprints for Nature's Wonderland in *Disneyland '61*; asked for Walt's autograph and "stole" his popcorn in *Disneyland After Dark*; escorted you to your reserved table in the Golden Horseshoe Revue; and brought Walt models in the Radio City CinemaScope intro to *Disneyland U.S.A.* I'd love to know her! Thanks, Dave! Joseph, Pasadena, CA

A —The same actress appeared in the lead-in for *The Horse Without a Head* on TV, and Walt called her Marla. The same name appears in production records for other shows: Marla Ryan.

Q In an episode of *Disneyland* entitled *The Story of the Animated Drawing*, there is a brief dramatization of Charles-Émile Reynaud working with his various inventions, including his Théâtre Optique. The Théâtre Optique that appears in the episode looks as though it's fully functional. Was this a re-creation of Reynaud's invention built by Disney staff? Or was it borrowed from a museum? Does this Théâtre Optique still survive today? Bradley, Laconner, WA

A —Disney licensed footage from a 1947 film, *Animated Cartoons— The Toy That Grew Up*, produced by Les Filmes du Compas and Roger Leenhardt, for that TV show. The Walt Disney Archives has no further information on that film, so they do not know if the Théâtre Optique still exists.

Q I recently purchased the Mickey Mouse Club Days of the Week five-piece ornament set from the Disney Store. They are being added to our Walt Disney Classics Collection Mickey

Mouse Club figurines—images I felt had been missing from the collection. The ornaments are painted in color. I watched the *Mickey Mouse Club* from 1955 through 1959 in black and white, and I know that the opening sequence was filmed in color, which we have on DVD. Were Mickey's "Days of the Week" greetings also filmed in color? I am curious about where the designers of the ornaments got the color references for Mickey's five different costumes. Clark, Lakeville, MN

A —The days of the week intros were filmed in color; you can see the color versions on the Walt Disney Treasures DVD, volume 9, *Mickey Mouse in Living Color, Volume 2*. Walt Disney often filmed his early TV shows, especially animation segments, in color, believing that they might have some future use.

Q In 1963, during the color-TV airing of *From All of Us to All of You* on the *Wonderful World of Color*, did it have a new Walt Disney introduction? Or did it have the old Walt Disney introduction from 1958? Matthew, North Hollywood, CA

A —Walt's lead-in for the 1963 airing contains some elements from the 1958 one, such as Tinker Bell reducing Walt to "cricket size," but in 1963 he talks about *The Sword in the Stone* and the upcoming *Mary Poppins*.

Q I was wondering how many educational Tomorrowland segments were made for the original *Disneyland* TV show. I'm a massive fan of *Our Friend the Atom* and am wondering how many episodes like it were made; I can't find the information anywhere. Dylan, Melbourne, VIC, Australia

A —Some others were *Man in Space*, *Man and the Moon*, *Mars and Beyond*, *Magic Highway U.S.A.*, and *Eyes in Outer Space*. Perhaps you can find a copy of Bill Cotter's 1997 book, *The*

Wonderful World of Disney Television, which details all the television shows.

Q **Has Disney ever released a DVD of season one of the TV series on ABC *The New Adventures of Winnie the Pooh*, which had thirty-two episodes? Steve, Gladstone, MO**

A —While entire seasons of *The New Adventures of Winnie the Pooh* have not been released on DVD, many episodes have been released through the Growing Up with Winnie the Pooh DVD series: vol. 1, *A Great Day of Discovery*; vol. 2, *Friends Forever*; vol. 3, *All for One, One For All*; vol. 4, *It's Playtime with Pooh*; and vol. 5, *Love & Friendship*.

Q **Dave, for the *The Best Doggoned Dog in the World* in 1961, did they replace the *Old Yeller* part of the program with scenes from *One Hundred and One Dalmatians*?**

A —*The Best Doggoned Dog in the World* was a 1957 TV show about man's special relationship with dogs that included scenes from *Old Yeller* (released a month later). However, when the TV show was rerun in 1961, the *Old Yeller* footage was replaced with footage from *One Hundred and One Dalmatians* to help promote the release of that motion picture.

Q **Will Disney ever release the full episodes of Walt Disney's Christmas shows? I've seen bits of them as DVD extras, but to my knowledge no DVD contains the full episodes. Carrie, Santa Barbara, CA**

A —*One Hour in Wonderland*, the first Disney Christmas show (1950), was released as bonus material on the Masterpiece Edition DVD of *Alice in Wonderland* (2004). The 1951 show (*Walt Disney Christmas Show*) has not been released, and I know of no plans to do so.

Q Why, oh why, can't I find a listing for an animated feature called (I think) *The History of Cats*? I seem to remember seeing it first in the 1970s, though it may have been produced earlier. I have tried and tried to find/acquire a copy, and it appears to have vanished into thin air! Do you know the item? Maureen, Tampa, FL

A —You may be thinking of an hour-long 1956 Disney TV show entitled *The Great Cat Family*; there was also a comic book of the same title. It relates in animation the history of cats from the days of the Egyptians to the present day, and explains how cats have been used in Disney films. An excerpt from the show appears on the 2008 Special Edition DVD of *The Aristocats*.

Q Hello, Dave! I am interested to know, for TV shows such as *One Hundred and One Dalmatians*, *Hercules: The Animated Series*, and *The Little Mermaid*, was there as much research done as for the original films, and to what extent were the characters made to be like themselves in the originals? Jay, Los Angeles, CA

A —The writers would have to do research for the stories, but the characters and their personalities are already established in the animated features. For TV series, the aim is always to have the characters look like and act like the ones in the original features, but sometimes a few revisions have to be made.

Q Hi, Dave. A really long time ago (1970s), back when Disney had their TV show *The Wonderful World of Disney* air on Sundays, I saw a Donald Duck cartoon about when Donald was born. He came out of his egg all hopping mad. I remember laughing and loving that particular cartoon. I have never seen it since. What is the name of that specific cartoon? Kristen, Pleasant Grove, UT

A —There is animation of the baby Donald coming out of an egg in the TV show *This Is Your Life, Donald Duck* from 1960.

Q When I was a kid in a small town in Saskatchewan with one TV channel in the 1960s and 1970s, we would always watch the Sunday Disney movie. One particularly stood out, as it took place in a swamp. I think it was about a kid who thought he saw a monster (dinosaur) in the swamp, and then he went in search of it. As an adult I went to Okefenokee Swamp because of the memory. It would be great to know the name of the movie. Margaret, Victoria, BC, Canada

A —You may be thinking of *The Strange Monster of Strawberry Cove* (1971), starring Burgess Meredith and Agnes Moorehead.

Q With the unfortunate passing of Annette Funicello, what items of hers does the Archives have? Avi, Irvine, CA

A —We have costume pieces of Annette's from her *Mickey Mouse Club* days and her red cape from *Babes in Toyland*. We also have all the books, comic books, paper doll books, and phonograph records that featured Annette, and lots of photographs.

Q I'm wondering if you could tell me if *Gravity Falls* is animated by hand. Daniel, Bergenfield, NJ

A —According to the show's creator, Alex Hirsch, it is, and it's produced for Disney by Rough Draft and Emation Digital in Korea.

Q I am trying to find more info on the Disney movie *Bride of Boogedy* and specifically a prop used in that movie. They refer to a "super-duper supernatural third eye." I was wondering if anyone had any idea what it looked like, and what it might have said. I know that the movie was on TV with no video release ever made possible. Would you have any info as to where those props ended up, or if anyone had a clear picture of the prop? Andrew, Miami, FL

A —In the script when they mentioned the "third eye," the characters Mr. Davis, Corwin, and Ahri plastered gag fake eyes to their foreheads. They said that the Lucifer Fall Festival was the only carnival with a "super-duper supernatural third eye."

Q Okay, Dave, here's a challenge for you. As a young boy (I'm sixty-two now) in the 1950s, we watched Disney every Sunday night, like most American families. I remember one program in particular, *The Legend of Andy Burnett*. He was a pioneer like Davy Crockett—another Disney favorite. I seem to remember he died or was killed at the end of the show (killing any chance of a sequel also). Unlike most Disney programs, I don't think this program was ever aired again. Any chance of getting a DVD or viewing it somewhere? Carl, Broughton, OH

A —That was *The Saga of Andy Burnett*, which aired in six parts in 1957–1958. It has not been released on DVD. By the way, Andy (played by Jerome Courtland) was not killed in the final episode, but one of his fellow mountain men, Jack Kelly (portrayed by Andrew Duggan) was.

Q My family recalls a Disney live-action flick called *Fuzzbucket*. However, we can only recall a scene of people floating on the ceiling and can find little information on the film. Any information would be great. Chris, Las Vegas, NV

A —*Fuzzbucket* was a 1986 Disney TV film starring Chris Hebert and Phil Fondacaro. It was released on DVD in 2011 in the Disney Generations Collection. Here is the plot summary from my *Disney A to Z* encyclopedia: "An invisible, furry creature befriends a boy who is insecure about the starting of junior high school and his parents' arguing. Causing trouble and havoc everywhere he goes, Fuzzbucket helps the boy overcome both school and family problems."

I recently came across a movie poster for "The Golden Horseshoe Revue" online. I'm familiar with the episode of *The Wonderful World of Color* **from the Walt Disney Treasures DVDs, and when I couldn't find any info about a theatrical release in the** *A to Z* **encyclopedia, I tried looking it up on** *IMDb.com*. **It didn't have a theatrical release listed, but the trivia page for the TV episode said it was edited down and released with** *The Monkey's Uncle*. **The movie poster has a copyright date of 1964, and since IMDb trivia isn't always accurate, I wondered if it was actually released with** *The Monkey's Uncle* **or** *The Misadventures of Merlin Jones*. **If there's any more information you can provide, it would be greatly appreciated. Thanks a lot! Braden, Idaho Falls, ID**

—The TV show was released theatrically in England in August 1963, only in London's West End, with *Miracle of the White Stallions*. In the United States, it got a theatrical release with a reissue of *So Dear to My Heart* in September 1964.

This may seem like a random question, but this is kind of my last-ditch effort to find what I am looking for. I have searched all over the Internet to find a list of videos of the old Disney musical clips that appeared between shows. The one in particular I am looking for is one that was about the moon disappearing and something about a werewolf. These were not animated and were sung by real people with an accompanying video. They were played during the 1990s. If you would be able to answer, or even direct me in the right direction, I would

greatly appreciate it! It's been driving me crazy, and I would like to at least know what these little skits were titled. Andrew, Thayer, IL

A —Disney released in 1984-1985 a series of five videocassettes called *DTV* (our version of the music videos on MTV) and later some TV specials. These music videos consisted of popular and golden oldies songs using clips of Disney animation. Perhaps the one you recall is the Creedence Clearwater Revival song "Bad Moon Rising," which appeared on the 1987 TV special called *DTV Monster Hits*.

Q I hope you can help me. There was a movie in the 1970s called *Child of Glass*, which was about a young boy who moves with his family to an old plantation home in the South. While living there, he befriends a young French girl ghost (who I think is played by Olivia Barash) who haunts him until he can find her doll that is hidden in an old well on the property. It is one of my favorite movies. I could swear this was a Disney film, but my husband doesn't think so. Tracy, Maple Park, IL

A —This was indeed a Disney film, a two-hour TV movie that we aired in 1978. Olivia Barash was in the cast, along with Steve Shaw, Anthony Zerbe, Nina Foch, Katy Kurtzman, Barbara Barrie, and Biff McGuire.

Q I remember around Halloween time when I was a kid the Canadian Broadcasting Corporation (CBC) here in Canada used to broadcast *The Magical World of Disney*, and also presented a special that had various Disney Halloween cartoon shorts. They would then play the Disney version of *Sleepy Hollow*. Was this a special that was put together by Disney, and if so, would it happen to be out on a DVD by chance? Brent, Vancouver, BC, Canada

A —*The Legend of Sleepy Hollow* actually appeared in a couple of Disney Halloween TV shows: *Halloween Hall of Fame*, first seen in 1977, and *A Disney Halloween*, in 1981. Neither of these has been released on video or DVD.

Q Hello. Around 1987 my family had a videodisc player, which sadly is the only medium in which I've ever seen the Disney cartoon *The Coyote's Lament*. I've been patiently waiting for its rerelease, but I haven't seen it as yet. All of my six children enjoyed it and still reminisce and want to share it with their children. Can you work your magic and speed up the process? Thanks in advance. Glenn, Fort Worth, TX

A —*The Coyote's Lament* was a Disney TV show, including a number of cartoons about a coyote, which first aired on March 5, 1961. It has never been released on videocassette, laser disc, or DVD. Perhaps you are thinking of a different cartoon.

Q What was the name of the kids' TV show with Alyson Michalka, who on the show was best friends with a boy whose family comes from another planet, and he went to school there while his dad was working on the time machine every day to try to get them back to their planet? Joe, Bethpage, NY

A —That was *Phil of the Future*, starring Alyson Michalka as Keely Teslow and Ricky Ullman as Phil Diffy. The show aired from 2004 to 2006.

Q Since you know all there is to know about Disney, and since I don't have your encyclopedia (yet), I'd like to know if the following Disney movies made in the 1970s were either theatrical feature films or made-for-TV films: *Run, Cougar, Run; Chandar, the Black Leopard of Ceylon; Mustang;* and *A Tale of Two Critters*. Thank you! Madelyn, Washington, D.C.

A —*Run, Cougar, Run* and *A Tale of Two Critters* were both initially released in theaters: *Chandar, the Black Leopard of Ceylon* and *Mustang* were originally shown on TV, both in two parts.

Q Hello! There are two episodes of the Disney TV anthology series (aka *Walt Disney's Wonderful World of Color*, etc.) that I hope you can help me find out more about. One of them concerns driving on what was then the new Interstate Highway System. I *think* it may have been the episode known as *Magic Highway U.S.A.*, but I'm not sure. The other episode is *Hurricane Hannah.* I believe it concerns hurricane forecasting, and I seem to remember missiles being fired into the hurricane for some reason. But after all these years, it's hard for me to be sure. Any sort of synopses of these two programs you can provide or link me to would be *very* deeply appreciated. I sincerely hope you're enjoying your retirement—you've earned it! Thank you! Tom, Fairview, TN

A —*Magic Highway U.S.A.*, from 1958, tells the history of the American road from its modest beginnings (using rare movie footage dating back to the turn of the century), an analysis of its current chaotic state, and a tongue-in-cheek view of what roads might be like in the future. *Hurricane Hannah*, from 1962, covers the incredible and stormy career of a major, destructive hurricane, from its birth at sea to the widespread damage wreaked when it comes ashore.

Q Dear Mr. Dave, many years ago, while watching Disney Channel, I saw a program about the making of *The Great Locomotive Chase*. This was a behind-the-scenes type of program showing the film cast and crew in Georgia. Is this available to the public (for sale)? Thank you for your time. Ernest, Cleveland, GA

A —The film you are referring to, *Behind the Scenes with Fess Parker*, first aired on the Disney TV show on May 30, 1956, and was later shown on Disney Channel. It has not been released on DVD.

Q Disney Channel did a special with Ringo Starr called *Ringo Starr—Coming Home*, in which Ringo takes you on a tour of his home city of Liverpool, England. Has this or will this ever be released on DVD, as I would love to see this program? Robert, Clermont, FL

A —The title is actually *Ringo Starr: Going Home*, and it aired on Disney Channel in 1993. It has not been released on DVD. *Going Home* was actually a series of specials on Disney Channel, including *Ashford and Simpson: Going Home, Boyz II Men: Going Home,* and *Travis Tritt: Going Home. Paul McCartney: Going Home* and *Gloria Estefan: Going Home* both won the CableACE Award for best musical show.

Q Many years ago, Mr. Walt Disney hosted *The Wonderful World of Disney* every week on TV. One week it might be about Johnny Shiloh; the next week, Charlie the cougar. One week, it was about a native Indian boy and the legend of the bald eagle. Mr. Dave, can you tell me what the name of that show was? It had something to do with getting an eagle's feather and bravery! Thank you. James, Tyler, TX

A —The featurette is *The Legend of the Boy and the Eagle*. It was first released in theaters in 1967, then shown on our TV show in 1968.

Q I would like to research a short-lived series called *Boys of the Western Sea*; does a copy of the film still exist? Where would I have to go to view it if it does? My impression is that the

231

original version exists in Norwegian. Thank you for your time and consideration. Richard, Trenton, NJ

A —*Boys of the Western Sea* was an eight-episode series that aired on the *Mickey Mouse Club* TV show in the 1956–1957 season. It was a Norwegian film, and some of the Mouseketeers helped dub the Norwegian dialogue into English. I know of no place where this film is available for purchase.

Q Around 1984 to 1986 on Disney Channel, there was a Winnie the Pooh show that was not animated. The characters were in animal suits and acted out the half-hour story. My daughters loved the show because they thought it was real, versus the animated show. I have been unable to find any copies or old videos of this show anywhere. Can you help? Robin, Sterling, VA

A —This show is *Welcome to Pooh Corner*, which aired on Disney Channel beginning in 1983. It has never been released on DVD, but it was on six volumes of VHS tapes available from 1984 to 1986. As I write this, some of the tapes are available on eBay.

Q At the beginning of *Phineas and Ferb*, Phineas's voice sounded a lot different than it does in more recent episodes. Was it a different actor, or was the current actor developing his voice for Phineas? Corey, West Palm Beach, FL

A —When *Phineas and Ferb* began back in 2007, Vincent Martella did the voice of Phineas, and he is still doing it today. When the series first began production, Vincent was fourteen years old. Now he is quite a bit older. No doubt his voice has changed over the years.

Q In the "Complete List of Disney Films" there is one missing: *Mosby's Marauders*, starring Kurt Russell and James MacArthur.

It was released sometime about 1966, and originally called *Willie and the Yank*. Why is it missing from the "Complete List"? Alan, Midvale, UT

A —It is not on the list of Disney theatrical features because it started out as a three-part TV show in 1967. It was only released in theaters abroad as a feature film, with the *Mosby's Marauders* name.

Q I am trying to get confirmation as to which show was the first to run on Disney Channel on April, 18, 1983. I know both *Good Morning Mickey* and *Welcome to Pooh Corner* ran that morning, but unsure which show actually owns the title "first show run on Disney Channel." Thank you! Kim, Natick, MA

A —According to the premiere issue of the *Disney Channel Magazine*, the very first show to air was *Good Morning Mickey*, followed by *Mousercise*, *Welcome to Pooh Corner*, and *You and Me, Kid*, in that order.

Q Please advise how I might obtain lyrics for the daily theme songs performed by the 1970s new *Mickey Mouse Club*. I am particularly interested in Monday's, "Who What Why Where When and How Day." Ed, Adelaide, SA, Australia

A —The lyrics, by Mark Ray, are: *It's a who what why where when and how day / Planet Mars and purple cow day / Holy mack'rel Mouseketeer day / Day for you and me. A how when where why what and who day / Shake a hand and how-dee-do day / Find the treasure in the cave day / Day for you to be. It's a who what why where when and how day / Anything your mind allows day / Stand right up and take a bow day / Let the whole world see.*

Q I recently discovered that Paul and Linda McCartney hosted an episode of *Disney Time* in the UK on Boxing Day

[December 26], 1973. Can you tell me anything about this series and episode? Can it be seen anywhere? Sharon, Glendale, CA

A —*Disney Time* was a series of holiday TV specials produced in England, with guest hosts presenting clips from Disney films. It began with a Christmas show in 1964. Most of the hosts were from British TV shows for kids. But there were also internationally known celebrities; besides Paul and Linda McCartney doing the Boxing Day show in 1973, other prominent hosts included Peter Ustinov, Bing Crosby, Shari Lewis, and Cliff Richard. The shows are not available for viewing.

Q **Does *Inside Outer Space* have footage from *Man and the Moon, Man in Space,* and *Mars and Beyond*? Matthew, North Hollywood, CA**

A —Yes, *Inside Outer Space*, starring Ludwig Von Drake, which aired on *Walt Disney's Wonderful World of Color* on February 13, 1963, used footage from *Man in Space* (approximately nine minutes), *Man and the Moon* (thirteen minutes), and *Mars and Beyond* (fourteen minutes). Since those three shows had earlier been aired only in black and white, this was the first color TV airing for the footage.

Q **On the series *Mickey Mouse Clubhouse*, they always sing the "Hot Dog" dance at the end of the program. Who wrote it, and did Uncle Walt have any input to my daughter's favorite song and dance? Paul, Marion, OH**

A —Walt Disney had nothing to do with the "Hot Dog" song. It was written and performed by the Grammy Award–winning alternative rock band They Might Be Giants and is featured in each episode of *Mickey Mouse Clubhouse*.

Q   **Did Walt Disney ever guest star on any of the 1950s or 1960s variety shows, game shows, or talk shows? Denny, York, PA**

A   —Among others, Walt appeared on the game show *What's My Line?* on November 11, 1956; he also appeared as a guest on Jack Benny's show on November 3, 1965, and on Ed Sullivan's *Toast of the Town* on February 8, 1953.

Q   **I'm a big fan of Disney Comics, especially about the ducks. There is a character called Ludwig Von Drake that is used in the comics. If I'm not mistaken, Ludwig appeared in a story by Don Rosa or Carl Barks. I think he also appeared in *Walt Disney's Wonderful World of Color*. In the comics he is from Vienna, and now I wanted to know if he really is from Vienna, or is that due to the German translation? Michael, Salzburg, Austria**

A   —Ludwig Von Drake has indeed been said to have come from Vienna. He first made an appearance on *Walt Disney's Wonderful World of Color* TV show in *An Adventure in Color* on September 24, 1961.

Q   **Can you think of a movie that I think we would have watched on Disney Channel back in the 1980s or early 1990s about a young girl living at a summer resort with relatives, who spent a lot of time recording the songs of whales in the ocean with them? (It's not animated.) Annie, Leo, IN**

A   —Might you be thinking of dolphins? In *A Ring of Endless Light* on Disney Channel, sixteen-year-old Vicky goes to visit her grandfather for the summer. She meets a boy studying dolphins, and while helping him discovers that she has a unique ability to communicate with the sea creatures.

Q Are *An Adventure in Color* and *Mathmagic Land* on the very first episode on *The Wonderful World of Color*? Matthew, North Hollywood, CA

A —Yes. *An Adventure in Color/Mathmagic Land*, introducing Professor Ludwig Von Drake, was the first episode of *Walt Disney's Wonderful World of Color*. It aired on September 24, 1961. This was Walt Disney's first color telecast, but he had actually started his TV show, originally called *Disneyland*, and airing in black and white, seven years earlier.

Q Dave, I am trying to get information on a movie about a lynx that Disney made. I believe it was for *Walt Disney's Wonderful World of Color* and was filmed in the 1960s. Part of it was filmed in Waterville, Washington. I am interested because I was in the crowd that was filmed. What are the chances that it will ever be offered on DVD, like *Charlie the Lonesome Cougar* and *The Yellowstone Cubs*? Thanks. Fred, Brewster, WA

A —*Lefty, the Dingaling Lynx* aired on our TV show in 1971. It has never been released on videocassette or DVD, and I know of no current plans to do so.

Q I remember as a kid (1980s) there was a short program on Disney Channel that would play between full-length programs every so often. It was fast-paced music with a guy who lived in a house filled with Mickey Mouse collectibles, and then he went to work in an office filled with Mickey Mouse things. I'm trying to find the title of this video; any help you could provide would be great! Thanks. Todd, Chicago, IL

A —The filmmaker was Mike Jittlov, and his stop-motion film was entitled *Mouse Mania*. It first appeared in the TV show *Mickey's 50* (for Mickey's fiftieth birthday in 1978), and was shown again with two other Jittlov films in another TV show, *Major Effects*. It was released on the Walt Disney Treasures DVD entitled *Mickey Mouse in Living Color Part 2* in 2004. Jittlov borrowed some early Disney products from the Walt Disney Archives to use in his films.

Q **Dear Dave, I used to have a certificate that listed me as an "Official Member of Mickey Mouse Club" dated 1959, but unfortunately it has gone missing over the years. I remember on the back were autographs of Jimmie Dodd, Cubby O'Brien, and Darlene Gillespie. As the story goes, the three MMC members made an appearance at a state fair in either Santa Barbara or San Luis Obispo counties. My parents took me to meet them (I was barely two years old), and evidently they had a table where a child could register and become an MMC member. My parents registered me and I got my certificate, an MMC badge/button and a pair of Mouse ears. My question is, in the Archives, is there a roster of the names of kids like me who signed up for the MMC, or was that registration formality more of a marketing promotion for the show? Leo, Santa Maria, CA**

A —No, there is no list of names. According to the TV show, anyone who watched the *Mickey Mouse Club* was officially a member. Membership cards and membership certificates were indeed a marketing promotion.

Q **Hi, Dave. I have two questions. I had the pleasure of having Diamond Level access to the Destination D—75 Years of Disney Animated Features event in 2012. During the Studio tour on day three, we had a presentation on the film media used during the history of Disney films. We were informed that many of the original films have been lost because of deterioration of the film stock. Have all of the *Walt Disney's***

Disneyland, Walt Disney Presents, and *Walt Disney's Wonderful World of Color* TV shows filmed when Walt Disney was alive (1954–1966) been restored to their original full color? Are there any plans to release these as "season volumes" on DVD or Blu-ray? The Blu-ray release of *Alice in Wonderland* contains a 1950 TV Christmas special that Walt Disney filmed entitled *One Hour in Wonderland.* I read that there was a second TV Christmas special from 1951 entitled *The Walt Disney Christmas Show.* Is *The Walt Disney Christmas Show* (1951) available on DVD or Blu-ray? Chuck, Columbus, OH

A —Disney has always been famous for taking care of its old films, while other studios let theirs disintegrate. So, no, there are not any Disney films that have been lost (except for some early Laugh-O-grams, Alice Comedies, and Oswald cartoons). Some nitrate prints have disintegrated, but they have all been backed up. Thinking ahead, Walt Disney filmed most of his early TV shows in color, even though they were being aired in black and white. Sometimes when the shows were later rerun, shown on Disney Channel, or released on videocassette/DVD, color prints were made from the original negatives. It is possible that some of the shows have never had a color print made. I know of no plans to rerelease the seasons of the TV series on DVD. The 1951 Christmas show has not been released on video or DVD.

Q I had heard that sometime in the 1980s Disney Channel was going to produce a TV show starring the Dreamfinder from the Journey into Imagination pavilion at Epcot. Did such a show exist? Matt, Austin, TX

A —The show, to be called *Dreamfinders,* was planned for Disney Channel, and announced in the first issue of the *Disney Channel Magazine,* but no shows were ever completed. The show would have featured a cast of children in a "real world" setting, confronted with a perplexing dilemma. Then Dreamfinder would whisk them away on a magic journey to "the Realm of Imagination." There, free of all worldly constraints, the children would use their ideas and dreams to find a creative solution to their problem. The show would have been an hour long, with a new episode each week.

Q **For the *Wonderful World of Color* episode *Disneyland* Goes to the World's Fair, who wrote the song on the history of fairs? Matthew, North Hollywood, CA**

A —The words and music for "The History of Fairs" were written by Mel Leven. Leven had also written several songs for *One Hundred and One Dalmatians* and worked with George Bruns on the music for *Babes in Toyland*.

Q **In the new Mickey Mouse cartoons on Disney Channel and *Disney.com* (produced by Paul Rudish), why is Mickey's voice provided by Chris Diamantopoulos, and not by the official voice of Mickey (since 2009), Brett Iwan? This is very curious to me, especially since the other characters in these cartoons (Minnie, Donald, Daisy, and Goofy) are all voiced by their current voice actors: Russi Taylor, Tony Anselmo, Tress MacNeille, and Bill Farmer, respectively. Fred, Placentia, CA**

A —The producers of the new cartoons were looking for a retro voice to match the vintage look of the cartoons.

Q **Several years ago I was watching Disney Channel late at night and ended up watching a show in black and white about the life and works of Tchaikovsky. The focus of the film was how he came to create the music for the *Sleeping Beauty* ballet. I was wondering what the name of this film was and if it was a part of some special series. I've never been able to find any**

information on it since, but I've always wanted to watch it again. Any chance it might be released to DVD eventually? Michelle, Orange, CA

A —The TV show you saw was *The Peter Tchaikovsky Story* (1959). It was released as bonus material on the 2003 Special Edition DVD version of *Sleeping Beauty*.

Q I believe this was on *The Wonderful World of Disney* back in the 1980s. There was a movie in which two boys find a biplane in a barn at an auction. An older gentleman teaches them to fly, and they take off to the skies. Can you tell me the name of the movie and if it is available anywhere? Thanks. Greg, Macy, IN

A —You may be thinking of the three-hour TV movie *Sky High* (1990), starring Damon Martin, Anthony Rapp, and James Whitmore. There was a similar 1975 TV show entitled *The Sky's the Limit*, about a boy and his grandfather fixing up and flying an ancient airplane. The grandfather and grandson were played by Pat O'Brien and Ike Eisenmann.

Q **Dave, where did the inspiration for Dreamfinder and Figment, the original hosts of the Journey into Imagination pavilion at EPCOT at Walt Disney World, come from? Was Walt Disney any influence? Paul, Apopka, FL**

A —For your answer, I turned to Steven Vagnini in the Archives, who has long been an expert on the attraction. Steven reports: "The characters that would become Dreamfinder and Figment originated as Professor Marvel and his dragon friend for a proposed, but never realized, area of Disneyland known as Discovery Bay. When that project was canceled, the characters became the symbols of imagination for the Journey into Imagination pavilion at Epcot. An early description of the Dreamfinder explained that the character is the Spirit of Imagination. 'He represents the practical and controlled side of the imaginative process. He may not be readily known to us, yet we've all met him every time we were excited by inspiration, thrilled by the art of creating, or felt the pride of having generated something new. It is his purpose to gather "ideas" because each one may be that spark which inspires new imaginings.' One might say that Walt Disney was one of the greatest 'Dreamfinders' of all; during the development of the Epcot character, Imagineers referenced many of Walt Disney's famous quotes to inspire the character's identity. Figment was Dreamfinder's foil: the childish side of imagination with a short attention span."

Q **I have a ten-and-a-half-by-fourteen-inch framed and matted photo of Walt Disney in a doorway with the shadow of Mickey on the wall. I can't seem to find any information on it. Can you help? Jeff, Loma Linda, CA**

A —We really do not have any information on this famous photograph, other than the fact that it was taken at Walt Disney's home in the early 1930s to be used as a publicity photo.

Q Who did the voice of Mickey Mouse for "Mickey and the Beanstalk" in the movie *Fun and Fancy Free*? The documentary *The Story of Fun and Fancy Free* says that Walt Disney did it, but I've read in a few books that Jimmy Macdonald did it. Who really did Mickey's voice in the movie? Justin, Appling, GA

A —They both did. It was midway through production of *Fun and Fancy Free* that Walt Disney got too busy with other duties to continue doing Mickey Mouse's voice, so he asked Jim Macdonald, from his sound department, to take over.

Q I lived in Kansas City for a while, and have visited the Hallmark Cards Museum there. Have always been curious as to the reason Walt Disney left Hallmark. Did he travel to California immediately after that part of his illustration history? Duane, Redlands, CA

A —Walt Disney never worked for Hallmark, though one of his earliest merchandise licensees (for greeting cards) was Hall Brothers (the forerunner of Hallmark) beginning in 1931. They produced a large number of greeting cards featuring Disney characters, but none were drawn by Walt Disney personally. Walt knew Joyce Hall, founder of Hallmark, as they both had roots in Kansas City. Walt left Kansas City because he wanted to be a part of the movie industry.

Q What were Walt Disney's favorite food and hobbies? Gabriel, Laredo, TX

A —Walt had simple tastes when it came to food, liking American comfort food, meat and potatoes. He was also partial to chili beans, and the Disney Studio commissary still serves Walt's chili to this day. Through the years he had a number of hobbies, including model railroading, the collecting of miniature furniture, playing polo, and lawn bowling. He also enjoyed traveling.

Q **My grandmother grew up in Hawaii in the 1940s and seems to remember meeting Walt Disney one day at the Outrigger Canoe Club in Honolulu. We were wondering if the Archives has any proof that Walt did visit the Outrigger Club in the 1940s. Thanks! Bret, Brea, CA**

A —We are aware of only one trip that Walt and his family made to Hawaii in the 1940s, but we do not know if the trip included the Outrigger Canoe Club. The family sailed to Honolulu on the SS *Lurline* on June 28, 1948, and stayed at the Royal Hawaiian Hotel until July 14.

Q **Did Walt Disney say this quote: "She believed in dreams, all right, but she also believed in doing something about them. When Prince Charming didn't come along, she went over to the palace and got him"? If so, when did he say this? And what was the interview about? Renee, San Gabriel, CA**

A —That quote is all over the Internet, but no source is given. We cannot prove that Walt Disney ever said it.

Q **Is The Walt Disney Family Museum only located in California or is there one at Walt Disney World in the Orlando area? Thanks. Zeke, Pharr, TX**

A —The Walt Disney Family Museum is located in San Francisco, California; it is not a Disney company project, but rather was created by Walt Disney's daughter, Diane, and her family, and displays memorabilia belonging to the family. At Walt Disney World, there is Walt Disney: One Man's Dream at Disney's

Hollywood Studios, an exhibit of artifacts and film clips telling Walt Disney's life story.

Q **I was looking for *The Walt Disney Story* by Diane Disney Miller, but I can't find it anywhere. Is it out of print? Or where could I find it? Sinead, Los Angeles, CA**

A —Diane's *The Story of Walt Disney* was originally published by Holt in 1957, after a serialization beginning in 1956 in the *Saturday Evening Post*. That original 1957 edition is quite rare, but Disney Editions issued a reprint in 2005, and you might be able to find that one. There was also a Dell paperback edition in 1959.

Q **Could you please tell me the true story (at least what you know to be true) behind Walt Disney's armed services experience. I have heard that he had joined the Navy and been discharged for fighting, but that is very difficult for me to believe. Thank you. Charles, Lynn Haven, FL**

A —Walt Disney was never in the military. Roy O. Disney was in the Navy, and Walt's other brothers were in the Army; but Walt was too young (only sixteen) to enlist. He did find a Red Cross unit that took seventeen-year-olds, and with a bit of clever forgery on his passport application, he became seventeen and was able to get in. He served in France right after World War I ended, celebrating his seventeenth birthday there, driving an ambulance, and doing other cleanup chores for about nine months as the troops were getting ready to come home.

Q **Why did Roy O. Disney want to change the name from Disney Brothers to The Walt Disney Company? Scott, San Marcos, CA**

A —This was a question that I asked Roy one of the first times I sat down in his office to talk with him, in 1970. He told me that since

Walt was the creative one, it was Walt's name that should be on the company.

Q **Two years ago I went to Walt Disney World for probably the nineteenth time. I noticed in Hollywood Studios, at one of the buildings showing displays about Walt, a Man and his dream [*sic*], a poster that was of the world with Mouse ears and one single tear. I assumed that this was published when he passed. This July I went back as I wanted to take a picture of this poster and it was gone. Can you please tell me who was the photographer or illustrator of this poster? Linda, Kings Park, NY**

A —When Walt Disney died in 1966, many editorial cartoonists created drawings using similar themes—either the world crying, or some of the Disney characters crying. One of the most common, which showed the world (with Mickey Mouse ears) crying and was in the Walt Disney: One Man's Dream exhibit, was by Karl Hubenthal of the *Los Angeles Herald-Examiner*.

Q **I read a Walt Disney book that had a picture of Walt standing next to an old car that I think said DISNEY STUDIOS and had a picture of Mickey Mouse on the door. What kind of car was it? I'd like to build a replica. Thanks. Gary, Nazareth, PA**

A —It was an American Austin coupe which we used in 1931 for promotional purposes. The American Austin Car Company, located in Butler, Pennsylvania, first produced cars for the 1930 model year and went bankrupt in 1934 (it was reorganized as American Bantam, continuing for another half dozen years). The most well-known photos of Walt Disney next to the car were promoting the Fanchon and Marco *Mickey Mouse Idea*, an elaborate live stage show, which played before the feature film in selected theaters around the country.

Q I work at Coney Island in Cincinnati, Ohio. We have a check signed by Walt; the owner of the park at that time, Ed Schott, did some consulting work for him. Is there any record in your archives from Walt's visit to Coney Island in 1955 or 1956? Thanks for any information you can provide. Tom, Cincinnati, OH

A —I have seen no evidence that Walt Disney visited Coney Island in Cincinnati, but he did send four of his Imagineers on a survey trip to look at amusement parks. On June 22, 1954, Bill Martin, Bruce Bushman, Bill Cottrell, and George Whitney Jr. visited the park. The only evidence I find of Walt in Cincinnati was on January 20, 1949, when he attended a local premiere of *So Dear to My Heart*.

Q I was wondering what Walt's association with DeMolay is? I have only seen it in one book, *The Vault of Walt* by Jim Korkis. Robert, Middletown, NY

A —Walt was a member of the Kansas City, Missouri, chapter of DeMolay when he was a teenager. The organization had been founded by Frank S. Land in Kansas City in 1919, and the chapter there was known as the Mother Chapter. Walt joined on May 29, 1920, when he was eighteen; he left Kansas City in 1923 to move to California.

Q Obviously, every Disney fan knows what became of brothers Roy and Walt, but what became of their two older brothers, Herbert and Ray, and their younger sister, Ruth? Did they ever go to any of their brothers' special events? I find the extended Disney family a very interesting and intriguing piece of history, yet one we don't often—if ever—get to hear about. Do you have any information about Herbert, Ray, and Ruth Disney? Amanda, Pismo Beach, CA

A —Of Walt's lesser-known siblings, Herbert was a mailman, living in Kansas City and Portland, Oregon; he died in 1961. Raymond was an insurance man, who at one time handled The Walt Disney Company's insurance needs. He died in 1989, at the age of ninety-eight. Ruth married Theodore Beecher, and lived in Portland until her death in 1995. The family had scattered when they left Kansas City in the 1920s; the only time I recall that they all came together was for a celebration of Elias and Flora Disney's fiftieth wedding anniversary in 1938.

Q I was curious about a small trophy I just acquired. It is a six-inch trophy, loving-cup, gold finish, oxidation/tarnish/patina present, brown Bakelite base (three-inch diameter), with one gold inscription ring, which reads RCC-EASTER PARADE-1937 BEST STRING POLO PONIES, WON BY WALT DISNEY. Maker's paper tag affixed to the underside reads HOLLYWOOD TROPHY CO, 6411 HOLLYWOOD BLVD. Walt played polo? Michael, Mount Laurel, NJ

A —RCC stands for Riviera Country Club. Here is my entry from *Disney A to Z*: "Walt Disney became interested in polo in 1932 and enlisted several Disney staff members and his brother Roy to join in. Walt eventually had a stable of seven polo ponies, named June, Slim, Nava, Arrow, Pardner, Tacky, and Tommy. The Disney team competed in matches at the Riviera Country Club against such luminaries as Spencer Tracy, Darryl F. Zanuck, and Will Rogers. The film *Mickey's Polo Team* reflected the Disney staff's interest in the sport."

Q I recently asked you on the *Disney Wonder* about whether Walt Disney had been to Pago Pago, American Samoa. If you learn something about this, please let me know. Lewis, Pago Pago

A —Walt Disney visited Pago Pago on October 22, 1962, while on a South Pacific cruise on the SS *Mariposa*. On that trip he also visited Bora Bora, Papeete, Nandi, and Honolulu.

Q At Christmas time in 1972 my family brought a limestone block to Disneyland. The block was salvaged from an old house on our farm in Ellis, Kansas. The house was once owned by Walt Disney's grandfather and had the initials of Roy Disney carved into it. Roy and Walt had spent time at this farm when they were younger. I am curious about the pictures of our farm that are in the Archives in Disneyland. I would like to bring my children and grandchildren to Disneyland to see these sometime soon. My wife and I now live on this farm and are proud to still have it in our family. A little bit of history and a lot of pride! Could you please let me know if the stone and pictures are still in Disneyland? Dennis, Ellis, KS

A —In the fall of 1912, Roy O. Disney traveled to the home of his uncle, William Harvey Disney, in Ellis to help with the harvest. Six decades later, I visited the farm and noticed the initials, and when I told Roy about them, he indeed recalled carving them. A few years later, when the building on the farm was being demolished, I requested the block of stone with the initials for the Walt Disney Archives. The family brought it with them on a driving trip to California, and it is in the Archives' collection in Burbank, California. They also have a few photographs of the farm. You can contact the Archives directly.

Q May I ask as to where Walt Disney learned art? I have heard that he studied at the Chicago Academy of Fine Arts. Do you know when he went there and what classes he took? Thank you. Richard, Council Bluffs, IA

A —When Walt was fourteen years old, he enrolled in children's art classes three nights a week at the Kansas City Art Institute. The next year, when he was fifteen, the Disney family moved to Chicago, and besides enrolling in high school, Walt attended night classes at the Chicago Academy of Fine Arts. There he studied pen technique, anatomy, and cartooning. But he learned the most from professional newspaper cartoonists teaching there, such as Corey Orr of the *Chicago Tribune* and Leroy Gossett of the *Chicago Herald*.

Q **I have heard that in Walt's formal office there was a bookshelf; I was told that some of those books later became Disney movies. Do you know which books later became movies? The one that I was curious about was the C. S. Lewis I heard he had. Dennis, Buena Park, CA**

A —The only C. S. Lewis book on Walt's office bookshelves was his *Poems* (Harcourt, Brace and World, 1962). Other books there that were made into Disney movies include Sterling North's *Rascal* (autographed to Walt), Robert Lewis Taylor's *A Journey to Matecumbe*, A. A. Milne's *Winnie the Pooh*, Upton Sinclair's *The Gnomobile* (autographed to Walt), P. L. Travers's *Mary Poppins in the Park* and *Mary Poppins A to Z* (autographed to Walt), Ernest Seton Thompson's *The Biography of a Grizzly* (autographed to Walt), The Gordons' *Undercover Cat* (autographed to Walt), and Paul St. Pierre's *Breaking Smith's Quarter Horse* (autographed to Walt).

Q **Hello, do you know where Flora and Elias Disney stayed when they honeymooned in Daytona Beach, Florida? I live near there and would love to see the hotel/inn/home where they stayed if it is still there. Fred, Port Orange, FL**

A —Elias and Flora married in Kismet, Florida, in January 1888, and actually lived for a time beginning that year in Daytona Beach; their first son was born there in December 1888. For a short time Elias operated and lived in Daytona Beach's Halifax Hotel. We do not know any other local locations where they lived. The next year, they moved to Chicago, where the rest of the Disney children would be born. Halifax Avenue was, and is, a major thoroughfare in Daytona Beach.

Q **There was a very famous meeting (famous in the space program community) between Walt Disney and John F. Kennedy about the work being done at the Disney Studios called *Man in Space*. (It is widely believed that Wernher von Braun also played a key role in meetings and information exchange.) Shortly after this meeting, Kennedy made his landmark speech about "sending a man to the moon and returning him safely to Earth." The Disney Archives has no record of this event. Would you kindly fill in the details of this meeting? Christopher, Crestline, CA**

A —There was no such meeting. Actually, it was President Dwight D. Eisenhower who contacted Disney after the airing of *Man in Space* in 1955 to request a print of the film, so he could show it to some of his people involved in the space program. Kennedy was not involved. We are unaware that Walt Disney ever met Kennedy, though the then-senator did visit Disneyland in 1959.

Q **I have noticed that Mr. Disney made many movies that have a background in England. For example *Mary Poppins*, *One Hundred and One Dalmatians*, and many more. Is it that the stories he wanted to tell were based in England, or he just liked the stories? Bob, Gibsonia, PA**

A —Walt loved England, perhaps because his early ancestors came from there, but it is also true that many of the beloved stories and folktales that he wanted to depict on the screen were set in England.

Q **Did Walt Disney ever celebrate his birthday at the resort? Emma, McLean, VA**

A —No, Walt Disney was not at Disneyland on any of his birthdays from 1955 to 1966. I checked the daily desk diaries from his office, which we have in the Archives.

Q In the 1950s, my grandfather took me and my younger brother to a Fourth of July fireworks display in the Northwestern University football stadium in Evanston, Illinois. My brother says that Walt Disney walked around the divided walkway, waving. The event may have been a promotion for Disneyland. Is my brother's memory correct? John, Centerville, UT

A —According to our lists of Walt Disney's travels, he traveled to Evanston in July 1957, to be in their Independence Day parade, along with Fess Parker (Davy Crockett) and Hal Stalmaster (Johnny Tremain), as well as various Mouseketeers and Disney characters. The event continued with a twilight show and fireworks at Northwestern's Dyche Stadium (now Ryan Field).

Q I have been reading a lot about Disney and Freemasonry and I was wondering, was Walt Disney a Freemason, and is Club 33 in Disneyland named after the thirty-three degrees of Freemasonry? Benjamin, San Diego, CA

A —Walt Disney was never a Freemason, though as a teenager he had been a member of DeMolay in Kansas City. Club 33 is named simply for its address on Royal Street.

Q What was Walt Disney's position or title with The Walt Disney Company at the time of his death in 1966? Larry, Tampa, FL

A —His title was executive producer.

Q I've always been under the impression that Walt Disney himself said, "If you can dream it, you can do it." But I've never been

able to find a source. Any idea if this quote was ever actually said by Walt himself? Todd, Chicago, IL

A —This is a very common urban legend. It is not a Walt Disney quote, but rather was written by Imagineer Tom Fitzgerald for the Horizons attraction at Epcot.

Q **What was the last day that Walt visited Disneyland? I worked with him on an October 24, 1966, Kodak and RCA shoot. Ben, Forest Grove, OR**

A —The last visit to Disneyland mentioned in Walt's desk diaries was October 17, 1966. He had other appointments on October 24, but perhaps could have squeezed in a quick trip to Disneyland, even though it is not mentioned.

Q **I've heard many stories about how wonderful and great Walt was, but I've also heard of him being a perfectionist. Do you know if Walt was ever difficult to work with? Avi, Irvine, CA**

A —Yes, Walt was a perfectionist, and that did indeed make him difficult for some artists to work with. (I always laugh at a statement Walt himself made regarding *Fantasia*: "I always thought I was the perfectionist until I met Stokowski.") The impression I get is that you needed to know how to work with Walt. For example, he didn't like to be reminded of things he was supposed to have said before. He didn't like being told that something he wanted could not be done. He didn't like to be told how much something would cost.

Q **I'm doing my History Day project on how Walt Disney's animation was a turning point for animation. I would like to know what you think the most significant thing he did for animation is. Anonymous, Mount Pleasant, SC**

A —There were in fact a number of significant things. Some of the more important were sending his artists back to school to learn how to draw better; emphasizing realism in animation, especially when it came to animal action in *Bambi* and later films; pioneering the use of Technicolor in animation; bringing personality to his characters; emphasizing story development; and helping to create the multiplane camera and the Xerox process for transferring drawings to cels.

Q **What was your favorite exhibit at the Reagan Library's Treasures of the Walt Disney Archives? Having viewed Walt's formal office from the Walt Disney Studios in Burbank, California, I wonder, what was the object/area in his office you found interesting, and why? Norway, Manteca, CA**

A —I am always most pleased seeing on display the items that I found for the Archives' collection, such as the handwritten letter from Ronald Reagan suggesting that a postage stamp be issued to honor Walt Disney. When I inventoried Walt's offices at the Disney Studio, the one item that impressed me the most was the original script for *Steamboat Willie*, which he had stashed in his desk drawer.

Q **I am one of several people working on a book about the history of the Connemara pony in America. According to our records, Walt Disney was given a Connemara pony at the Dublin premiere of the movie *Darby O'Gill and the Little People*. I am trying to follow up on what happened to this pony—was it imported to the United States, did it become a member of the Disney family, etc.? No one in the American Connemara Pony Society seems to know, and I stumbled upon your name while trying to find some other information about the pony via the Internet. Hope you can help. Thanks for your time. Stephanie, Middletown, OH**

A —Several years ago, Roy E. Disney gave me an article by Stanislaus Lynch, the man who obtained the pony for Walt in Ireland. He was a two-year-old silver-gray colt, whose sire was PCiarain and dam Knockranny Beauty. The colt was presented in the Round Room of the Lord Mayor of Dublin's Mansion House in Dublin. According to Lynch's November 1959 article, the colt was by that time at Disneyland Park. I found no further information.

Q **Dave, have you personally met Walt Disney? Larry, Tampa, FL**

A —Yes, I met him briefly when visiting Disneyland as a teenager around 1957. Of course, neither he nor I realized then that a decade and a half later I would be sitting in his office preparing an inventory of everything there.

Q **Did Walt Disney make his famous Disneyland promise on the Park's opening day telecast? Paul, Evanston, IL**

A —If you are asking about the "Disneyland will never be completed, as long as there is imagination left in the world" quote, Walt did not say this on the opening day TV special. He made the statement to a reporter.

Q **Walt Disney had his first success with cartoon films through the Laugh-O-gram Films company in Kansas City. Though this event was a catalyst to his move to California and developing the Walt Disney brand, I wonder what ever became of the Laugh-O-gram business. Did it continue after Walt's departure, or was it folded in his pursuit of bigger and better things? Brad, Indianapolis, IN**

A —After Walt Disney left Kansas City for Hollywood, the Laugh-O-gram company filed for bankruptcy and went out of business. Walt Disney was not personally involved in the bankruptcy case.

Q **I'm trying to find information about the aircraft Disney owned and used. I'm a retired aircraft mechanic. John, Des Plaines, IL**

A —At various times, Walt Disney owned three planes: a Beechcraft Queen Air, a King Air, and a Grumman Gulfstream I.

Q **What was Walt Disney's last project(s) that he was working on before his death in 1966? Larry, Tampa, FL**

A —Besides the films *The Jungle Book* and *The Happiest Millionaire*, he was working on such projects as Walt Disney World/EPCOT, Mineral King, CalArts, and an update of Tomorrowland in Disneyland.

Q **Do you know where I can find photos and information on Walt Disney's brothers and sisters, because I can't seem to find any photos or information anywhere. Veronica, [No city provided], TX**

A —Walt Disney's biography by Bob Thomas (*Walt Disney: An American Original*) includes photographs of and information about Walt's brothers Herbert, Raymond, and Roy, and his sister, Ruth.

Q **Hey, Dave! Just had a quick question. While visiting Walt Disney World a few years back, a Cast Member told me that Goofy was Walt Disney's favorite character. This surprised me, because one would naturally think Mickey to be his favorite. Is this true? Or did Walt actually have another character in mind as his favorite? Thanks! Kyle, Mountain Brook, AL**

A —I do not recall Walt Disney ever talking about his favorite character; that would be like asking a parent which was his favorite child. Obviously he had a soft spot in his heart for Mickey Mouse, because he was the character who put Walt's company on the map, and besides, he did Mickey's voice for two decades.

Q **Hello! I was wondering whose family crest is found on the Disney castles around the world? I have heard that it is the Disney family crest; however it looks slightly different from the official Disney crest. Any help would be appreciated! Thanks! John, Orlando, FL**

A —They are all the Disney crest. Heraldry is not an exact science, and the Disney crests at times have been portrayed in different ways.

Q **Where would I be able to find a Walt Disney autograph? And how much is it worth? Tylor, Auckland, New Zealand**

A —There are autograph dealers who occasionally have Walt Disney autographs for sale. One reputable dealer who specializes in Walt Disney memorabilia is Phil Sears (*www.phil-sears.com*). A simple signature can bring a couple thousand dollars. Because of the high value, forgeries do come on the market.

Q **I am doing a presentation on Walt Disney for my college class on California history. In searching the web for information, it seems that there are conflicting reports surrounding Walt's high school education. Did he graduate high school, and did he ever go to college? Leslie, Chowchilla, CA**

A —Walt Disney only attended one year of high school, at McKinley High School in Chicago. He did not go to college.

Q **Did Walt Disney ever wear a pair of the famous Mickey Mouse ear hats? Paul, Evanston, IL**

A —There is at least one image that appeared in a magazine of Walt Disney wearing the Mouse ear hat; you can see it on Pinterest or Google Images.

Q **Hi, Dave. Back in 1992, I visited The Walt Disney Story in the Opera House at Disneyland and was disappointed to discover that the original Oscar given to Walt in 1932 for the creation of Mickey Mouse was no longer on display. A Cast Member told me then that Lillian Disney removed it as a response to the new R-rated movies being produced by the Disney Studio's subsidiary, Touchstone Pictures. Is there any truth to this story? Brad, Palmyra, VA**

A —All of the awards won by Walt Disney were personally owned by Walt; they were turned over to the Disney family at their request in the mid-1980s and are now on display at The Walt Disney Family Museum in San Francisco. The story about Lillian Disney's role is untrue.

Q **Hi, Dave. Why does Disney not talk about Walt and Roy's Canadian connection? Their aunt, uncle, and grandparents lived right outside my small town of Goderich, Ontario, Canada. There are lots of photos and documents in our library relating to the Disney family; if you take an aerial shot of my town and one of Disneyland, the layouts match. There are photos suggesting that Walt flew over here as a young person. Can you give me any information that you have about this? Sarah, Goderich, ON, Canada**

A —Walt Disney's biographies all mention the Disney family's connection to Canada. Walt's father, Elias, was born in Bluevale, not too far from Goderich. Elias's grandfather had settled in the Goderich area years earlier, where he operated a gristmill. Elias frequently talked fondly about life in Ontario, and Walt wanted to go there some time with his father, but it never worked out. The only time Walt visited was on a car trip with his wife in June 1947. He never flew over the area, nor did he ever say he considered the layout of Goderich when he was planning Disneyland. I visited Goderich, at the request of Roy O. Disney, to check out the Disney family's roots in 1971.

Q **What significant events changed Walt Disney's life? Georgia, Chicago, IL**

A —My guesses as to the most significant events in Walt Disney's life would be these: his travel to France with the Red Cross in 1918, his trip to California in 1923 to start his company, his marriage to Lillian Bounds and the births of his two daughters, the creation of Mickey Mouse in 1928, *Snow White and the Seven Dwarfs* in 1937, his first TV series in 1954, Disneyland in 1955, and *Mary Poppins* in 1964.

Q **What personal or professional relationship, if any, did Walt Disney have with Ronald Reagan? Although going on to become president of the United States, Ronald Reagan was a former Hollywood actor and soon-to-be governor of California at the time of Walt's passing. Did their careers or personal lives ever intersect beyond the grand opening ceremony of Disneyland in 1955? Brock, Dartmouth, MA**

A —Then California governor-elect Reagan said in a December 15, 1966, radio interview that though he had never made a picture with Disney, he had known Walt as a "friend"—sounding very distraught over the news of Walt's passing. Based on personal correspondence between them, it's clear that Reagan had much respect for Walt, and valued his help at the beginning of his political career, when Walt had supported him. Reagan was also an early proponent of issuing the Walt Disney commemorative postage stamp in 1968, saying that because of Walt "the world is a richer, better, place."

Q **Walt Disney revolutionized the animation industry by having the first full-length color movie, *Snow White and the Seven Dwarfs*, and his inventions like the multiplane camera and the storyboard. How else did he revolutionize the animation world? How did people respond/react to his works? Jasmine, Lowell, AR**

A —Walt also pioneered synchronized sound in animation (with *Steamboat Willie*). But his key accomplishments were not just in technology but in story and artwork. He hired excellent writers and artists who were able to bring his ideas to life on the screen. He spent the necessary funds to train his artists, supply them with the best equipment, and give them the time they needed to come up with the highest quality product possible. He was gratified by the response from theater audiences, and by the multiple awards his films won.

Q **First let me thank you for sharing your knowledge and love of all things Disney. We loved your interview at the fortieth anniversary for the Archives and again all the treasures you talked about at Destination D. We are wondering about this: you said that the family had access to Walt's office for about a year before you went in to do an inventory. How was it decided which items belonged to his family and which ones belonged to the company? There seems to be some "sharing" between the family museum and the Archives; how is that done? We are so glad you are taking care of the history of the magic! Thank you! Karen, Mesa, AZ**

A —Thank you for your kind comments. While Mrs. Disney did remove a very few personal items from Walt's offices, the family

did not have unlimited access. Walt's secretaries worked
in the offices for about a year to clear up the files, handle
correspondence, etc. Most of the items in the offices remained,
and are now a part of the Archives. One exception is the
awards won by Walt, which were always deemed to be his
personal property. One of the offices is displayed, with its
original contents, in Walt Disney: One Man's Dream at Disney's
Hollywood Studios.

Q **I'm a lawn bowler, and was surprised to learn that Walt lawn
bowled. What is the story about Walt and lawn bowling? Ian,
Niagara-on-the-Lake, ON, Canada**

A —Walt Disney was passionate about lawn bowling in the later
years of his life. He bowled at the Smoke Tree Ranch in Palm
Springs, where he had a vacation home, and even helped lay out
the ranch's bowling green. He also bowled at the Beverly Hills
Bowling Club, of which he was an early benefactor, and in 1964
participated in the United States Lawn Bowling Championships
at Buck Hill Falls, Pennsylvania.

Q **When Walt first opened his studio in 1923, how many
employees did he have? Anonymous**

A —When he first opened his Studio in October 1923, it was only
Walt, his brother Roy, and an inker-painter named Kathleen
Dollard. By the end of the year, there was one more staff
member added.

Q **Hi, Dave! Supposedly my great-grandma, Anna Czekala, was
the Disney family doctor (according to my mom and family
stories). This would have been in Chicago, and I'm not sure if
it was the first time they lived in Chicago or the second time.
She worked out of St. Anne's Hospital in Chicago. I'm looking**

to confirm this, obviously. She was one of the first female doctors of her time. This would be really cool, as I'm a Disney freak! Diane, Oswego, IL

A —The Disneys lived in Chicago when Walt was born in 1901, moving to Marceline, Missouri, in 1906. The family returned to Chicago from 1917 until 1919. I know of no way to prove a connection between the physician and the Disney family, unless a search of Chicago city directories would indicate they might have locations in close proximity to each other. The Disneys lived on Tripp Ave.

Q In *Saving Mr. Banks*, when P. L. Travers goes to Disneyland with Walt Disney, Walt is met by a group of fans wanting autographs. But instead of hand-signing everything for them, he hands out pieces of paper with his autograph already on them. Did Walt really do that, and if so, were they authentic signatures? Avi, Irvine, CA

A —Walt found out that when he started signing autographs at Disneyland, he got this huge crowd around him, and he was unable to get his work done. So he made a point of hand-signing pages from his notepads, and he would hand them out to guests on request. The signatures were authentic. I should also note that Walt and P. L. Travers never visited Disneyland together; instead, the head of the Disney story department, Bill Dover, led the English author around.

Q While researching information on dude ranch vacations, I came across a brochure from one of the ranches. In the brochure they mentioned that Walt Disney had vacationed at the ranch. Do you have any information about a dude ranch vacation that Walt may have taken? Larry, Lincoln, CA

A At various times, Walt Disney had two different vacation homes at the Smoke Tree Ranch in Palm Springs, California.

Q What was Walt's favorite color? Kaori, Tokyo, Japan

A —It was blue. He gave this answer in response to a questionnaire he received in 1964.

Q When Walt Disney gave his wife, Lilly, a puppy in a hatbox as a Christmas present, which inspired Lady's introduction in *Lady and the Tramp*, is it known what the puppy's name was, and if so, who named it, Walt or Lilly? Emily, Selden, NY

A —The puppy in the hatbox was a chow named Sunnee; we are not aware of who named her. The Disney family had Sunnee for a number of years, though in the 1940s they got a large poodle named Duchess Disney.

Q My question is a simple one. Do you think Walt would be proud? Molly, Port Orange, FL

A —I have no doubt that Walt would be proud of the company today. There were so many more things he wanted to do when he died prematurely at age sixty-five.

Q Growing up with Disney from the 1950s to the present, we often saw Walt with a cigarette burning or a pack in his pocket. I have read a few of the books pertaining to Walt, but can't ever recall anything ever being said about his brand of cigarettes or how much he smoked. Can you shed any light on this? Just curious, as almost everything has been asked over the years, but I never saw this question. Thanks. Ron, Ocoee, FL

A —Walt Disney smoked Lucky Strikes in the 1940s and French cigarettes, Gitanes, later in his life, but he never wanted to be photographed with a cigarette as he felt it set a bad example for children. He was a heavy smoker, and in fact died of lung cancer.

Q Hi, Dave. I remember reading a while back that Roy O. had sent you on a trip to gather up some family history. I was wondering if you have or if you will ever write about your experience. Eric, Lemon Grove, CA

A —There is a report on that trip in the *Disney twenty-three* magazine from summer 2010 ("In Search of Disney," by Dave Smith as told to Steven Vagnini).

Q Can you list all of the Disney "sites" across L.A. County and where they are located or if they even exist? Examples are: Walt Disney's house, Carthay Circle Theater, Disney's first studio (before they built in Burbank, California), etc. Josh, Lancaster, CA

A —There is an article by Michael Crawford on this subject in the Summer 2014 issue of *Disney twenty-three* magazine. Also check out an interactive map on *D23.com*.

Q Hey, Dave! My question is, what was Walt Disney's religion? I've heard lots of rumors about him being a Mason or something of that nature, but I have never seen any evidence to this or to allude to him having any religion. Megan, Summerville, GA

A —Walt Disney was raised in the Congregational church. He was never a Mason, but was in DeMolay briefly as a teenager.

Q Hi, Dave! I read Bob Thomas's book on Walt Disney and he mentions (on page 190) that when Walt found out one of his animators was arrested on a homosexual charge, he said, "Let's give him a chance; we all make mistakes." This certainly seems like a big thing at the time, considering LGBT people could be and were prosecuted around the country. As a gay man, it would mean a lot to me if I knew Walt was supportive (or at least not condemning) of LGBT people. . . . Do you have any information

from the Archives supporting this claim? Thank you! Scott,
Anaheim, CA

A —We have nothing other than the statement in Bob Thomas's
book. Bob probably got the story from one of the many people
he interviewed.

Q If my memory serves, Tom Hanks was not the first person to
play Walt Disney in a motion picture. I am remembering a film
that ran in the Magic Kingdom's Main Street Cinema in the
1990s, where Roy E. Disney appeared as his uncle. Can you
verify and identify this production? Jason, Redmond, WA

A —The 1991 film starring Roy E. Disney as Walt was initially titled
Mickey's Audition, and later *Mickey's Big Break*. But the first
film to have an actor playing Walt Disney was actually *Once
Upon a Time* (Columbia, 1944); Walt was portrayed by Walter
Fenner.

Q Have any of Walt's relatives worked at the Parks? Camille,
Pawtucket, RI

A —Some have worked at the Disney Studio, but I am unaware
of any working at the Parks. The closest we come is Roy
Patrick Disney who, while he was working in Film and TV Post
Production at the Studio, helped staff several attractions at
Disneyland during cast Christmas parties.

Q How many rides was Walt Disney personally involved with?
How many ideas did he come up with for future projects?
Mitchell, Hudson, NH

A —Since Walt Disney was intimately involved with everything that
was created at Disneyland, that would have included all the

attractions that were built there (1955–1966) during his lifetime. In addition, Walt was involved in the planning stages for later attractions, such as Haunted Mansion, Country Bear Jamboree, The Hall of Presidents, and Pirates of the Caribbean.

Q **Was Walt Disney afraid of mice? I read somewhere on the Internet that Walt Disney was afraid of mice, but I know there are a lot of false rumors spread about him, so I was hoping you could shed some light on the subject. Thanks! Carson, Nashville, TN**

A —No, he was not, though that is a common urban legend. Several sources have reported that he had pet mice that played around on his drawing board in Kansas City.

Q **I have seen things in the old *Disney Magazine* and others that say Walt never set foot on the Florida property; then in the fall 2011 issue of *Disney twenty-three* magazine, page 8, there is a photo with Walt and Joe Fowler with a caption that says they traverse part of their newly acquired property during Walt's first on-site inspection in November 1965. Is it true that Walt did walk on the property? John, Watervliet, MI**

A —Yes, archivist Steven Vagnini's article in the Fall issue of the magazine is correct. Walt Disney did have an opportunity to survey the Walt Disney World property about a year before he died. Perhaps the articles you remember refer to Walt's not being able to see the finished Walt Disney World, which is true.

Q **Has the Disney Company ever thought of making an Audio-Animatronics figure of Walt Disney? Avi, Irvine, CA**

A —The suggestion has been made many times, but nothing has come of it. Some speculated that the Disney family might not approve of an Audio-Animatronics figure of Walt.

WALT
DISNEY
IMAGINEERING

Q A few weeks ago after purchasing the book *Walt Disney Imagineering*, I heard about a traveling show on Imagineering. Could you tell me more about this exhibit? Eric, Cumberland, [No state provided]

A —*The Architecture of Reassurance: Designing the Disney Theme Parks* displayed concept art for the Disney Parks. It opened at the Canadian Centre for Architecture in June 1997. It also traveled to such venues as the Walker Art Center in Minneapolis, the Armand Hammer Museum of Art in Los Angeles, and the Cooper-Hewitt National Design Museum in New York, where it ended its tour in 1999. Flammarion published a book of artwork from the exhibition, edited by Karal Ann Marling.

Q Ever since I was in first grade, I have wanted to become an Imagineer. I am in high school now, and I am trying to find out which college I should go to and what classes I should take to fill the requirements of the job. Please help! Gavin, Auburn, IN

A —You should pick the discipline that you like, Gavin, and for which you have talent. Walt Disney Imagineering is one of the most creative organizations in the country, and it hires in many different fields, such as architecture, model making, design, art, filmmaking, drafting, special effects, engineering, and show writing. One thing you might look into is their ImagiNations Design Competition for students. Some of the winners have gone on to internships and even full-time positions at Walt Disney Imagineering.

Q I've always wondered when I read articles about what Imagineers (i.e., John Hench, Kim Irvine, Marc Davis, etc.) get to do at Disney, because all of them seem to have pretty cool jobs—even if it is designing what a garbage can looks like at the Parks—and I'm curious to know how they get their positions. Do most Imagineers have college degrees in one field or another?

Do they work their way in to them? Does it take more than raw talent, imagination, and creativity to become a Disney Imagineer? Misty, [No location provided]

A —As with most large companies, at Disney Imagineering, workers in many disciplines are needed. Imagineers are selected for their talents in the needed fields. Naturally, Walt Disney Imagineering tries to hire the best candidates for the jobs that they can find, so they can keep up the tradition of excellence, which is so strongly associated with the company.

Q How often do the Imagineers visit the Parks? Melanie, Northfield, OH

A —Some Imagineers actually have offices within the property of the Disney Parks, but others try to visit the Parks as often as they can, to see what is working and what is not. When they start designing and building a new area, such as Cars Land, they may eventually spend every day at the Park for months.

Q As a gift to my husband and my mother-in-law, I am trying to locate pictures, information, anything I can on Allen Mckenzie Smith, born December 18, 1918. Allen was an Imagineer/ architect and worked very closely with Walt Disney on New Orleans Square and It's a Small World. He and his wife, Ginger, were even flown out to the World's Fair with Walt Disney to do research on rides. There are so many great stories about this man, but he left Disney to work for Sid and Marty Krofft, and then sadly passed away January 1, 1982. I have already contacted The Walt Disney Company, and the Archives department could only supply dates employed; even the photo department could not really help. I know many great people worked for Walt Disney, I also know a few of them

slipped between the cracks; could you help me find out if Allen Smith is one of them? Jennifer, Ojai, CA

A —You have contacted the right people. The fact is that only a very small percentage of the thousands of people who worked for Disney ever had their photos taken at work. Sorry you were unsuccessful.

Q I'm aware that Marc Davis had a hand in helping to develop certain attractions (or, rather, the overseas counterparts of existing attractions) for Tokyo Disneyland—there exists a bit of concept art of extra scenes for Tokyo's Haunted Mansion, such as a crypt containing the tombs of famous horror figures such as Dracula and Jack the Ripper. Does his involvement in Tokyo Disneyland (or anything in Disney Parks beyond the 1970s) expand beyond the Mansion, and was any of his conceptual work during this period realized? Andrew, Snellville, GA

A —We know that Marc Davis consulted on World of Motion in Epcot and for attractions such as Haunted Mansion, Pirates of the Caribbean (including the skeletons in the grottoes), Jungle Cruise (including animals in the African veldt), It's a Small World, and Western River Railroad (dinosaurs in Primeval Diorama) in Tokyo Disneyland after his retirement in 1978. His distinctive artwork from throughout his Imagineering career has been maintained at Walt Disney Imagineering, and it is still consulted by Imagineers. Marc died in 2000.

Q I love the songs created by X. Atencio for Pirates of the Caribbean and the Haunted Mansion. Is there a reason or story behind why his first name, Xavier, was shortened to X., or was it just his preference? Thanks very much! Chad, North Las Vegas, NV

A —In an interview, X. commented that he was given that nickname by friends in high school, and the nickname stuck when he went on to work at Disney in 1938. His full name is actually Francis Xavier Atencio.

Q **Hello! I recently went to Disney Legend Bill Martin's estate sale and picked up a bronze plaque. It features Mickey Mouse, with the initials B.G., which I assume is Blaine Gibson. It says THANK YOU BILL along the top, and WED MAPO along the bottom. Can you tell me anything about this plaque, and why it was given? Anything you could tell me would be appreciated! Oh, and this thing is *heavy*! Extremely heavy. Stefan, Pasadena, CA**

A —Without seeing a picture, I would assume that this is a plaque given to Bill on his retirement. He retired from WED Enterprises (now Walt Disney Imagineering) in 1977.

Q **Does the Archives contain any plans for Disney Parks that never came about? If so, is there anything you can share with us about those plans? Joe, Midland, TX**

A —The plans for unbuilt parks and attractions are maintained by Walt Disney Imagineering, not the Walt Disney Archives. As you are no doubt aware, preliminary design work is done on hundreds of parks and attractions that end up never being built.

Q **I love Disney and especially Disneyland. When I had to give a speech in my English class about roller coasters, I was amazed to learn that Disneyland's Matterhorn Bobsleds was the first roller coaster in the world to feature tubular steel tracks. That got me thinking, what are some of the other Disneyland "firsts"? Cody, Buellton, CA**

A —Disney Imagineers have received many patents for Disneyland attractions. Besides the Bobsleds, there were others for such things as the Jungle Cruise boat-guiding apparatus, the Submarine Voyage boats, several safety control systems, the It's a Small World boat guidance system, and the ride vehicles in a number of attractions.

Q **I was wondering about Disneyland attractions that have been removed from the Park. When an attraction is slated for removal, for instance Adventure Thru Inner Space, does WED document the attraction with film (stills) and movies? Would they create a catalog of the ride? Richard, Bradford, ON, Canada**

A —Yes, Walt Disney Imagineering does document the attractions in various ways before they are removed, but this documentation has probably been more comprehensive in recent years than in the 1950s or 1960s.

WALT
DISNEY
WORLD

Q We go to Walt Disney World at least once a year and have done so since Epcot has opened. One of our favorite attractions is Impressions de France. Are there any plans to release either the music as a sound track or the movie as a DVD? Are there any plans to restore it as part of the France attraction? Joan, Lewisville, NC

A —Impressions de France is a mainstay of the French pavilion in Epcot's World Showcase. I also love the film, and make a point of stopping to see it every time I am in Epcot. The combination of the striking images of France and the beautiful music of the country's most famous composers creates a fantastic film. I have heard of no plans for restoring or changing the film, and I would be personally disappointed if it were changed. Since it was filmed in a special five-camera format, it would not be possible to release the film on DVD. Nearly ten minutes of the sound track have been made available on CD (*Walt Disney World Official Album*) for sale at Walt Disney World and on iTunes.

Q In the 2007 revamp of the Walt Disney World Haunted Mansion, did they replace the original Madame Leota ball to make it float? And if so, is the original in the Archives? Patrick, [No location provided]

A —Yes, the floating Madame Leota crystal ball that was installed in the 2007 refurbishment uses an internal projection to make the effect more realistic, so the former prop was replaced. It is now part of the Archives.

Q I am currently reading some books about Walt Disney World's history and keep on hearing about different attractions and their being replaced. Is there a place where I can find a complete list of Walt Disney World attractions past and present? Melanie, OH

A —I am unaware of a complete published list of present and former Walt Disney World attractions. However, most of them can be found alphabetically under their individual names in my *Disney A to Z* encyclopedia.

Q **I am a self-proclaimed Walt Disney World expert and was wondering why Hollywood Studios was named Disney-MGM Studios before they switched the Park's name. Grace, Stamford, CT**

A —When Disney was planning a movie-themed park, CEO Michael Eisner felt that the MGM Studio was much better known for its live-action films than Disney was, and he accordingly arranged a licensing contract with MGM so that we could use their name, as well as their characters and music in the Park to help enhance the guests' experience. The Park opened in 1989 as Disney-MGM Studios Theme Park.

Q **What happened to the Audio-Animatronics figures used in the show Food Rocks at Epcot? Brenan, St. Petersburg, FL**

A —Most of them were declared surplus property by Walt Disney World and sold on eBay by a private seller. The Walt Disney Archives was able to salvage several costumes from the show.

Q **I am a big Muppet fan, and I have read that Muppet performer Dave Goelz provided the voice of Figment in the most recent version of Journey into Imagination at Epcot. Is this true? Fred, Placentia, CA**

A —Yes, Dave Goelz provided the voice of Figment in the Journey into Imagination with Figment attraction. He is best known for his voices of the Great Gonzo, Bunsen Honeydew, and others on the Muppets TV series. The original voice of Figment, in the 1983 version of the attraction, was provided by Billy Barty.

Q **In 1991 my wife and I met a Disney artist named Harry Holt at Magic Kingdom. He was doing pencil drawings of the Wizard's Assistant at the Emporium on Main Street, U.S.A. He autographed one of them for us. I have searched for information about him but have not come up with anything. Anything you could provide would be appreciated. Albert, Boyertown, PA**

A —Harry Holt was an animator who was hired at the Disney Studio in 1936, remaining for twenty years. Later he became a sculptor and art director for WED Enterprises (now Walt Disney Imagineering). He retired in 1982, but he loved meeting Walt Disney World guests, so an animation desk was set up for him in the Magic Kingdom in 1987 and he continued doing drawings for Park guests for several years. He passed away in 2004.

Q **In the 1970s or 1980s, I belonged to the Magic Key Club at Disney World. I could buy a book of Key Club Tickets and I could use each ticket, A through E. I wanted to know how long the Magic Key Club was around and what the requirements for getting a membership were. I don't recall how I got it, whether it was because I was a stockholder (two shares) or because I frequented Walt Disney World. Joe, Titusville, FL**

A —The Magic Kingdom Club was established in 1958 so companies and organizations near Disneyland, and later Walt Disney World, could offer memberships, a magazine called *Disney News*, and discounts to the Parks. They had their own ticket books until 1982, when Disney stopped using ticket books. The Club ceased operation in 2000.

Q **Were there ever plans for Dreamfinder and Figment beyond the Journey into Imagination attraction and related souvenirs (such as a movie, TV show, books, etc.)? Megan, Columbus, OH**

A —I asked archivist Steven Vagnini, who is a big fan of Journey into Imagination, to provide an answer. He told me that, outside of being the original hosts of Journey into Imagination at Epcot, the beloved Dreamfinder and Figment characters found themselves in various roles over the years. Figment, the playful dragon, hosted a series of films offered to schools and institutions through Disney Educational Productions, including *Reading with Figment and Peter Pan* (a fantasy in which Figment helps to convince Peter how important reading is) and the *Language Arts Through Imagination* series. Meanwhile, Dreamfinder was going to be in his own proposed series for Disney Channel called *Dreamfinders*, planned for April 1983, but it never aired. In 2014, the characters were featured as the stars of the Figment comic series from Disney Kingdoms.

Q **What is the story of the Osborne Family Spectacle of Lights, and how did Disney acquire them? Teresa, Weymouth, MA**

A —Jennings Osborne and his family began their Christmas light spectacular at their home in Little Rock, Arkansas, in 1986. Over the ensuing years, the display grew and grew, until it became so large that it became a major tourist attraction, with much traffic congestion. Several neighbors sued, and eventually Mr. Osborne was ordered by the state Supreme Court to shut it down. Because of all the publicity, Disney inquired about moving the display to Walt Disney World. In 1995 the Osbornes decided to share their display and the Disney-MGM Studios (now Disney's Hollywood Studios) became its new home, where it delighted guests through the 2015 holiday season. Mr. Osborne passed away in 2011.

Q **Where do the trees for Christmas go when they are taken down in the Parks, meaning, are they thrown away? Wesley, Macon, GA**

A —Almost all of the trees are now artificial trees. They are dismantled after the holiday season and stored in a warehouse until the next year. The warehouse at Walt Disney World is known as the Holiday Services warehouse.

Q **In the narration for the Tomorrowland Transit Authority in the Magic Kingdom, the narrator describes the Carousel of Progress as following "four families." However, most other sources, including *disneyworld.com*, call it one family. Which is correct? Dave, West Haven, CT**

A —Descriptions of the family have not always been consistent. Generally, it is felt to be a single family, as it might be portrayed in different eras, and the family members have the same names. But, if you want to be technical, it could not really be the *same* family, because its members hardly age. Plus, the show covers a period from the turn of the twentieth century to modern day—well over a hundred years.

Q **What is the original version of the Electrical Water Pageant music called? And why did they change it? Thank you for your time and energy. Carol, Fort Washington, PA**

A —When the Electrical Water Pageant began at Walt Disney World in 1971, it used the piece "Baroque Hoedown," by Jean-Jacques Perrey and Gershon Kingsley. That music was transferred to the Main Street Electrical Parade (Disneyland 1972, Walt Disney World

1977), so new music had to be created for the water pageant. Over the ensuing years, the music has been changed a number of times as the themes of the floating structures have changed.

Q **The four singing busts in the Haunted Mansion in Walt Disney World look very familiar. I think I remember these gentlemen from the *Wide World of Disney* [sic] with Walt Disney back when I was a kid. Who are they, and what was their part in the Disney company? Suzanne, Lawrenceville, GA**

A —There are five busts there. The lead bass, Thurl Ravenscroft (the one who is often confused with Walt Disney), is backed up by Chuck Schroeder, Bob Ebright, Jay Meyer, and Verne Rowe. These were not Disney employees but rather singers who were hired for this particular task.

Q **In the Carousel of Progress, in the scene in which Sara is ironing, there is a little girl helping her. Who is this girl? We know there are two children in every scene in the carousel. She is not named in the scene and it has always bothered me. Debbie, Hamilton, NJ**

A —This is a frequently asked question. As you saw on Facebook, where I see you also commented on this, there really is no answer. The little girl was evidently just created by the attraction's designers because they felt they needed another female child in that one scene. I guess you could also ask, Why doesn't the father ever age? Since the scenes cover almost a hundred-year time span, it is obvious that liberties were taken with plausibility when it comes to the members of the family in each scene and their ages.

Q **I was curious about the Haunted Mansion ride here in our Orlando park and if the ride itself was larger in square footage**

than the original one in Disneyland. Thanks very much. Kim, Orlando, FL

A —Because the ride layouts are so different in the Haunted Mansions in the two parks, it would be difficult to determine which is larger. The actual path for the Doom Buggies is about 175 feet longer in Florida than in California.

Q A friend of mine recently found at an auction a giant ten-foot-tall black metal chair with large red hearts on it and the outlined faces of Mickey and Minnie facing each other on the back part (I have some photos of it). Any idea where this chair came from and what it was used for? Anonymous

A —According to Becky Browne Allen of Global Retail Store Development Production at Walt Disney World, that particular chair was designed and built for the display windows at the World of Disney store in the Downtown Disney Marketplace, for the store's grand opening in 1996.

Q My parents and I regularly travel to Disney in Florida. We were told that within the castle is a penthouse where Walt Disney used to stay when he visited the Parks. Is this true? Scarlett, Haworth, England

A —A Disney family apartment was considered at one time for Cinderella Castle at Walt Disney World, but it was never built. Walt Disney died five years before the Park opened. A suite was added to the castle as part of the Year of a Million Dreams in 2007, with lucky families selected to spend the night there.

Q I saw a sign for DISNEY WILDERNESS CENTER near Poinciana, Florida. Is this part of Walt Disney World holdings? What is it? Jim, Myersville, MD

A —The Disney Wilderness Preserve, with its Conservation Learning Center, was established in south Osceola County as a wetlands mitigation project. The property was purchased by Disney and donated in 1993 to the Nature Conservancy to offset lands affected by the development of Walt Disney World. Work began immediately on returning the drained ranchlands to their original state as a natural habitat. The area opened to the public in 1999 and includes self-guided nature trails from which guests might spy such creatures as bald eagles, sandhill cranes, red-cockaded woodpeckers, storks, bats, and tortoises, as well as plants native to cypress swamps, freshwater marshes, and longleaf pine forests.

Q **Have any of the Florida Disney hotels been renamed? I seem to remember a different name for the Port Orleans Hotel. John, Malden, MA**

A —Originally, for ten years from their opening in 1991, there were two resorts, the Port Orleans Resort and the Dixie Landings Resort. The two resorts were combined under the Port Orleans name in 2001. The original Port Orleans became Port Orleans French Quarter, with Dixie Landings becoming Port Orleans Riverside. Other renamed hotels were Shades of Green (formerly The Golf Resort and The Disney Inn), Disney's Saratoga Springs Resort and Spa (formerly The Disney Institute), Disney's Grand Floridian Resort and Spa (formerly Disney's Grand Floridian Beach Resort), and Disney's Old Key West Resort (formerly Disney's Vacation Club at the Walt Disney World Resort). Besides these Disney-owned resorts, the hotels in the Lake Buena Vista area have gone through many name changes.

Q **Are Pluto's doghouse and the Old Cornelius Coot statue from Mickey's Toontown Fair at the Archives? Ryan, Annapolis, MD**

A —Yes, both are in the Archives. It took several hours to painstakingly uninstall and carefully remove each one from the site, with Disney archivist Steven Vagnini there to oversee the work for the Archives.

Q **I went to Walt Disney World in the mid-1980s, and there was a shop on Main Street where you could dress up in costumes and have your picture taken. No one else remembers it, and I can't find any information on it. Am I wrong? Or was there really such a place? Anonymous**

A —Beginning in 1979, when Polaroid became the sponsor of the Camera Center on Main Street, U.S.A., guests were given the opportunity to pose in an "authentic nineteenth-century costume" aboard a replica of a turn-of-the-century presidential railroad car. Guests received their eight-by-ten-inch picture a minute later. The railroad car featured the Walt Disney World Railroad logo. Polaroid ended its sponsorship in 1984.

Q **Where is/was the Preview Center that was used as an attraction while Walt Disney World was being built? It was a very small building with a theater and no seating, just standing, with rails. Is it still standing, and exactly where is it in relation to Walt Disney World Park now? It showed the progress of the Park and how the roads and highways were to grow. I especially remember the driveway along the entrance lined with topiary Disney character plantings. Leon, Indiantown, FL**

A —The Walt Disney World Preview Center, which was open from January 1970 to September 1971, was located on Preview Boulevard, now Hotel Plaza Boulevard, near the intersection of State Road 535 and Interstate 4. The building is still there, on the north side of the boulevard between the Wyndham Lake Buena Vista Resort and the Best Western Lake Buena Vista

Resort; it is now the national headquarters of the Amateur Athletic Union.

Q

My dad often talks about our family trips to the Magic Kingdom back in the 1970s. Whenever I mention an upcoming trip to Disney World with my family, his first question is, "Are you going to have 'Space Burgers' for lunch?" He may be referring to the burgers at Cosmic Ray's. Were the burgers called "Space Burgers" or is that something he just made up? Colleen, Buffalo, NY

A

—Perhaps he was thinking of the offerings in the old Tomorrowland Terrace, the former name of Cosmic Ray's Starlight Café. Besides a Space Dog and a steak sandwich, back in the late 1970s guests could order a Moon Burger (a cheeseburger) for 95¢, an Orbit Burger (a regular hamburger) for 80¢, or a Gemini Burger (double beef patties) for $1.25.

Q

I have heard that there is a video clip of Roy E. Disney portraying his uncle, Walt Disney. Have you heard of this video and is it on DVD anywhere? Scott, Remlap, AL

A

—That short film was first called *Mickey's Audition*; then the name was changed to *Mickey's Big Break*. It was made in 1991, and has been shown in several places at the Walt Disney World Resort: in a temporary attraction in a soundstage at Disney-MGM Studios (now Disney's Hollywood Studios), and in the Magic Kingdom in the Main Street Cinema and the Town Square Exhibition Hall (now Town Square Theater). It is no longer being shown, and has not been released on DVD.

Q

Could you provide a breakdown by percentage of Disney World's land that is used, available for future expansion, and preserved? Thanks, Dave. Gil, Lyon Township, MI

A —No exact numbers have ever been officially published, but roughly half of the vast Walt Disney World property is composed of wetlands and other protected environmentally sensitive areas.

Q I was reading the *Disney A to Z* encyclopedia, and I came across the fact that the *Voyage of the Little Mermaid* show replaced a show called *Here Come the Muppets*. I was just wondering what that show was about. Allison, San Ramon, CA

A —*Here Come the Muppets* was a live show at Disney-MGM Studios that operated from May 25, 1990, to September 2, 1991. It featured walk-around versions of the Muppets and was superseded by a different show, in another venue in the Park, called *Muppets on Location—The Days of Swine and Roses*. That show lasted until 1994.

Q I was reading the book *The Imagineering Field Guide to Disney's Hollywood Studios* and noticed something interesting. It mentions that they have a program in which a guest can have lunch with an Imagineer in the Hollywood Brown Derby Bamboo Room. Is this program still going on? If not, is there another way to meet and talk with an Imagineer? Anonymous

A —This program is still being offered at the Hollywood Brown Derby at the Disney's Hollywood Studios. For more information check: *http://disneyworld.disney.go.com/dining/dine-with-an-imagineer/*.

Q I have two coins (one gold and one purple) from the twentieth Anniversary Surprise Parade at Walt Disney World. I received the coins when I was about four years old from Cast Members in the parade. I was wondering if they give out these coins at every parade during the celebrations or only at certain shows? Heather, Miami, FL

A —These coins (there were also green ones) were first given out by parade Cast Members, along with strings of colored beads, during the Party Gras Parade at Disneyland, which ran during most of the year in 1990. A similar parade for the twentieth anniversary of Walt Disney World using the floats from Disneyland, named the Surprise Celebration, began in the Magic Kingdom in the fall of 1991 and continued until 1994. That parade had different coins, in gold, blue, and green.

Q **So I used to work in Marceline, Missouri, home of Disney, and have been there many times. Are there any places at Walt Disney World that mention Marceline? Joyce, Brookfield, MO**

A —There are references to Walt's life in Marceline in the Walt Disney: One Man's Dream attraction at Disney's Hollywood Studios, in both the exhibit and the film. Walt Disney World offers a guided tour entitled "Walt Disney: Marceline to Magic Kingdom."

Q **I know there were once two steamboats that cruised the Rivers of America at the Magic Kingdom. What happened to the one that was decommissioned? Anonymous**

A —The *Admiral Joe Fowler* was one of the two riverboats; it was retired from service in the fall of 1980 and not retained.

Q **A friend of mine loved to visit Top of the World at the Contemporary Resort at Walt Disney World from 1972 until its closing. Can you give me a list of stars who performed there over the years? Also are there photographs of the band that played there? Deborah, Orlando, FL**

A —The Archives does not have a complete list of the performers at the Top of the World supper club, but they included such celebrity artists as Phyllis Diller, Peter Marshall, Shari Lewis, Frankie Avalon, Cab Calloway, Johnny Ray, Sammy Davis Jr., Donald O'Connor, Diahann Carroll, Patti Page, Jack Jones, Carol Lawrence, Billy Eckstein, Rosemary Clooney, and Kay Ballard. After a decade, the celebrity performers were phased out and replaced by a show entitled *Broadway at the Top*. I have seen band photos on the Internet.

Q

Is the Florida Orange Bird an official Disney character? Also are there any plans to bring the bird back to the Parks? Samantha, Athens, TN

A

—The Orange Bird is an official Disney character, who was designed under the supervision of Disney Legend Bob Moore. The character was conceived as a mascot of the Sunshine Pavilion at the Walt Disney World Magic Kingdom, which was sponsored by the Florida Citrus Commission. After the commission ceased its sponsorship in 1987, the Orange Bird left the Magic Kingdom. D23 members were the first guests to see the Orange Bird's return to Sunshine Tree Terrace on April 17, 2012; the character was then featured on the marquee to the location, and the original Orange Bird static figure that was once found above the terrace's counter was refurbished and reinstalled. In March 2015, Sunshine Tree Terrace switched locations with Aloha Isle Refreshments. A series of Orange Bird merchandise products—including a poster, pins, T-shirts, and even Orange Bird versions of the Mickey ear hats—have been available for sale.

Q

Certain aspects of the Pirates of the Caribbean ride were changed at Disneyland and Walt Disney World after the release of the films. Were any other rides or attractions changed after the release of a particular film? For instance, since the Haunted Mansion ride predates the 2003 film, did any aspect of it change to reflect the film? Ian, Lakewood, OH

A —I don't believe there were any changes to Haunted Mansion to match the film, though the original Madame Leota now floats (as the film version of that character did). At one point, the world of Tron was incorporated into the PeopleMover at Disneyland. There is Tarzan's Treehouse, which took the place of Swiss Family Treehouse at Disneyland after the release of the Tarzan film. Tom Sawyer Island received a pirate overlay, becoming Pirate's Lair on Tom Sawyer Island, tied in with the release of *Pirates of the Caribbean: At World's End*, and the Submarine Voyage became the Finding Nemo Submarine Voyage. Iago and Zazu were featured in the Tropical Serenade attraction at Walt Disney World for many years, and at Epcot, Timon, Pumbaa, and Simba host Circle of Life: An Environmental Fable at The Land, while The Living Seas is now The Seas with Nemo & Friends.

Q **When Disney first purchased the property down in Florida for the future Walt Disney World Resort, what structures or unusual items were found on the land and where were they located? Do any of these still exist? Jim, Auburn, MA**

A —There were several structures and interesting items found throughout the property that would later become Walt Disney World. On my spring 1971 trip to the construction site, I was shown perhaps the most unusual item discovered, the "Lawnmower Tree," which was located at Fort Wilderness near the Wilderness Trading Post and Marina. A manual lawn mower was left by someone at the base of a tree, which eventually grew around and through it. Nearby, on Riles Island (later Discovery Island), Bob Foster and others working on the land acquisition discovered an abandoned house (along with a dock and an operating solar water heater), which Bob describes as "a strange assemblage of rambling rooms" that had belonged to former resident "Radio Nick" Nicholson. Aside from an abandoned packing house along Bay Lake near today's Fort Wilderness Resort—and a "not too well constructed house" located along the Orange and Osceola County line—another structure on the property was a "fairly newly built house" located near an airstrip and what would become the Lake Buena Vista Club. The house, formerly owned by a relative of Florida state senator Irlo Bronson, was visited by Walt Disney on his 1965 visit to the property and later inhabited by Phil Smith, legal counsel and the first Walt Disney World Cast Member, and his family until 1968. Their stories of living in the house and on the property are told by Steven Vagnini in an article in the summer 2010 issue of *Disney twenty-three* magazine.

Q **Every time I go to Walt Disney World, I always enjoy the many numerous ride sound tracks. However, with rides and attractions like Splash Mountain, the Haunted Mansion, Country Bear Jamboree, and Pirates of the Caribbean, I have never been able to find copies of the songs on these rides. Has Disney ever released the sound tracks to said rides on a CD or in another digital format? Ben, Atlanta, GA**

A —Songs or medleys from all of these attractions are included in the latest 2013 *Walt Disney World Official Album* (available on CD and from iTunes). On the *Musical History of Disneyland* six-CD set (2005), complete ride-through sound tracks for the Haunted Mansion, Pirates of the Caribbean, Country Bear Jamboree, and Disneyland's version of Splash Mountain are included. A digital format of the original Country Bear Jamboree record album is available for download on iTunes. The complete ride-through for the Haunted Mansion is also included in the 2009 CD release *The Haunted Mansion* from Walt Disney Records (also available on iTunes). Likewise, the Parks have recently sold a *Pirates of the Caribbean* theme park album that has a sound track (2006; also on iTunes).

Q Hi, Dave! I was wondering if you knew where the video of Walt Disney's plan for EPCOT was. I originally saw this video, *Walt Disney's Plan for EPCOT Part 2*, on YouTube, but I am searching for the original source, which I hoped to find in the Disney Archives. Christy, Sunnyvale, TX

A —Walt Disney's EPCOT film, produced in 1966, was released on the Walt Disney Treasures DVD, volume 11, *Tomorrowland*, in 2004.

Q Hi there! I am hoping you can help with my quandary. The first time I visited Walt Disney World was in about 1979 or 1980. I was wandering around and stumbled upon a little side street. I noticed a door, which led into a small theater. I sat down to watch the "show." The two things I remember most are "Alice in the Flower Garden" and Cinderella—first in her rags, and then the lights went down, and when they came back up, she was in her ball gown. It was on a revolving stage, and it was done with Audio-Animatronics figures. I also have a postcard of Alice with the flowers. Can you please help me with this? Lisa, Elyria, OH

A —You may be thinking of the Mickey Mouse Revue, which was in Fantasyland at Walt Disney World's Magic Kingdom from 1971 to 1980; the theater is now home to Mickey's PhilharMagic. The Mickey Mouse Revue later moved to Tokyo Disneyland, where it remained until 2009.

Q My favorite Disney theme park is Disney's Hollywood Studios, so I'm always looking for information about it! While digging around the Internet, I found some conflicting reports about the Theater of the Stars, the original one on Hollywood Boulevard before Sunset existed. The question I have is, what are the shows that were shown there? I can't find anything official pre—*Beauty and the Beast* in 1991, a whole two years into its existence. Shaun, Orlando, FL

A —The Theater of the Stars opened on May 1, 1989, with a show entitled *Hollywood, Hollywood!* That show continued until August 31, 1991. There were three other shows that performed there concurrently—*Swing, Swing, Swing* (April 7-18, 1990), *Dick Tracy Starring in "Diamond Double Cross"* (May 21, 1990-February 16, 1991), and *Hollywood's Pretty Woman* (September 24-November 3, 1991). *Beauty and the Beast—Live on Stage* opened at the theater November 22, 1991. This is the full list of shows and their dates, based on the weekly entertainment programs for that period.

Q Hi, Dave. We really appreciate your taking the time to continue to answer our questions. From various books and magazine articles, I know that Walt Disney visited the site that would become Walt Disney World only once. Is it known exactly where he walked and what is located there today? Robert, Kissimmee, FL

A —On his trip to Orlando in November 1965, Walt did visit the site. There are some photos, but since no work had begun, it is difficult to determine exactly where Walt went. We do know he was at a house that was near where the Saratoga Springs Resort now stands, and he rode in a boat on Bay Lake.

Q When was the first year that the icicle lights were displayed on Cinderella Castle? It's been less than ten years, I'm sure of that. Julie, Orlando, FL

A —The shimmering "ice" lights were added on Cinderella Castle at Walt Disney World in 2007, and they have been a great success ever since. They had actually debuted earlier on *Le Château de la Belle au Bois Dormant* at Disneyland Paris.

Q This may sound like a strange question, but I was wondering; when did the Mickey Premium Bar first hit the Disney Parks? Samuel, Faribault, MN

A —The Mickey Premium Bar (ice cream) is a Nestlé product; Nestlé first joined Disney to sponsor The Land at Epcot in 1992. Before that ice cream bar, there was an earlier one, with only the Mickey Mouse ears covered in chocolate. Gold Bond Ice Cream was licensed in 1975 for a Mouseketeer Bar; Gold Bond was acquired by Good Humor in 1989, and they continued selling the bar as part of their Mickey's Parade line until Nestlé came out with theirs.

Q Who voiced Captain Nemo in the former 20,000 Leagues attraction at the Magic Kingdom? I've heard that it was Pete Renaday (Renoudet) or Paul Frees. Erica, Kissimmee, FL

A —Pete Renaday, who also provided the voice for Henry in Country Bear Jamboree and narrated The Walt Disney Story, among other roles, did the voice of Captain Nemo in the attraction.

Q My husband remembers a Hawaiian Hot Dog served in Adventureland at Walt Disney World, most likely in the 1970s. I can't seem to find a mention of it on old menus. Do you have record of it or, even better, have a recipe so I can re-create it at home for him? Craig, Van Nuys, CA

A —I found that a Hawaiian Hot Dog was indeed served at the Adventureland Verandah in the Magic Kingdom; it had sweet-and-sour sauce to make it "Hawaiian." It sold for $1.35 in 1977.

Q There is a sign outside of the Pecos Bill Cafe at the Magic Kingdom that says HERRICK'S PILLS. Can you tell me the origin of that sign? I know many names you see around the Parks are those of Disney employees, but I haven't found reference to a Herrick. Just curious, because that's my last name. Our family stops there for a photo every visit! Susan, Mansfield, TX

A —There was an actual product called Herrick's Pills sold in the 1850s.

Q Good afternoon, Mr. Smith. I would like to know when the actual groundbreaking for Walt Disney World in Orlando was. Jim, Bethel, AK

A —There was no groundbreaking ceremony in Florida, just as there was none for Disneyland in California. Initial work on the project began in October 1965 with the clearing of part of the land and construction of drainage canals. Major earth-moving operations began in April 1969.

Q I am from Scotland, UK, and I am trying to find out facts and figures about the Soarin' ride at Epcot, please. I can't find anything anywhere. Can you help? Kevin, Jedburgh, Scotland

A —The attraction originally opened at Disney California Adventure, as Soarin' Over California, in 2001; it was added to The Land at Epcot in 2005. Guests are lifted up to forty feet in the air, and surrounded by a giant projection dome, giving the feeling of flying. One of the Imagineers, Mark Summer, came up with the idea for the unique ride system by building a model with an erector set he had at home.

Q One of my most treasured memories is watching my mom and my two children watch the Tapestry of Dreams Parade at Epcot in 2000 (I believe). It was their first trip to Walt Disney World. I watched with tears in my eyes as my kids stared in amazement and wonder. And as my mom watched, she looked over at me and we were both moved to tears by the magic of the moment. Why was the Tapestry of Dreams Parade done away with? How long was its run? Are the any plans to bring it back? Stacy, Laurel, MD

A —The parade in World Showcase at Epcot started as Tapestry of Nations on October 1, 1999, and switched to Tapestry of Dreams on October 1, 2001. It continued until March 1, 2003. Disney parades are periodically changed so that guests can have new experiences when they visit the resorts. I am aware of no plans to bring back Tapestry of Dreams.

Q Hi, Dave. A friend of mine gave me a copy of an employee handbook entitled *Walt Disney World and You.* It has an insert entitled "The Walt Disney World Look for Hostesses." Is this a rare find? The back is numbered WDW-395. Thanks. Chuck, Griffin, NC

A —I would not exactly call it rare. Such booklets were given to all new Walt Disney World Cast Members when they went through orientation on their first day of work. The booklets went through many different editions.

Q Who did the music for Epcot's opening ceremonies? I want to say John Williams; some of it sounds so close to *E.T.*, Orlando, FL

A —The fanfare, written by Disney music director Steve Skorija, is called "We've Just Begun to Dream." At the D23 Epcot thirtieth event, he mentioned that he had used eleven notes from a reconstructed thirty-seven-note Greek song (thought by some to be the world's oldest piece of extant notated music) to create the Epcot piece.

Q Dave, I was wondering what ever happened to the magic stores that were in the Magic Kingdom? One was located right on Main Street and the other was behind the castle, as you walked through from the hub; it was located to the right. They sold all kinds of tricks and had great masks there that you could buy. My first trip there, I bought the Gorn mask from *Star Trek* and a great Wolfman mask and Wolfman hands; that was thirty-nine years ago. Thank you for your time. Scott, Somerset, PA

A —Merlin's Magic Shop was in Fantasyland at the Walt Disney World Magic Kingdom from 1972 to 1986. It became Mickey's Christmas Carol, and then Sir Mickey's. The House of Magic (1971–1995) on Main Street, U.S.A. closed to make room for the Main Street Athletic Club store and later the Hall of Champions.

Q We took a picture for the Leave a Legacy in Epcot a few years back. We cannot find the picture ID number to find it on the wall. Can you locate it? Wayne & Emily are the names on our card. Carolyn, Bellefontaine, OH

A —You can look up the location at Epcot the next time you are there, at the Leave a Legacy Locator in the Camera Center under Spaceship Earth.

Q How many presidents have lent their voices to The Hall of Presidents attraction? Avi, Irvine, CA

A —The first president to provide audio for his Audio-Animatronics figure in The Hall of Presidents at the Magic Kingdom at Walt Disney World was Bill Clinton, when his figure was added in 1993. Both George W. Bush and Barack Obama have continued the tradition.

Q I've been fortunate to meet Disney people like yourself at Disney events. Nearly twenty-five years ago I met Disney animator Harry Holt at Walt Disney World, where he was signing pictures. I have his scene from *Bambi* framed on my wall. I've read where some people say that these are pencil drawings, some say they're photostatic copies, and others say a combination of the two. Could you please clarify? Thanks as always. Lou, Rego Park, NY

A —I passed this question on to former Walt Disney World artist Russell Schroeder, who worked with Harry Holt, and here is his reply: "When Harry Holt first started drawing in the Park, he did completely original pencil sketches for guests. Because of the high demand and to reduce guests' wait time, he soon created an assortment of original sketches that were then printed on quality paper, but he left a space for something hand-drawn to be added. Guests could also get the art framed at that location. If Lou's copy has multiple characters in it, it is likely one of those combination printed and hand-drawn pieces."

Q Hi. What is the name of the band that plays in front of Grizzly Hall in Walt Disney World? I have pictures and video of them multiple times but can never find the name. Thank you. Alex, Indianapolis, IN

A —The Notorious Banjo Brothers and Bob are three musicians and mischief-makers who have performed slightly irreverent and comedic sets throughout Frontierland in the Magic Kingdom over the past dozen years. Another live entertainment offering there is the Frontierland Hoedown, which features several of the Country Bears, Brer Bear, Brer Fox, Brer Rabbit, and a group of Frontierland dancers.

Q I wondered if you could divulge the name and some history concerning the Walt Disney World resort located between the Magnolia and Palm golf courses? It is my understanding that it is currently a resort for individuals in the military and other service fields. This was one of our family's favorite resorts; my mother even redecorated our home from its inspiration in the mid-1980s! Colleen, Hubbard, OH

A —This resort first opened in 1973, known initially as The Golf Resort. The name changed to The Disney Inn in 1986. In 1994, the resort was leased to the United States government, named Shades of Green, and henceforth utilized for rest and relaxation by military personnel. In 1996, the government purchased the hotel, with a hundred-year lease on its land.

Q Could you please tell us about the history and development of Figment and the Dreamfinder, originally from the Future World attraction of Journey into Imagination in Epcot? Brock, Dartmouth, MA

A —Dreamfinder and Figment originated as Professor Marvel and his green dragon friend at the proposed, but never built, Discovery Bay expansion of Disneyland. When Kodak signed on to be the sponsor of Epcot's Journey into Imagination, the characters were re-imagined. Professor Marvel became the Dreamfinder, and his green dragon became Figment, who adopted a royal-purple pigment. Dreamfinder was developed as the kind, wise spirit of imagination (with the attitude of Santa Claus or the Wizard of Oz), and Figment became just the opposite—the curious and childish sidekick with a short attention span.

Q The props and sets in the Tower of Terror are amazing! I've heard that the Mission Inn in Riverside, California, and the Biltmore in Los Angeles provided some of the inspiration for the design. Are there any other buildings that inspired this beautiful attraction? Todd, Locust Grove, VA

A —The Imagineers looked at photographs of many elaborate buildings from the right era for their design ideas, then scoured Hollywood auction houses for the actual props. Some came from lavish estates of the biggest names in the entertainment industry. One set of chairs was four hundred years old; other chairs came from the exclusive Jonathan Club, a well-known Los Angeles landmark built in the 1920s.

Q **There is a song from Disney that I believe was at the original Innoventions, where we sat and saw a computer "behind the scenes." The lyrics to a repetitive portion of the song are, "*That's why I'm a rooter of the computer, everybody needs a friend!*" I would love to know, who is singing that? Diana, Melbourne, FL**

A —The attraction in CommuniCore was the Astuter Computer Revue (1982–1984), with "The Computer Song," written by the Sherman brothers and sung by Ken Jennings, portraying Earlie the Pearlie. Jennings was selected for the role after performing Tobias in *Sweeney Todd* on Broadway.

Q **On my first trip to Walt Disney World about ten years ago there was a parade that took the kids off the sidewalk and let them interact and dance with the characters; what was it called? Any information would be great thanks. Bridget, Brooklyn, NY**

A —You are likely thinking of the Share a Dream Come True Parade, which premiered with the 100 Years of Magic celebration in 2001. The parade invited guests to participate with characters along the route in a series of "show stops" for a number of years. The last version of the parade, Celebrate a Dream Come True, adopted a new theme, did not incorporate show stops, and was replaced by the Festival of Fantasy parade in 2014.

Q When I was younger I remember loving a ride called Dreamflight in Tomorrowland at the Magic Kingdom. Why did they close such an interesting flight simulation ride, and when? Teresa, Chester, NY

A —The attraction opened as If You Had Wings, sponsored by Eastern Airlines (1972–1987). When Delta took over as the sponsor, they changed the title to If You Could Fly for nineteen months while they designed a new attraction. That new attraction was Delta Dreamflight, opening in 1989. When Delta discontinued sponsorship in 1996, the attraction was renamed Take Flight, until it was removed in 1998 so Buzz Lightyear's Space Ranger Spin could take its place.

Q In 1988, I was in Walt Disney World with my mom and dad. At that time there was only the Magic Kingdom and Epcot. I believe Disney-MGM Studios opened the following year. I think I remember Fantasmic! being at Epcot. Is that possible? If so, where was it? Michael, Manassas Park, VA

A —Fantasmic! was never at Epcot. You may be remembering Laserphonic Fantasy, which ran from 1984 to 1988, when it was superseded by Illuminations. Fantasmic! was created in 1992 at Disneyland and opened at the now Disney's Hollywood Studios in 1998.

Q In 1989 my family and I visited what was then Disney-MGM Studios, and I convinced everyone to go on the Animation tour rather than The Great Movie Ride. It was late, just before the Park's closing. I remember it being quite a walk, with TVs and video explaining what happened in the area that was behind large panes of glass. Well, I managed to go on the tour again a couple years ago. This time it was during the day. We were let into a theater and given an intro. Then we went on the tour . . .

but it was *much* shorter than I remember, and there were no large panes of glass showing a large room where the animators worked. I was wondering when the attraction was changed, and was it because of advances in technology? Amanda, Portage la Prairie, MB, Canada

A —The Magic of Disney Animation tour opened in 1989, and at that time Walt Disney Feature Animation had a studio there doing actual animation for the Disney features. Guests could watch the animators at work through large windows. The Florida studio closed in 2004, so there were major renovations and changes to the tour that year, including the addition of the interactive Animation Station exhibit area.

Q Is there a list somewhere listing all of the animals carved in the Tree of Life? I've searched high and low and can't seem to find one. Thank you. Kaitlyn, Mount Holly, NJ

A —Disney has not put out a list of the animals, because they want guests to have fun trying to find as many as they can. There are a total of 325 animals, according to the Walt Disney World Web site.

Q We recently had the pleasure of going through Spaceship Earth after many years of avoiding it. Is Juliet Mills the voice that we heard on our journey? It was so much more fun than it used to be. Leslie Ellen, Defiance, OH

A —The current narrator of Spaceship Earth since December 2007 is Dame Judi Dench. The attraction received extensive renovations that year.

Q Hi, Dave. In 1995, I visited an exhibit at Epcot, Universe of Energy. This was so interesting and the Disney World Screen

Saver I purchased at Walt Disney World in 2000 has a picture of the dinosaurs also labeled Universe of Energy. Have not seen this exhibit in quite a few years . . . have been to Walt Disney World every year and sometimes two times yearly since 1973 . . . and would like to know what happened to the exhibit. Also, I think in 1995, I rode a great ride, seats moving only, at Epcot, where we traveled through the body and had great health food and drinks after the ride. Wondering . . . what has happened to this exhibit, as well? Thank You. Judy, Leland, NC

A —The Universe of Energy, with its dinosaurs, is still in Future World at Epcot. It was updated in 1996 to incorporate Ellen's Energy Adventure, starring Ellen DeGeneres. The ride through the human body was Body Wars, an attraction inside Wonders of Life. That pavilion closed in 2004, to be open henceforth only seasonally and for special events. Most recently, the pavilion space has been used as a festival center for the Food and Wine and Flower and Garden festivals; however, the pavilion's original attractions have not been featured.

Q Dave, I have a small pin, the type that might go on a tie. It is in the classic shape of Mickey's head and in capital letters it has the word DREAM on it. The person who gave it to me explained it was a pin Walt had made for only a special few and that they were all lost. Seven years ago, when it was given to me, is when the man told me someone at Disney came across them by accident. Can you tell me anything about this pin, please? Thanks. Jill, Garden Grove, CA

A —The information you were given is incorrect. The pin was made in 1987 and distributed to more than six thousand Cast Members at Walt Disney World. DREAM stands for "Disney Resorts Experiences Are Magic," and it was part of a campaign to encourage Cast Members.

Q **In the Magic Kingdom at the Walt Disney World Resort, the barbershop had an old National cash register. Is there any history on this register? Where is it now (as it is no longer in the barbershop)? Any documentation for the register? John, Plattsburgh, NY**

A —Until the mid-2000s, a mechanical antique cash register was used to ring up sales at the Harmony Barber Shop on Main Street, U.S.A. in Magic Kingdom Park. The register dated from 1912. It was replaced by a terminal that allowed guests to pay with credit cards and charge to their hotel bill; additionally, the new terminal was integrated with the Emporium's network. The old cash register was sold at a Cast Member sale.

Q **I've seen the little theater with the Buddy Ebsen dancing figure at Walt Disney World and read about its history. But nobody ever seems to mention if it ever actually worked. Did they ever run it, and if so, is there any film of it in action? Donald, San Jose, CA**

A —The dancing-man figure, on display in the Walt Disney: One Man's Dream attraction at Disney's Hollywood Studios, did indeed work, but only in a testing stage. I do not recall ever seeing any film of it in operation.

Q **Was the Liberty Tree in Liberty Square at Walt Disney World inspired by the Liberty Tree in the 1957 movie *Johnny Tremain*? Justin, Appling, GA**

A —Yes, it was. The huge live oak tree, now 175 years old, was found on another part of the Walt Disney World property and transplanted to Liberty Square. You can imagine how impressive a task it was to move a thirty-five-ton full-grown tree without damaging it.

Q Aloha, Dave. Several years ago I bought two VHS videos during the holiday season at my local Walmart store. These videos are *Walt Disney World at Home—At Home for the Holidays* and *Walt Disney World at Home for Kids—Holiday Crafts & Treats*. Were these ever released on DVD, and if not, will they be released on DVD? They are both very entertaining and show some inside looks at how Disney gets ready for the holiday season. Serena, Pahoa, HI

A —Those two videos were produced by Walt Disney Attractions as an exclusive for sale at Walmart in 1996; they have not been released on DVD.

Q When did the holiday version of the Main Street Electrical Parade run in the Magic Kingdom in Walt Disney World? I have seen video of it from 1999, but no one knows for how long it ran. Jeremiah, Kissimmee, FL

A —The Main Street Electrical Parade returned to the Magic Kingdom in 1999 after a hiatus of eight years. For the first time, it ran year-round beginning in May 1999 until April 2001. So the only two years that it would have run during the Christmas season were 1999 and 2000.

Q I heard that when Disney came to Florida, he had two places in mind for the location of Disney World, Ocala and Orlando. What made Disney choose Orlando over Ocala? Dominique, Ocala, FL

A —Walt Disney and his staff made intensive surveys of Florida, looking for the right amount of available and affordable land, proximity to interstate highways, ease of access, etc. It was deemed that the area between Ocala and Orlando experienced a significant decline in minimum winter temperature; because cold nights tend to have an adverse effect on attendance and landscaping, the region south of Orlando was more appealing. It was the Orlando area property that fulfilled their needs.

Q **I have seen pictures and been told of an abandoned part of Walt Disney World. Where was that, and why was it shut down and abandoned? Bayley, Sacramento, CA**

A —There are only a few areas of Walt Disney World that have been closed down, such as River Country and Discovery Island. Both closed after being superseded by larger and more elaborate attractions elsewhere at the resort.

Q **When Epcot's original Test Track closed in 2012, did the Walt Disney Archives acquire any pieces from the attraction that we might recognize? Robert, Kissimmee, FL**

A —The Archives saved a number of pieces, such as a crash-test dummy, the height-measuring tool, a marquee, and a memorable road hazard sign picturing a cow.

Q **Hi, Dave! Today I purchased a great find at a local library book sale: *Walt Disney's EPCOT Center: Creating the New World of Tomorrow*. Inside just happened to be an old Kodak guidebook of EPCOT Center, a ticket, and a passport. I was able to do some research on the guidebook and ticket, but was unable to find a whole lot of information on the passport. I know the one I found was from the World Fest event, when Mexico was celebrated in 1985. I was just wondering if you perhaps knew the history of the passport. When did they first issue them? Thanks, Dave! I appreciate it! Lauren, Sacramento, CA**

A —The passport, such as you found, was among several versions produced during World Fest in 1985. World Fest was an event that spotlighted individual countries in World Showcase during the spring and summer months. The passports were meant to be stamped in each Showcase country. In later years, more elaborate passports were sold as merchandise items in Epcot.

Q **Are there any items in the Hollywood Tower Hotel in Hollywood Studios that were actually used in the *Twilight Zone* series? Or any replicas? I know when I was in the library I saw the fortune-telling machine from the episode "Nick of Time" on the top shelf. Megan, Rome, GA**

A —There were replicas created to represent props used in particular episodes of the *Twilight Zone* series, but no original props were included. The fortune-telling machine you saw was one of them.

Q **I'm interested in the music of the Parks. Not just the attraction and parade music but the background music played in each area of the Parks and Resorts. Are those produced "in-house," or are they purchased for use? Are they available for purchase? Nothing would put me at ease more than being able to listen to the background music of Old Key West, Fort Wilderness, or the Wilderness Lodge. Bill, Leola, PA**

A —Much of the background music for the Disney Parks is licensed to Disney, but some is written and recorded specifically for its particular use. It is normally not available for purchase, though occasionally tracks have been included on official Park albums.

Q **Every time I went to Walt Disney World, I would always slip into the old theater on Main Street to visit the character mural hidden there. Since no one ever really went back there, it felt like my private Disney experience, particularly as it was pretty much the only place to find Basil of Baker Street in the whole park. Now I find it replaced by a character-greet queue. Why**

was it not left as part of the queue? Please tell me Bill Justice's artwork has not been destroyed! Linda, Yatesville, PA

A —The mural, originally painted by Bill Justice for The Walt Disney Story in 1973, had additional characters from more recent films later added by Disney artist Russell Schroeder. The mural has been saved, and is in the Walt Disney Archives.

Q Are there any parts or references from the old Snow White attraction used in the new Mine Train ride? Jonathan, Pawtucket, RI

A —Yes, there are. The two vultures on the crane near the mine entrance of the Seven Dwarfs Mine Train originally appeared in the Snow White's Scary Adventures attraction, as did the figures of Grumpy, Doc, Bashful, Sleepy, and Happy seen in the cottage near the end of the attraction. New figures of Snow White, Dopey, and Sneezy were created for that latter scene.

Q Why did Treasure Island, also known as Discovery Island, close? Was there something wrong with the island? Elizabeth, [No city provided], IL

A —Discovery Island closed in 1999 soon after the newly opened Disney's Animal Kingdom provided a better venue for showcasing animals.

Q My friend has an original paper Disney ticket that was worn around the neck with tear-offs that I believe were part of a multiple-day option. Is this type of ticket considered to be more collectible than usable at this point? Larry, Marion, IN

A —Early park admission tickets are still good for admission, unless marked otherwise, so your friend's ticket value, if unused, is the current admission price. There is little or no additional collectible value associated with the tickets.

Q I heard a rumor that the horse with the ribbon on its tail at Prince Charming Regal Carrousel in Walt Disney World is Cinderella's favorite. Is that true? Megan, Rome, GA

A —There are now eighty-six horses on the Carrousel, with horse No. 37 nicknamed by Magic Kingdom Cast Members as Cinderella's horse (Cindy). It is the only horse with ornamentation on its tail. Horse No. 20, next to it, is named King, though Cast Members call it Prince Charming's horse.

Q I previously attended Disneyana Conventions that were held in Orlando, and during the events there was a venue entitled Mickey's Attic where you could purchase relics of the Park. At one of those conventions I purchased a stained-glass panel approximately six feet long and twenty inches wide with the inscription THE NEW CENTURY CLOCK SHOP that was billed as having been used in the Park. I have been searching photos and cannot locate a photo where this sign was displayed in the Park. Can you help? Thank you. Joseph, Tunkhannock, PA

A —The New Century Clock Shop was located on Main Street, U.S.A. at the Walt Disney World Magic Kingdom from 1971 to 1986. There were similarly named shops at Disneyland and Tokyo Disneyland.

Q Were there any specific factors that led to the abandonment of the original EPCOT concept (The City of Tomorrow), or was it just simply Walt Disney's death? Did they legitimately try to do it in the years after his death, or did the enthusiasm and vision die with Walt in December 1966? Kenny, Lithonia, GA

A —EPCOT was indeed Walt Disney's pet project, and after he died Disney executives were unsure of what to do about the project. Walt had been unable to refine his ideas. When the executives began studying Walt's ideas of a community where people would actually live and work, questions arose as to possible problems with trying to regulate the lives of residents, essentially having them "living in a fishbowl." It took almost a decade for the Imagineers to come up with something they felt would really work.

Q **Are the first three scenes in the Carousel of Progress the same today as they were for the 1964–1965 New York World's Fair? If not, are there pictures of those first three scenes as they were originally composed? Tim, Cordova, TN**

A —It is primarily the last scene that has been updated; the first three scenes have remained about the same, though with some tweaks over the years. Some photos can be found online.